Ecumenical Beginnings
in
Protestant World Mission

ECUMENICAL BEGINNINGS

IN

PROTESTANT WORLD

MISSION

A History of Comity

BY

R. PIERCE BEAVER

THOMAS NELSON & SONS

Edinburgh   NEW YORK   *Toronto*

In Memoriam
ARTHUR VALE CASSELMAN

Friend to many missionaries
Staunch advocate of comity and cooperation

Contents

Preface

THE past century and a half of continuous and steady growth in missionary cooperation and the movement toward unity and union among young churches issued out of, and were built upon, the almost universal practice of comity in the foreign missionary enterprise. The repudiation of comity in some quarters and the questioning of it in others after World War II have come as a surprise and even a shock to missionaries and administrators. There is but one other alternative to comity than chaotic competition between churches, and that is more effective cooperation in strengthened unity. In fact, one who has studied the history of the rise of the young churches can scarcely reach any other conclusion than that there is really no other alternative to comity but that which most pioneer missionaries and the first national pastors believed to be its goal and natural consequence, namely, a united but diversified church in each land which would be far different than the churches of Europe and America.

The new tensions became urgent of solution about 1951 or 1952. Preparatory to further discussion of them, the Assembly of the Division of Foreign Missions of the National Council of the Churches of Christ in the U.S.A. committed a study of the subject to its Staff Council. That was, in effect, assignment of the study to the Director of the Missionary Research Library and Research Secretary of the Division. The author of this book then held that office. The desire at the time, according to a consensus of the secretaries of the boards, was a handbook of comity agreements in every land with an historical introduction and an appraisal of the contemporary situation. Data were gathered, but it was soon apparent that while references to comity agreements might be discovered by the hundreds, actual comity agreements were hard to find. They were frequently only verbal compacts that had never been reduced to writing, or if written, seldom sent to the headquarters of the boards and societies. The writer, moreover, joined the faculty of the Divinity School of the University of Chicago, and other matters seemed immediately more pressing.

However, the tensions and questions over comity have increased and the future of the ancient principle and practice must be resolved. A full history of the practice, with an explanation of its intent, ought to contribute toward that end. Moreover, since the whole development toward unity and cooperation came out of comity, its story is in urgent need of telling. That has never been done. Two admirable books have dealt with missionary cooperation. *Ecumenical Foundations,* by William Richey Hogg (New York: Harper, 1952), has most adequately told the story of the rise of the system of functional cooperation through councils. This book reveals the concern of the councils for comity matters, but does not deal with the origins in comity practices and concerns. More recently there has been published Henry P. Van Dusen's interesting and valuable book, *One Great Ground of Hope* (Philadelphia: Westminster Press, 1961), which demonstrates how "the Christian world mission has been both the precursor and the progenitor of the effort after Christian unity." This book indicates that comity was an early form of cooperation and that the furtherance of it was a major objective of the early councils. Having read Dr. Van Dusen's book and referred again to Professor Hogg's work, this author came to the conviction that there was urgent need for a book on comity in foreign missions which, with those two books, would complete the story of cooperation. This book then is an effort to reveal the foundations in comity on which the whole structure of cooperation rests and out of which also came the first impulses toward union in the mission fields. Since, as Dr. Van Dusen states, the foreign mission has been the progenitor of the effort after unity, comity may be regarded as the first concrete step in the evolution of the ecumenical movement.

A handbook of comity agreements, such as was projected almost a decade ago, could be prepared only after an exhaustive field study in each country, and it could not justify the enormous amount of labor and expense that would be involved. Such studies belong to the field of local church history. The extensive travels of the author in recent years have, however, provided many opportunities for investigating general developments with respect to comity and current attitudes toward the practice. Detailed accounts of local agreements, which would make dull reading, are not necessary to the setting forth of the essential features of the story. Nor need every region be brought forth in the book for minute scrutiny, for that would be exceedingly repetitive. This would produce in writing overlapping similar to the overlapping in territory that comity strove to prevent. There are, for example, but a few passing references to Burma, where the American Baptists so long had the country to themselves that they spread over it and have always dominated the scene. Later entering missions were resented by some Baptists, but they made place for them, yet with consequent overlapping. Some missionaries and nationals, who know intimately the history of their areas, therefore may feel that their particular region has been slighted, and that they could add many details. It is hoped that this book may stimulate such persons to record all pertinent information and to undertake the highly important task of collecting and preserving the source material of local church history.

This book endeavors to show what comity is, what its intent has been, how it came to be the almost universal practice of the missionary societies, what the chief differences were in regional developments and emphases, and what the factors are which have created the tensions and uncertainties of the present. It does not attempt to duplicate ground already covered by others in books readily available nor to describe the developments in cooperation and unity, excepting as aspects of these cannot be divorced from comity.

The secretaries of many mission boards and societies answered inquiries about the comity practices of their boards and missions when the earlier study was contemplated. Many missionaries and administrators have verbally given valuable information; and officials, pastors, and laymen in the young churches have generously voiced their views and opinions. The warm thanks of the author is extended to them all, and he acknowledges his indebtedness to them as well as to the sources specifically quoted or cited, and to the publishers of those works. The rich resources of the Missionary Research Library alone made the study possible, and the books, periodicals, and reports listed in the Bibliography are but a small part of the many hundreds of items which had to be examined there in the search for data. The author is grateful for the help of the staff not only in this work but also in many other research projects over the years. A special word of gratitude is due my colleague, Professor James H. Nichols, for reading the manuscript and offering valuable criticisms and suggestions.

R. Pierce Beaver

The University of Chicago
September 8, 1961

Ecumenical Beginnings
in
Protestant World Mission

Introduction

What Is Comity?

THE practice of comity in foreign missions antedated the use of the term by more than sixty years. The word began to be used in the 1880's, and became current through its employment in the papers and discussions at the Centenary Conference on the Protestant Missions of the World in London in 1888. Thereafter its place was fixed in the vocabulary of the Protestant foreign missionary enterprise.

The missionaries and the directors of their boards and societies eventually came to use the term very loosely and to make it cover a wide range of cooperative practices. It even came to designate the prevailing spirit of unity. This development will become apparent in the following chapters. However, comity always meant, basically and essentially, the division of territory and assignment of spheres of occupation including delimitation of boundaries, on the one hand, and noninterference in one another's affairs, on the other.

Nevertheless, noninterference always had a far more positive aspect than mere avoidance of competition. It involved mutual recognition and common agreement on employment of workers, their salaries, standards of membership for the churches, transfer of membership, the adoption of similar standards of discipline, and respect of each other's discipline. Noninterference was assured by delimitation of territory, the consequent elimination of differences which could be the cause of rivalry and confusion, and the creation of boards of arbitration for the settlement of differences with regard to boundaries and infringements of accepted practice.

Comity, then, was the creation of denominationalism by geography. Yet its fundamental purpose was not that by any means. Comity through delimitation of territory and assignment of spheres of occupation sought to assure the responsibility to specific missionary agencies for the speedy evangelization of every region of the earth and every district in each region, to the end that the Kingdom of God might spread through the whole world and that a great Church of Christ might arise in every land through the combined efforts of the separate societies.

The system of comity which evolved was an attempt by Protestant missionary agencies to achieve voluntarily, through spiritual obedience and under the guidance of the Holy Spirit, by a democratic process, a responsible and speedy evangelistic occupation of all heathendom similar to that in Roman Catholic missions planned and administered by the central authoritative missionary organ of the Church, the Sacred Congregation for the Propagation of the Faith. This is the real reason why comity could not be static, and why it bred ever-greater expressions of unity and gave rise to increasingly effective cooperation. It was so successful that eventually it was taken for granted and regarded as being only "negative cooperation" or the lowest form of cooperation. Nevertheless, it was always primary and fundamental. The Rev. H. A. Grey, writing a pamphlet during the Kikuyu Controversy, stated:

> Comity may be taken in a wide sense to comprehend every degree of friendly relationship; or it may be taken as the primary stage alone. It must then be distinguished from other degrees of friendly relationship. We should perhaps graduate the degrees by such terms as Organic Unity, Inter-communion, Federation, Co-operation, &c., Comity standing for the lowest and least defined relationship.[1]

[1] *Comity in the Mission Field*, p. 1.

"Effective occupation" is the key to understanding what impelled the missionaries to create the system of comity. The meaning of this term includes both the preaching of the gospel to every man and the effective nurture of the national church, which was affirmed to be the ultimate evangelistic agency in every place. Missionaries generally agreed that Robert E. Speer had given the definition of "adequate missionary occupation" which pleased them best. It is this:

> The presence in a given field of Christian missionary agencies, whether foreign or native or both, whose numerical strength, geographical distribution, adaptation of methods, and vital spiritual character give promise under the blessing of God, first, of establishing within a reasonable time an indigenous Church, which through its life and work will propagate Christianity and leaven the nation or field within whose borders it stands; and second, in cooperation with this Church, of presenting Christ to every individual with such clearness and completeness as to place upon him the responsibility of acceptance or rejection of the Gospel. And any effort to say which of these is first—because in any arrangement you must name one first and the other second—will displace the other, and will certainly disarrange and throw out of proportion our missionary activity. Both these things must be dominating aims.[2]

[2] China Continuation Committee, Milton T. Stauffer, secretary and editor. *The Christian Occupation of China; a General Survey of the numerical strength and geographical distribution of the Christian forces in China,* made by the Special Committee on Survey and Occupation, China Continuation Committee, 1918–1921. Shanghai, 1922; reverse of title.

Chapter I

Comity and Unity

THE Protestant missionary enterprise was characterized from the very beginning by an extraordinary sense of unity across national and denominational lines. Comity can be understood only in the context of that unity, of which it is one of the earliest fruits even as at the same time it was the creator of still greater unity and cooperation.

The origins of Protestant missions are complex. Many streams intermingled to produce the great movement of the nineteenth century, and by that time the common mission had a history of almost two centuries. There is no break in continuity from the first efforts at evangelism by chaplains of the Dutch East Indies Company and the inauguration of the American Indian missions by the Mayhews and John Eliot. It was the American Indian missions especially that provided stimulus and continuity, but interaction between all elements is evident. Some of the theologians of the "Second Reformation" in the Netherlands, who were concerned about missions, influenced thought in England. The jurist Grotius certainly did also. Some early German thinking had impact in Sweden, and Svedburg's interest was aroused by the American Indians. Leibnitz's views on missions had effect in many quarters. Increase Mather in Boston and Professor Leusden in Utrecht corresponded about the missions, and each acknowledged the inspiration in their homelands of the missions in the "East" and "West" Indies. Cotton Mather carried on correspondence with August Hermann Francke in Halle and the missionaries in Tranquebar. He publicized their work and collected gold in Massachusetts for the institutions in Halle and India. Churchmen

and dissenters together in England organized in 1649 for
the support of the American Indian missions the first, and
still existing, missionary society, the Society for the Propagation of the Gospel in New England. It has continued
throughout its history to prize this association of Anglicans
and others.

When Pietism brought into being the first German stream
of missions, the Danish king sent to Tranquebar the men that
Francke inspired and trained at Halle. An interconfessional
group in London publicized their efforts, and when the mission failed of Danish support, the Anglican Society for
Promoting Christian Knowledge came to the rescue. The
S.P.C.K. had been founded by Dr. Thomas Bray along with
two other organizations, the Society for the Propagation of
the Gospel in Foreign Parts (S.P.G.) and Dr. Bray's Asso-
ciates, for missionary activity by the Church of England in
America among the settlers, Indians, and pagan Negro slaves.
The Society in Scotland for the Propagation of Christian
Knowledge was also organized for support of the Indian
missions in New England and the Middle Colonies.

The Scots who supported that Society were responsible
for the Quarterly Concert of Prayer. Jonathan Edwards, the
greatest American theologian of the time and missionary to
the Stockbridge Indians, wrote his book, *A Humble Attempt
to Promote Explicit Agreement and Visible Union among
God's People, in Extraordinary Prayer for the Revival of
Religion, etc.*, and that gave power to the movement as well
as relating it to the missionary vision. The English Baptists
made the prayer movement a Monthly Concert, and the ideas
connected with it influenced William Carey and his brethren.
The London Missionary Society (L.M.S.) made it the
Monthly Concert of Prayer for Missions, and it became on
both sides of the Atlantic the most potent means of missionary education and support.

Moravian missions introduced still another stream of missionary action and inspiration that mingled with the others. Having undertaken an enterprise too large to support, even by their unstinted devotion, the Moravians were soon aided financially both by a small new Moravian community in England and by a society of friends of the work, the London Society for the Support of Moravian Missions. Bishop Spangenberg created its counterpart in America in 1745—the Society for the Furtherance of the Gospel among the Heathen. It fell into abeyance and was reorganized in 1787 by Bishop Etwein as the Society for the Propagation of the Gospel among the Heathen. The Moravian missionaries and their converts among the American Indians were harassed by the white settlers, but by the end of the eighteenth century they had become a powerful inspiration to missionary zeal. William Carey was influenced both by Brainerd and the Moravians, and the Moravian missionaries made a great impact on John Wesley.

All of these influences and streams of missionary endeavor coalesced into the mighty new surge of Protestant missionary endeavor at the end of the eighteenth century and beginning of the nineteenth. The works of Claudius Buchanan and the *Letters* of Melville Horne spurred efforts on both sides of the Atlantic. The renewed interest of the Scottish Society in the American Indians stimulated the chartering in Boston in 1787 of the Society for the Propagation of the Gospel among the Indians and Others in North America. When William Carey and his friends established the Baptist Missionary Society in 1792 and went to Serampore, Americans were thrilled and stimulated by his reports. American Congregationalists and Presbyterians contributed more to the Serampore work than did the Baptists. The London Missionary Society (L.M.S.), founded in 1795, was a union effort of British evangelicals in four or more communions, although it eventually became principally a Congregationalist organ. It resolved "not to send Presbyterianism, Independency, Episcopacy, or any other form of Church Order and Government . . . but the glorious Gospel of the Blessed God to the Heathen." It made a powerful impact in America, and was a major factor in the foundation of the New York, Massachusetts, and Connecticut Missionary Societies, and a dozen others. Had not the international difficulties created by the War of 1812 intervened, the American Board of Commissioners for Foreign Missions might have been auxiliary to it, and also the American Baptist Foreign Mission Society auxiliary to the Baptist Missionary Society in London. J. T. Vanderkemp founded the Netherlands Missionary Society as auxiliary to the L.M.S. The Church Missionary Society (C.M.S.) was established by evangelicals in the Church of England, not because they were dissatisfied with the L.M.S., but because they were convinced that there had to be a genuine foreign missionary organ within the Church of England.

The same group of evangelicals, across the lines of the societies and the communions in Great Britain, founded the London Society for the Promotion of Christianity among the Jews (later becoming Anglican), and were responsible for the creation of such auxiliaries as the Religious Tract Society and the British and Foreign Bible Society. Their counterparts in America created the Bible societies, the education societies, and the tract societies as necessary agents in support of missions. They were responsible, too, for the moral reform societies and a host of philanthropic projects.

The C.M.S. and the L.M.S. employed Germans, Swiss, and Swedes, both Lutheran and Reformed. Jänicke's seminary in Germany supplied men for British and Dutch societies. The Basel Missionary Society (1815) united in a common venture Lutherans and Reformed in Switzerland and Germany, as did the Evangelical Missionary Society of Paris in France. Basel not only sent its people directly, but supplied missionaries for the C.M.S. and L.M.S. and pastors for Reformed, Lutheran, and Evangelical churches in the United States.

American German Evangelical churches sent the contributions from their annual "Missionsfest" to Basel and to Barmen (Rheinische Mission), which was also a union Lutheran and Reformed society. The Swedish Missionary Society, later to be the official organ of the Church of Sweden, despite its solidly Lutheran constituency, appointed Moravians and English Wesleyans to its governing board and for more than a decade made grants to the Basel, London, Wesleyan, and Moravian societies. Methodist influence on Scandinavian missions is freely acknowledged. The United Foreign Missionary Society for New York and the Middle States, was created by the official action of the Presbyterian, Reformed Protestant Dutch, and Associate Reformed Churches as their joint organ. When it merged with the American Board in 1826, that institution became the union missionary organ of the Congregationalists, Presbyterians, Dutch Reformed, Associate Reformed, and later the German Reformed Churches in America. It was the common concern of all these supporters of the mission on both sides of the Atlantic which was chiefly responsible for the establishment of the Evangelical Alliance in 1846.

Every missionary society published news about the activities of the others in its magazine. These accounts were read in the Monthly Concert of Prayer for Missions. Thus the early participants in the Protestant missionary enterprise were drawn together, influenced each other, supported each other, and felt a sense of unity and brotherhood not known to the other clergy and laity in the churches in a time of denominational isolation. The very battle against indifference, inertia, and official opposition which they had to wage for recognition of the missionary privilege and obligation sharpened their sense of unity and common purpose.

Moreover, it was not the directors of the missionary societies, the secretaries, and the missionaries alone who felt this sense of unity and common purpose, for it was widely

shared throughout the rank and file of those who supported
and promoted the foreign mission. It is a note often repeated
in American missionary sermons and books in a time of sharp
denominational rivalries. Baron Stow, in the preface to his
book, *The Missionary Enterprise,* wrote: "The Spirit of Missions is the spirit of Concord. The keynote was struck on
the plains of Bethlehem; and all who have sympathy with
the angelic announcement, are sure to think, feel, utter, and
act in concert, both with the heavenly host, and with one another." [1] Archibald Alexander in a sermon on Acts 11.18 in
1830 stated:

> It also affords good ground for joy and thanksgiving that
> there has arisen no discord among the friends of foreign mis-
> sions, to distract their counsels and paralyze their efforts.
> Both in Europe and America, the utmost harmony has pre-
> vailed among those,—however different in denomination,—
> who have been engaged in the missionary operations of the
> day. The little, narrow feeling of party and sect, which has
> on other occasions, operated so balefully, has no influence
> here. The missionaries, attached to different societies, and
> belonging to different denominations, meet in foreign lands
> as brethren of the same family. They feel that they are labor-
> ing in the same cause, and serving the same glorious Master.
> With hearty goodwill and mutual confidence, they are accus-
> tomed to counsel and assist one another, in the prosecution
> of their arduous work. Nowhere upon earth does the genuine
> spirit of catholicism more prevail, than among missionaries,
> and the ardent friends of missions.[2]

The first great unofficial missionary conferences were
manifestations of the bond of unity that united men and
women across denominational boundaries. The circular containing the call to the Union Missionary Convention in New
York in 1854 declared that this public assembly was to be an

[1] P. iv.
[2] Alexander, A., *Sermon on Acts XI:18,* p. 27. (1830).

illustration of "the practical unity of the Church," and stated that if men charged with the work at home manifested the same catholic spirit as was exhibited by the missionaries aboard, it would strengthen the hands of those missionaries. It reminded the brethren that "the approach of the time for the larger outpouring of the Holy Spirit will certainly be marked by a desire to seek for and magnify Christian unity." Loud applause greeted the chairman's remarks at the closing session, when he said: "It is a matter of grateful reflection and of high congratulation that Christians of every shade of denominational opinion can here find a common ground of Christian philanthropy, and for Christian cooperation and work." [3] The London Conference of the same year considered as one of its three topics the subject "The Essential Unity and Aim of All Evangelical Missions." It was not hyperbole when the Liverpool Conference of 1860 resolved that: "Though belonging to different sections of the Church of Christ, they rejoice in that close union to each other and that practical co-operation which have so largely prevailed among the agents of Missionary Societies, both at home and abroad." [4]

The prevailing sense of unity and common purpose was strengthened by its total concern with the whole world of men outside of the then definable Christendom. The evangelical promoters of missions in Great Britain were indeed zealous for social reform at home and abroad, but it is not clear to this writer how much they recognized the existence of a single evangelistic task at home and abroad. Great Britain and Protestant Europe were generally considered to be Christian. Far in the future American delegates to the Willingen Conference of the International Missionary Council in 1952 would come home with the awareness of having

[3] *Union Missionary Convention, New York, 1854, Proceedings of* –, pp. 8–10, 22.
[4] *Conference on Missions Held in 1860 at Liverpool,* p. 12.

seen a glorious new vision of a single world mission of the
church of Christ to all the world. Yet that same vision had
inspired, animated, and sustained their forefathers a century
and a half earlier. The people who founded the many American missionary societies between 1787 and 1820 had a vision
of one total world mission encompassing evangelism to
nominal Christians and unchurched people in the seaboard
states; the christianizing of society through philanthropic
and reform organizations and movements (all to the glory of
God); the providing of ministers, churches, schools, and literature for the new frontier settlements where the people were
in danger of paganization; the evangelization of the heathen
on their doorstep, that is, the American Indians; witness to
the pagans and the nominal Roman Catholics in Latin
America; and missions to the heathen at the ends of the earth.

The mission was a kind of total concern that in Germany
would combine "inner" and "foreign" missions in one organization, such as Bethel under von Bodelschwingh. It was also
a vision that, to the participants in foreign missions, really
demanded the commitment of every last member of the
Church, and included many emphases which are now thought
to be of contemporary origin. For example, take the present
stress on the evangelistic office of every layman and the
effort to enlist laymen going abroad in business and profes-
sions as voluntary agents in the mission. This was a popular
idea in the United States in the 1830's. One of the most
interesting documents of foreign missions is the call by the
Sandwich Island Mission to the whole American people in
1836.[5] Had it been heeded there would not have been left
in the land a single professed Christian layman, pastor,
theological professor, or even member of the Prudential Committee of the American Board! Similarly, there was discussion

---

[5] [American Board of Commissioners for Foreign Missions, Sandwich
Islands Mission], *The Duty of the Present Generation to Evangelize the
World;* see also Dibble, S., *Thoughts on Missions,* ch. V, pp. 111ff.

of the same subject of lay participation by the missionaries and lay guests at the Punjab Missionary Conference at Lahore in 1862–63, where the consensus was expressed in the words of Lt. Col. E. J. Lake: "Laymen must identify themselves more with missionary cause; and to do so effectively, they must, in some sense or other, be themselves missionaries." [6]

It might be remarked parenthetically that the services of laymen in providing transportation and local assistance on the field, in evangelism and teaching, in influencing governments, as well as in the practical organization, administration, and financial support of the societies and boards at home have never been sufficiently recognized and their story told. Without a solid base among the laity in the several demoninations, the world mission could never have prevailed against the indifference and hostility of a great part of the clergy. It should be noted, too, that the great faith missions, beginning with the China Inland Mission, and the women's societies, beginning with the British Zenana and Bible Missionary Society and the American Women's Union Missionary Society, which were nondenominational, but called themselves, and thought of themselves, as interdenominational, were far more lay organizations than the denominational societies. They believed themselves to be of the Church, and they had none of the antagonism toward churches shown by many of the recently organized faith missions. They were part of the one mission of the Church, and long participated in the common consultations, conferences, and comity agreements.

One of the most important things to notice with regard to the general sense of unity, and the factor which above all else made comity possible, was the mutual recognition which almost all in the missionary enterprise made of the truth that God was no discriminator among them, and that the

[6] *Punjab Missionary Conference, Lahore, 1862–63, Report of the* –, p. 97.

Holy Spirit effected the same fruits through the labors of each and every mission. Missionary speakers in the early years of the nineteenth century drew for illustrations upon the whole range of missionary agencies and literature. The spiritual "adoption" of the missionaries of one society by the people of many denominations made for a marvelous practical experience of the Communion of Saints. Alexander Duff was treated as if he belonged to all the churches when he visited the United States in 1854. Missionary biographies were read across communion lines. There were many subscription editions of Livingstone's works in America. Professor Walter Freytag wrote in a paper prepared for the Willingen Conference that signs of the unity of the Church are to be discerned in the fact that "through the work of missions which themselves differ most widely in character, in some mysterious fashion a single achievement is accomplished," and also that "the work of different missions can bring forth one and the same fruit, which bears the marks of Christ's own people." [7] This truth had been recognized for a century and a half at least. Even a purely confessional conference could not ignore that fact. Thus Bishop E. Graham Ingham and Eugene Stock, secretaries of the section on missions at the Pan-Anglican Congress of 1908, reported that this conference "has manifested the essential oneness of missionary work everywhere, even amid all the diversities of fields, climactic, racial, political, social, religious, and with all the varied lines and methods of missionary organization." [8] At an earlier Church Congress in 1897, Bishop Edgar Jacob stated that Anglicans would gladly recognize the fruits of the Spirit in the missionary labors of others throughout the world, and quoted a resolution of a recent Lambeth Conference:

That in the Foreign Mission Field of the Church's work, where signal spiritual blessings have attended the labours

[7] "Mission and Unity," pp. 2, 3.
[8] *Pan-Anglican Congress, 1908*, vol. V, p. xxvi.

of Christian missionaries not connected with the Anglican Communion, a special obligation has arisen to avoid, as far as possible without compromise of principle, whatever tends to prevent the due growth and manifestation of that unity of Spirit which should ever mark the Church of Christ.[9]

The evidence of the common work of the Spirit in all missions, the apparent necessity of unity for the prosecution of a world-wide mission, and a love of Christ that found its highest expression in mission produced the bold antisectarianism of the first half of the nineteenth century (which became much more timid in the late years of the century); the emphasis upon stressing the essentials of the faith over against denominational particularities; the questioning of the fitness of the historical denominational differences of Europe for the churches of Asia and Africa; and most important, the mutual recognition by the denominational agencies of one another's churches as valid branches of the one Church of Christ. A good example of the principle of early antisectarianism is shown in Thomas S. Skinner's *Thoughts on Evangelizing the World*.[10] The writer congratulated the young churches of the mission fields on the opportunity to grow to maturity in a time when it was being recognized that every church and every Christian should have as supreme object the discipling of the nations and the evangelization of the whole world, according to our Savior's command. Working together toward this great object, all should seek to propagate "substantial Christianity," rather than any sectarian form of it, preaching that on which they agree, not the differences; laying their plans to further this end, not sectarian goals; looking toward the coalition of all Christians in the work. As to the second, the stressing of the essentials over against denominational particularities, the grand statement of the L.M.S. quoted at the beginning of this chapter is

[9] *Church Congress, Nottingham*, p. 1.
[10] New York, 1836.

the classic expression. It can be matched by similar statements of the C.M.S., for example, the 1871 declaration:

> The Society's great and primary and ultimate object is there-
> fore not the extension of any particular Church, however
> desirable that may be, but the glory of God in the propaga-
> tion of the Gospel and the salvation of souls. To this principle,
> interpreted indeed by their own fallible judgment, but with
> earnest prayer for Divine guidance, the Committee have
> steadfastly adhered, notwithstanding strong opposition and
> pressure.[11]

Beside this statement of an evangelical society can be
placed the views of the Anglo-Catholic Bishop of Lebombo,
stated at the General Missionary Conference of South Africa
at Johannesburg in 1904, when he called for: "In necessariis
unitas, in dubiis libertas, in omnibus caritas"; declared that
the differences on organization, sacraments, and worship
were "as nothing as that which separates us from the
heathen"; and called for common action in teaching.[12] With
respect to the third, the questioning of European and American denominational forms, let Joseph Mullens of the L.M.S.
in Calcutta be the spokesman. "Was it a very necessary thing
that the very systems . . . that came out of the struggles,
contentions, and controversies of the Reformation [and the
political conflicts] are what we should take and fix, like cast-
iron matrices, in which to mould without necessary adapta-
tion, the varying minds and circumstances of American
Indians, Africans, Asiatics, and the inhabitants of the numerous islands of the Pacific?"[13] He and many others gave a
negative answer.

Most of the Protestant churches, including the established
state churches, so universally recognized each other's validity

[11] *Church Missionary Intelligencer,* New Series, vol. VII (June, 1871), pp.
163–164; from report of C.M.S. 72nd anniversary meeting, 1871.
[12] *Report of Proceedings,* pp. 136–139.
[13] *Conference on Missions Held in 1860 at Liverpool,* p. 16.

in the mission fields, even though they might not be in communion in the homelands, that there is little point in giving documentation. The Anglicans varied. The C.M.S. bishops and missionaries were almost without exception generous in this regard. The S.P.G. personnel took varying attitudes from time to time and place to place, becoming more aloof as the nineteenth century progressed. In earlier years most would go along with their colleague, G. V. Pope in India, who said that Protestant missionaries agree sufficiently to regard each other as fellow workers, to rejoice in one another's success, and to regard each other's fields as brought under Christian teaching.[14] Many Anglicans would agree with the statement of Bishop Jacob of Newcastle:

> What does "comity" of missions mean? It is obviously a misnomer to those who believe that there is no common ground between the Church of England and other Christian bodies, for it implies at least a relationship of courtesy and friendliness. But I wish to go to the root of the matter, and say that it has a doctrinal basis which I shall state under two heads. First, when in the presence of heathenism, two missionaries belonging to different Christian bodies can agree in heartily and thankfully saying, "We love Him, because He first loved us," there is an agreement of faith which no outward differences, however important, can frustrate. I may state this in other words by saying that the holding, in its natural sense, of the great Christian doctrine of the Trinity, including the doctrine of the Incarnation of our Lord Jesus Christ, very God and very Man, constitutes a bond of union so strong that in the presence of heathenism differences, even of doctrine, are small in comparison. And secondly, I shall state, without attempting here to enlarge upon the truth, that baptism in the Name of the Father, the Son, and the Holy Ghost, by whomsoever administered, implies incorporation

[14] *South India Missionary Conference, Ootacamund, 1858, Proceedings of* —, p. 334.

into the one Church of our Lord Jesus Christ, so that no question whether any particular body of Christians does or does not constitute a valid branch of the Church can so unchurch the baptized Christian as to represent him as outside the Church of Christ. Admission by baptism into one society, however divided that society may be, and the holding of one faith in the Father, the Son, and the Holy Ghost, seems to me the doctrinal basis of missionary "comity." [15]

The Bishop's insistence upon the recognition of the essential unity symbolized and manifested in the evangelical message was repeated innumerable times throughout the nineteenth century, and this above all made comity possible among agencies which accorded with Rufus Anderson in regarding "preaching" as the grand means divinely appointed for the spread of the gospel throughout the world. One of the later statements, by N. G. Clark, a secretary of the American Board, in 1887, stresses the relationship of the union message to the system of comity.

A strict adherence to the message as that in which all evangelical Christians are agreed will secure mission comity at home and abroad. No one mission board will feel at liberty to enter upon a field already occupied by another, least of all to introduce its peculiar views of doctrine, ritual observance, or polity, so as to distract and disturb the minds of believers, to interfere with the growth and development of self-supporting institutions of the gospel, or to appropriate the results of the expenditure and toil of others.[16]

It is important to note that there was such trust in those who manifested obedience to the Great Commission that they were usually ready to accept each other's message as "evangelical" if its foundation was the doctrine of the Trinity and

[15] *Church Congress, Nottingham, 1897,* pp. 161–162.
[16] *The Message and the Messenger,* p. 7.

the Incarnation. Beyond this there was at most a desire for explicit acceptance of the ecumenical creeds. There was on the part of the missionaries of the regular agencies no wish to press for a minute spelling out of the basic doctrines in particular forms, as is often the case at the present moment. "Evangelical" had no sectarian meaning, and "Evangelicals" were not a partisan group jealous of sharing the name with others. The Roman Catholic and the Orthodox churches were usually the only ones excluded from the designation. Missionary obedience was the best proof of being "evangelical."

The missionaries and their constituency in the homelands were quite convinced about the "reflex influence" of missionary unity upon their supporting churches. A typical assertion is that statement by William Warren:

> One of the good things that have come to us from foreign missions is the strengthening of the bond of Christian brotherhood in the churches at home. This world-work has brought Christian hearts and wills nearer together. In proportion as the work of Christ and of the Kingdom has expanded, the hearts engaged in that work have been brought into closer Christian bonds. The influence of Christian missions has been to soften the superiority of sect, and thus promote Christian charity the world over.[17]

Furthermore, it was generally agreed, following Rufus Anderson and Henry Venn, that the work of foreign missionaries in any land was temporary and their methods all subject to the one goal of raising up the great agency for the effective proclamation of the gospel—the native church. The missionaries were to be evangelists, not pastors and rulers of the churches. They were to get out when their work was done and go to "the regions beyond." The young churches, self-

[17] *These for Those*, p. 320.

governing, self-supporting, and self-propagating, were expected to take up the evangelistic task with an effectiveness
the missionaries could never hope to have. Mr. Pope told the
Ootacamund Conference in 1858 that the missionaries must
look forward to the day when there will arise a Church of
India differing in many respects from any Christian community in Europe or America.[18] Four years later at the
Punjab Conference at Lahore, the Rev. John Newton of the
American Presbyterian Mission at Lahore brought in a paper
on "An Indian Catholic Church," which received hearty
assent.[19] He argued that spiritual unity required visible unity,
that an Indian catholic church was feasible, and that it could
combine essential Congregational, Presbyterial, and Episcopal elements, yet allow liberty for indigenous development.
Any obstacles would come from Europe and America, not
from India. The plan was sound in conception, but did not
allow for enough indigenous initiative in shaping the emerg-
ing church. The proposal was warmly seconded by an Anglican, who said that "the future Church of India will be a
church of its own type." The vision was never lost in India
and a long series of mergers resulted in the formation
eventually of the Church of South India and in the current
negotiations for a comprehensive united Church of North
India. The aspirations in India can be matched in China and
elsewhere.[20] The capture of missionary thought by "the
colonial mind" and the increase of confessionalism, which
were behind the timidity about organic union in the discus-

[18] *Op. cit.*, p. 334.
[19] *Punjab Missionary Conference, Lahore, 1862–63,* pp. 299–317.
[20] An example from China: an extract from an article, "Church Organization in China," by a presbyter, in the *Chinese Recorder,* Vol. XVI, No. 1
(January–February, 1885), p. 31: "In conclusion, a Church of the living God
is being builded in this Empire. It is to be of Chinese, for Chinese, and,
sooner or later, to be controlled and governed exclusively by Chinese. Faithful
missionaries of Christ desire nothing so much as to see their part of the work
done, and the young Church, and vigorous, turned over to those who, under
God, are to be its natural guardians."

sions at the Ecumenical Missionary Conference in 1900,
delayed the emergence of that independent church that
would be one and different, but the nationals championed
the cause when some of the missionaries lost courage. Bishop
Azariah of Dornakal was not timid about speaking his mind
to Western churchmen. At the Lausanne Conference in 1927
he made that famous statement: "Unity may be theoretically
a desirable ideal in Europe and America, but it is vital to the
life of the Church in the mission field. The divisions of
Christendom may be a source of weakness in Christian countries, but in non-Christian lands they are a sin and a
scandal." [21] At Edinburgh ten years later he declared: "We
want you to take us seriously when we say that the problem
is one of life and death to us." [22]

For all these reasons then: because the missionaries and
their societies were held together from the beginning in a
bond of unity which increased with continued participation;
because they regarded themselves as together engaged in the
conquest of the whole world for Christ, were cognizant of
the presence and fruit of the Holy Spirit in the work of all
missions; because they mutually recognized each other as
truly belonging to the Church of Christ, preached one message of salvation; and because they regarded themselves as
temporary and expendable agents in the fostering of an
indigenous Church that would be self-governing, self-supporting, self-propagating, and "different"—the world mission
of the Protestant churches would not be a totally chaotic
multiplicity of overlapping and competing agencies, although
it would always be hampered by the jealous sovereignty of
the sending churches. There would always be some measure
of consultation, adjustment, and cooperation.

[21] *World Conference on Faith and Order, Lausanne, 1927, Proceedings
of —*, edited by H. N. Bate, pp. 53–54.   1137
[22] *The Second World Conference on Faith and Order, Edinburgh, 1927*,
edited by Leonard Hodgson, p. 49.

Comity and Its Fruits

Moreover, the keen awareness of the meager resources in men and money for so vast an undertaking sharpened the sense of need for agreement about a division of the regions and peoples of the world among the existing societies and the delimitation of local territory for responsible evangelistic occupation. "Economy" was almost an obsession with the directors or board members and the secretaries. "In reference to a division of the unevangelized world among different missionary societies, such a division has been proposed in order that no part of the world be long neglected and that proper comity be observed among different societies." "Comity between different missionary organizations, as well as economy, requires that the entire field should be so distributed as to prevent any waste of material through two or more societies occupying the same field or any portion of the same field." [23] This continuing concern for faithful stewardship of men, money, and all resources will be noted in the following chapter. Comity, "denominationalism by geography" within a total world mission, proved to be the scheme that was developed for relating the separate denominational societies and boards to the total world-wide task.

In *One Great Ground of Hope* Dr. Van Dusen has shown how "the Christian world mission has been both the precursor and the progenitor of the effort after Christian unity." [24] None of that story needs to be duplicated. He divides Christian collaboration in the Protestant mission into six types: consultation; comity; cooperation in joint action; federation;

[23] Clark, N. G., *Missionary Comity. Methods and Means for Carrying Forward the Work in the Foreign Field* (1886), p. 1, and *True and False Economy in Missions* (1891), p. 3.
[24] Van Dusen, H. P., p. 17.

union institutions; and organic church union. This chapter will be concluded with a few words relating comity to these several forms of collaboration.

Consultation came largely out of the arrangement of comity agreements. Some of the earliest international consultation was between the secretaries and directors of societies about areas of the world that were to be chosen for their missions and about more local territorial problems, as in the correspondence between the L.M.S. and the American Board about the Washington Islands, Singapore, and Madras, which led to a general agreement about comity. Even earlier and continuing for a long time—in fact, never having ceased—newly arriving missionaries scouting for locations sought the help of missionaries residing in the port cities or areas of entrance. Dr. George W. Carpenter called attention to the fact that until the railroad was built, every newcomer to the Congo had to walk overland from the seacoast to Stanley Pool before he could begin the up-river boat trip, and for a minimum of four days he enjoyed the hospitality of the Bas-Congo stations. The residents gave him advice about the journey, factors to observe in beginning work, and above all where to locate his new mission. Such were the simplest beginnings of consultation. Next there were discussions and agreement with neighbors about boundaries. Then came local, regional, and eventually national conferences for consultation. They had to do with language study, decisions on theological terms, orthography, and information about customs, cultures, religions, and methods. But, most important for the whole future course of cooperation, they dealt with matters made urgent by the comity agreements effected between the missions, questions which would render futile the delimitation of territory if they could not be solved. Members and inquirers moved about, and unless there were standards for admission and transfer the discipline of adjoining missions could be undermined. Without uniform schedules of pay for workers and careful inquiry about applicants, evangelists, teachers, and servants could move from mission to mission, forcing competition for their services. These matters were the heart of the subject matter of the early conferences. Having met once for such matters, and having found it good, the tendency was to meet repeatedly at intervals and to set up an association to call and arrange meetings. Moreover, disagreement about comity matters which could not be settled by conversations between two missions, required wider consultation, and associations either began as instruments of arbitration or set up boards of arbitration. Down to the Edinburgh Conference of 1910, comity matters including arbitration were the chief factor stimulating the establishment of continuing associations, and after that date the new committees or associations, largely brought into being through the efforts of the Continuation Committee under John R. Mott, gave much attention to the furtherance of comity and arbitration where the development in this had been slow. The decisions made with regard to comity matters and the creation of boards of cooperation were the first steps in actual cooperation. By the time of the Edinburgh Conference so much progress had been made beyond this that comity was regarded as "negative cooperation" or the primary stage of cooperation. Yet it was essential. Delimitation of territory had given the denominations security. Consultation and decisions about comity matters acquainted the missionaries with one another, taught them that they could trust each other, and induced them to take the first common actions together.

There was plenty of informal, unofficial cooperation at the very beginning of the Protestant missionary enterprise. There was even official cooperation such as the establishment of the United Foreign Missionary Society in the United States by the authoritative action of three national church judicatories in 1816. On the fields it was comity that led to the first concrete steps in official cooperation, as has been indicated. Agreements about such things as discipline and employment were speedily followed with cooperative measures respecting literature production, printing presses, publications, and distribution of literature. These matters were often called "comity in printing." Such agreement was extended to adoption of a common version of the Bible. Then came "comity in medical institutions," "comity in education"—meaning usually as the first project, a union training school for pastors and evangelists. So even before some fields had embarked on the process of division of territory into spheres of occupation, in others comity had taken on the meaning of cooperation in union activities and institutions. With the eventual establishment of the National Christian Councils, which administer union programs and projects, the two lines of consultation and cooperation which arose out of comity merged.

The federation of missions, in contrast to consultative national missionary conferences and councils, was the accompaniment of comity plans for a whole country in the Philippines and Puerto Rico, and these were transformed into federations of churches with the rise of evangelical denominational bodies. Four Presbyterian Missions in Korea federated upon the establishment of comity agreements with the intention of creating one national church, and after the comity agreement with the Methodists a General Council of Evangelical Missions came about. All national missionary conferences which had programs of common action before 1910 were federations which had their roots in the efforts to achieve and maintain comity. Those after that time, however, were the result largely of Dr. Mott's efforts under the authority of the Continuation Committee. Federation of churches ought to have been easily built upon denominationalism by geography, and it was the natural development in Puerto Rico and the Philippines. Moreover, it was a theoretical achievement in the Congo and certain Latin

American countries, where a single name was used for all the churches and a common transferable membership honored, but the judicatories for implementing it were never established and the national federation was a federation of missions until the recent creation of true National Christian Councils. Comity in Kenya resulted in a thoroughgoing effort to achieve organic union, and when it failed through "High Church" intervention, a federation was attempted; and when that failed, there was a federation of some of the missions. The Kenya Christian Council was late in formation.

It was indicated earlier in this chapter that denominationalism by geography was expected, by many of the missionaries at least, to lead directly to an independent, truly national united church when the missionary era came to an end. One great purpose of delimitation of territory was the isolation of denominational differences in order to prevent confusing and distracting the native Christians. There was almost universal mutual recognition of validity, and transfer of membership was supposed to be an integral part of comity. The English Presbyterian and American Reformed Missions in Amoy established one church at the outset. L.M.S. and American Board churches tended to favor participation in church unions. The "colonial mind" which stressed the necessity of long tutelage under missionary control, the strengthening of denominationalism in the sending churches during the second half of the nineteenth century, and the later rise of world-wide confessionalism joined in frustrating the fulfillment of the early vision. Robert E. Speer inveighed against the concept of an indigenous self-governing church that allowed the incorporation of the young churches into the denominational structures in the Western nations, although even in his own church they were held as presbyteries and synods under an American General Assembly. When that phase passed, Presbyterian and Reformed Churches also became pioneers in church union movements. Nevertheless, despite the long delays, organic church union had its roots in the practice and the assumptions of comity.

It is difficult to see how the effective missionary occupation of all lands that were open could have been achieved without the practice of comity. Without it cooperation would also have been delayed indefinitely. Comity is the bedrock foundation on which there has been built throughout Asia, Africa, Latin America, and the Pacific a Protestant Christian community conscious of its unity, and into which, by that reflex influence in which the missionaries placed much hope, the Western sending churches have gradually been incorporated. Remarks of two archbishops of Canterbury might be recalled. Archbishop Lang said:

> The existence of the ecumenical movement, as expressed in the three conferences at Oxford, Edinburgh, and Madras, might justly be described as "a wholly new fact in Christian history." It reveals the possibility of a unity of Christians which transcends barriers of race and nationality and brings to the rescue of the world the saving energies of the kingdom of God.[25]

And the better-known statement of Archbishop Temple:

> As though in preparation for a time like this, God has been building up a Christian fellowship which now extends into every nation, and binds citizens of them all together in true unity and mutual love. No human agency has planned this. It is the result of the great missionary enterprise of the last hundred and fifty years. . . . Almost incidentally, the great world fellowship has arisen; it is the great new fact of our era. . . . Here is the one great ground of hope for the coming days—this world-wide Christian fellowship, this ecumenical movement. . . .[26]

[25] *The Oxford Conference* (*Official Report*), ed. by J. H. Oldham, p. 22.
[26] Temple, W., *The Church Looks Forward*, pp. 2–4.

But one who knows the missionary literature of the end of the eighteenth century and the first half of the nineteenth century must be aware of the fact that this development has not been so "incidental" and so completely without planning. This was a vision and a hope which animated and inspired many who were devoted to missions.

Plans should be such as would admit the coalition of all Christians, whatever may be their sectarian names and opinions.

THOMAS B. SKINNER

All show extraordinary harmony—avoiding monotony of unison, but seldom a discordant note.

The Spirit of Missions is the spirit of Concord. The keynote was struck on the plains of Bethlehem; and all who have sympathy with the angelic announcement are sure to think, feel, utter, and act in concert, both with the heavenly host and with one another.

BARON STOW

CHAPTER II

The Rise and Acceptance of Comity

The Beginnings

THE spirit of fellowship and cooperation that characterized
the Protestant missionary enterprise from its inception was
more than a vague sense of unity. It manifested itself from
the earliest days in policy and in practical measures. The
denominationalism by geography that was effected through
comity was one of the earliest and most universal evidences
of the fact that the foreign mission carried on by a number
of independent agencies was essentially a common concern
to those engaging in it. Comity came about because the
directors of the mission boards and societies were zealous for
the total evangelization of the world and wished to see their
meager resources in men and money applied effectively
toward that goal, and because their missionaries in the field
wished to eliminate all elements of denominational rivalry
and contention which might hamper speedy evangelization
of the area. When a few of the leading societies had adopted
the policy of delimitation of fields and noninterference in
the affairs of others, most other agencies followed them.
Thereafter the missionaries initiated and carried through a
countless number of local agreements, seldom referring them
back to the society's or board's headquarters, excepting perhaps in the course of a general summary of the year's activities.

It seems that the idea of local or regional comity was an
early fruit of the intimate fellowship and constant consultation enjoyed by the representatives of the several societies

who almost simultaneously took up residence in the great port cities and national or provincial capitals. Yet at the same time the directors of the societies at home were thinking of dividing the whole world after the same fashion. These places were large enough in size and population so that missionaries of three or more societies might locate in them and yet, with a little care, avoid trespassing on each other's work. They could decide upon location of buildings, spheres of endeavor, the employment of teachers, translators, and servants; and also join forces in language study, Bible translation, literature production, and in a common front before the local government. When missionaries of new societies arrived, scouting for a suitable place to begin a new mission, the older residents generously gave them lodging and advice.

These missionaries in the ports and capitals came together informally for many years in order to pray, study, and have fellowship together. However, since Anglo-Saxons in general and Americans in particular have a tendency toward organization, they eventually formed local missionary associations. Continental European missionaries, when present, were also naturally drawn into them. The earliest local association of which there is record is the Bombay Missionary Union, founded in 1825. The success of the local unions led to regional and ultimately to national associations. The earliest informal, unofficial comity agreements were largely by-products of the friendly consultation among members of a local association or among the missionary residents in ports where an association had not been formally created. Other agreements about delimitation of territory resulted from the advice given the scouts of new missions by the residents of the ports. Thus the American Board in opening a mission in South Africa was directed to Natal by Dr. John Philip of the London Missionary Society (L.M.S.) in Capetown, and the initial party of missionaries sent out in 1834 were directed to go to him for advice and aid.[1] The local associations never took formal action with respect to territorial agreements or new locations, because they had no legislative or administrative authority and the members would have thought such formal action ill advised. Early agreements were verbal, not written, and even in a later day they were seldom committed to writing or referred back to the headquarters of the societies and boards. They became unwritten tradition, passed on to each new generation of missionaries and national pastors, and were accepted as binding by nearly all. The regional and national associations of a later time found themselves responsible for administering a vast system of unwritten agreements and had to provide the means of arbitrating disputes. Such procedure was scarcely needed until a large number of agencies had entered a field and sometimes inadvertently got in one another's way. Such local action was both the cause and result of the policy or attitude of the societies.

The practice of comity first appears clearly in the missionary literature in the decade of the 1830's, but it is apparent that it was already being applied to the hinterland of the ports and that the boards and societies were already endeavoring to apply the underlying principle in their expanding operations. The first recorded example of a comity agreement, however, occurred in the South Pacific, far from a major commercial or administrative center. This was the compact made in July, 1830, between the Wesleyan missionaries, Nathanael Turner and William Cross, on the one hand, and John Williams and Charles Barf of the L.M.S., on the other. By this agreement Tonga and Fiji were to be occupied by the Methodists and Samoa (the Navigators) by the L.M.S.[2]

[1] American Board of Commissioners for Foreign Missions, *Annual Report, 1834*, p. 145; Groves, C. P., *History of the Planting of Christianity in Africa*, vol. I, pp. 263–264; Smith, E. W., *Life and Times of Daniel Lindley*, pp. 49–51, 64–65.
[2] Williams, J., *A Narrative of Missionary Enterprises in the South Sea*

Williams and Barf had arrived at Tongatabu while en route to the Fiji Islands, the New Hebrides, and the Navigators or Samoa. Tonga had been the scene of the ill-fated pioneer venture of the L.M.S. in 1797, which had ended in failure. However, a native evangelist had later established a mission there. Denominational and institutional distinctions meant nothing to this evangelist, and when Wesleyan missionaries appeared he and his people invited them to settle among them. The Methodists upon arrival found three or four hundred Christians awaiting them. The mission prospered. John Williams reported that in the course of their conversation Messrs. Turner and Cross suggested to the visitors that Fiji was closely related to Tonga while Samoa had somewhat similar connections with the other areas of L.M.S. missions. Considerations of proximity, politics, and linguistics, therefore, they said, made a division of responsibility desirable. Tonga and Fiji should be recognized as the area of Wesleyan operations, while the L.M.S. should add Samoa to its present territory. Williams and Barf gave hearty agreement. They stipulated only that when the Wesleyan reinforcements arrived on Fiji they should receive as their own the two native evangelists whom the L.M.S. then had working there and take over the direction of their work.

The word comity would not be devised until another half a century had passed, but four men in a friendly conference on a South Pacific island had contributed decisively to the formation of a pattern that was coming to prevail over wide areas. This particular compact was of the utmost importance because it led to official acceptance of the principles of comity by the societies which the men represented. John Williams explained his intention in these words:

Islands, pp. 301–302; Lovett, R., *History of the London Missionary Society, 1795–1895*, vol. I, pp. 284–285; Findlay, G. G. and W. W. Holdsworth, *History of the Wesleyan Methodist Missionary Society*, vol. III, pp. 295–296.

And here I may just remark upon the desirableness of every Society having a distinct sphere of labour among a heathen people. Much as I should rejoice in being associated with an Episcopalian, a Baptist, or a Methodist brother, who did not attach primary importance to secondary objects, yet the interests of every Mission, especially in the early years of its progress, seem to me to require another line of conduct. The natives, through comprehending very imperfectly our objects, would at once discern a difference in the modes of worship, and their attention would of necessity be divided and distracted. Being also of an inquisitive disposition, they would demand a reason for every little deviation, which would lead to explanations, first from one party, and then from the other, and thus evils would arise, which might otherwise never have existed. There would have been another great inconvenience, in the present instance, had we both gone to one group of islands, from the circumstance of the Wesleyan Missionaries having adopted a different orthography and alphabet, as well as different elementary and other books. I do therefore sincerely hope, that the directors or conductors of all Missionary Societies, will ever be ready in this way, to sacrifice denominational peculiarities, to the great object of their institution.[3]

As one might have expected from their general conduct of affairs, both the Wesleyan Methodist Society and the L.M.S. saw this problem from the same point of view as John Williams, when he reported the agreement to them during his visit to London. The Methodists accepted Williams' statement without waiting for verification from Turner and Cross, and in February, 1836, the two societies formally ratified the compact made on the field for the delimitation of territory in the South Pacific.[4]

This influential precedent later had an unhappy sequel,

[3] *Op. cit.*, p. 303.
[4] Findley G. G. and W. W. Holdsworth, *op. cit.*, vol. III, p. 347; Lovett, R., *op. cit.*, vol. I, pp. 284–285, only repeats Williams and does not document the action in L.M.S. records.

which demonstrated the inferiority of a verbal compact to a written agreement. Since most comity agreements were similar verbal assents, it is astounding that there was in general so little disagreement about them. In this particular instance Nathanael Turner, when later questioned, denied that such a definite and specific agreement had been made. He could recall only a general understanding that overlapping and competition should be avoided.[5] Conflict resulted because other Wesleyan missionaries, not knowing about the agreement, had begun work on Samoa. They withdrew upon receiving instructions from their Society in London, but Samoan converts attached to the mission refused to accept the transfer to the Congregationalists.[6] Several attempts were made at intervals to effect a union, but in vain. When after some decades it became apparent that the division was permanent, the Australian Methodist Church took the Samoans under its care. It sent them a missionary in 1857. Subsequent efforts to bring the two bodies together were also fruitless.[7]

The officers of the L.M.S. chanced to be engaged in other questions of comity at the time of the ratification of the agreement with the Methodists. Correspondence was then being carried on with its sister board across the Atlantic, the American Board of Commissioners for Foreign Missions. Some major principles of comity emerged clearly from these discussions and were embodied in a statement of policy by the American Board. This influenced the other contemporary missionary societies toward a consensus on fundamental policy which became the unwritten rule observed by most of the home base agencies and the warrant for the countless local comity agreements that were made around the world.

The officers of the American Board in Boston had requested

[5] Findlay, G. G. and W. W. Holdsworth, *op. cit.*, p. 296.
[6] *Ibid.*, pp. 348ff.
[7] Burton, J. W., *Modern Missions in the South Pacific*, pp. 84–85.

the Sandwich Island Mission to send one of its missionaries
in Hawaii on a tour of exploration to the Washington Islands,
as the Americans then called the northern group of the
Marquesas Islands. The Rev. C. S. Stewart accordingly visited
those islands in 1829. When he made his report, his brethren
in Hawaii wrote to the L.M.S. missionaries at the Society
Islands, informing them that they contemplated establishing
a mission there. The English brethren replied on February 1,
1832, that they did not distinguish the northern cluster of
islands as distinct from the Marquesas, that one of their
number had visited the group and had left several native
teachers there, and that they had already recommended that
the London headquarters send out immediately a party of
six missionaries. Three other members of the Sandwich Island
Mission were then dispatched as a deputation both to visit
the Washington Islands and to confer with the English Congregationalists on Raietea, Huahine, and Tahiti. The Englishmen informed their visitors, who profited greatly by the
consultations, that they desired that the Americans should
defer further action until they should hear from their directors in London, but, nevertheless, should such a delay
seem inexpedient to the Americans, they would cheerfully
relinquish all claims to the northern islands. Apparently the
local men believed that they enjoyed freedom of decision in
such matters. When the deputation returned to Hawaii and
made its report, the Mission voted to proceed at once, but as
no physician was available at the time, the departure of the
missionary party was postponed until the following year.[8]

Meanwhile the Prudential Committee of the American
Board had received an account of these proceedings. Having
considered the matter, the Committee made the pronouncement that: "It is contrary to their general principles to inter-

[8] American Board of Commissioners for Foreign Missions, *Annual Report,*
1833, pp. 87–88.

fere with other missionary societies; and besides it is found that a mission to the Washington Islands can be more conveniently sustained by the London Missionary Society than by the Board."[9] The Sandwich Island Mission was advised to take no further steps unless decisive measures had already been carried forward before the reception of these instructions. The party had, indeed, already left Honolulu on July 2, 1833. However, it encountered grave difficulties and returned the following May.[10] The area was then left to the L.M.S.

It was at this very time that the new American mission in Natal was assisted in location and settlement by Dr. Philip and the L.M.S. brethren in South Africa, and that an adjustment was being made at Madras. The American Board's Prudential Committee voted in 1834 to establish the press for its Tamil Mission at Madras.[11] The press was established, and then the missionary of the L.M.S. at Madras, on the grounds of the need for concentration of efforts, proposed that the Americans take over Black Town from the L.M.S. for more general work. This was done.[12] But about the same time the London brethren declared that American activities at Singapore conflicted with their interests. Singapore had been selected as the central station for all American Board missions in East Asia, and missionaries moved from Canton to that place in July, 1834. Missionary personnel at that station numbered ten in 1836. The major activities there were to be a press and a seminary for training native workers for all the Asian missions. However, by 1841 Singapore had been abandoned because of difficulties and more especially because of the objections of the L.M.S.[13]

[9] *Ibid.*, *1833*, p. 88.
[10] *Ibid.*, *1834*, p. 93.
[11] *Ibid.*, *1834*, p. 84.
[12] *Ibid.*, *1837*, pp. 72, 146, 147.
[13] *Ibid.*, *1835*, p. 68; *Ibid.*, *1836*, pp. 74–76; *Ibid.*, *1837*, pp. 89–90; *Ibid.*, *1841*, pp. 35, 144.

The Singapore venture called forth the fullest statement that has been found regarding the common view that the great ports should be regarded as common ground.[14] The passage in the *Annual Report* of the American Board for 1837 reads:

Singapore, Calcutta, Madras, Bombay, Smyrna, and perhaps a few other great marts of commerce, must necessarily be, to some extent, common ground to the different Protestant missionary societies. They are the natural entrances to great fields of missionary labor. In them printing on a large scale can be performed most economically and most advantageously. It is believed, indeed, that claims should not be asserted by missionary societies to the exclusive occupation of any large sea-ports, which will oblige other societies to transport by land their heavy printing apparatus and materials to interior places, or to send them to places where the property will be endangered, or the operations of the press restricted, from any cause. The occupation of these places for printing establishments should not be regarded as an encroachment of one society upon the field of another. And the reasons which make it proper for the printing establishments of different missionary societies to be placed in these marts of commerce, make it proper to connect with the establishments whatever is necessary to render them in the highest degree effective. Missionaries should reside there who are conversant with the different languages in which books are to be printed, and they should have the assistance of learned native helpers; and these missionaries and their helpers should be allowed to find such employment among the inhabitants as may be necessary to diversify their employments; give helpful exercise to their bodies and minds; acquaint them with the native character, manners, customs, and literature; perfect them in the native languages and dialects; and, in short, prepare them for their work as authors and editors, and make them feel that they are usefully em-

[14] *Ibid.*, 1837, pp. 87–90.

ployed and laboring to the best advantage. Of course, they should be permitted to have schools, to preach to native congregations, and to perform all other kinds of missionary labor within reasonable territorial bounds.

This right to mutual occupation by a number of agencies in the case of the great ports and capitals is frequently asserted by many societies.[15]

The American Board at its annual meeting the previous year, 1836, had called all missionary societies to a kind of global comity arrangement in order to speed the total evangelization of the whole world. Its pronouncement was one of the long series of policy statements that came from the pen of its secretary, Rufus Anderson, the foremost American missionary statesman.[16] All the evangelical churches, it is asserted, certainly have in view the publishing of the gospel to the whole unevangelized world. All the followers of Christ should look upon this as feasible *now* through human instrumentality and as a work to be accomplished without delay. All the societies should look upon the task as a whole in which they act on behalf of evangelical Christianity. To this end they ought to accept definite spheres of responsibility, calculate the resources in men, money, and labor needed, estimate the length of time required to carry to completion each particular agency's allotted responsibility. "Each would then have its own work clearly in view; would compare its means with the extent of the enterprise; would measure the progress made towards the desired result; and would press onward with singleness of purpose, with well directed exertions, and with animation and hope, till the earth should be FILLED with the knowledge of the Lord." The English

[15] Existing cities of great size were always "open" to occupation by more than one mission; problems arose only when a new city was founded in what was formerly a rural area. See the final chapter.

[16] *Ibid.*, 1836, pp. 108–117; *Outline of a Plan of Missions for the Board* (1843), pp. 17ff.

brethren were at present undertaking more than the Americans, and the French and German churches were beginning their missionary enterprise but could be expected to be little more than auxiliary to the "grand spiritual armies of England and America." Therefore: "Acting on the principle of not interfering with other evangelical missionary Societies, and with the evangelical churches of other portions of Christendom—since there is room enough for all—the American Board will direct its efforts to specific portions of the great field." The Board's specific responsibilities within the world-wide mission were then set forth: there would be two lines of advance in Africa, penetrating the interior from Cape Palmas on the west coast and Port Natal in the south. When these two met there would be a continuous line of stations some 4,500 miles long! One line of missionary advance would run from Macedonia through Constantinople, across northern Asia Minor, thence through Persia and Afghanistan and turn south through western and southern India to Ceylon: while a second Asian missionary frontier would begin in Greece, cross southern Asia Minor, Syria, Palestine, and end in Mesopotamia. A third Asian line would advance northward from Indonesia to China and Japan. Finally, the Board would be responsible for an advance in the Pacific from the base in Hawaii.

The following year the same Board, pursuing its grand vision, resolved that in encouragement to, and in unity with, other socieites striving for the total evangelization of the world, it would "endeavor to promote the best understanding at home and abroad between their agents and missionaries and our own." [17]

The secretaries and directors of the L.M.S. responded to the American Board's overtures in a letter dated February 7, 1838.[18] This letter asserted that the principle set forth by the

[17] A.B.C.F.M., *Annual Report, 1837*, p. 30.
[18] *Ibid.*, 1838, p. 32.

American Board was one that commended itself to everyone
with a knowledge of the practical operations of missions and
one on which the English societies had long acted. The L.M.S.
accordingly welcomed the American missionaries at Canton
and Madras, and would be glad to see them enter the other
presidencies in India. There were in those places opportunities and ample scope for the efforts of all. The letter
stated further:

> We have already adverted to our having acted on the prin-
> ciple of regarding certain stations as common ground; and, in
> relation to other British societies, we have added another
> principle, which we should be happy to extend to our co-
> operation with yourselves; under the assurance that, if prac-
> ticable, it cannot but prove agreeable and beneficial, viz.
> When any section of the missionary field is occupied by one
> society, it is deemed highly advantageous and suitable that
> another society, contemplating operations in the same section,
> should, in the first instance, communicate with the society
> already in the field.

Recent rapid expansion of the English societies has required
frequent application of this principle, and it has produced
satisfactory results. Therefore, "we [i.e., the British societies]
are now engaged in revising regulation for its application
to be sent to the brethren abroad, connected with the several
societies, among whom we hope the benefits resulting will
be equal to those which we have experienced at home."

The Prudential Committee considered the communication
of the L.M.S., and on its behalf Rufus Anderson brought
before the next full meeting of the Board a paper entitled
"Interference of Different Missionary Societies With Each
Other's Proceedings." [19] Anderson pointed out that six
denominations were then engaged in missionary programs,
including Congregationalists (apparently the term covers

[19] *Ibid.,* 1838, pp. 32-34.

both Congregationalists and Baptists), Presbyterians, Lutherans, Methodists, Episcopalians, and Moravians; some of these comprising several divisions that were carried over into missions. There were eighteen missionary societies then in the field: eight British, five American, one French, and four German. Since every part of the heathen world is equally accessible to all of them, geographical considerations cannot be expected to draw one society to this area and another to that, and thus keep their operations distinct and apart. As a matter of fact, many important fields are already jointly occupied, not counting the great ports which are common ground. Instances in which the American Board is involved with others are given, such as Cape Palmas, Zululand, the Peloponnesus and Attica, Constantinople, Bombay, Jaffna, and Bangkok. There are remarkable cases of complete non-interference, such as the Baptist mission in Burma, the Church Missionary Society's work in Egypt and Abyssinia, and the American Board missions to the Armenians and Persian Nestorians. When G. T. E. Rhenius and his colleagues left the Church Missionary Society (C.M.S.) and applied to the L.M.S., the latter refused to accept them unless they should surrender Tinnevelly and remove elsewhere. The American Board had inadvertently interfered with the L.M.S. work at the Washington Islands and Singapore, but in no other instance has it ever been guilty of interference. There is no necessity for such interference. It may be avoided, the statement adds, if four simple rules are observed by all. First, each society should claim no more territory than it can occupy without long delay and undertake no more work than it can do thoroughly. Second, certain great "centers of human society and marts of commerce" should be regarded as common ground. However, this rule should be qualified by a proviso recommended by the L.M.S., namely, that even here a geographical division be undertaken in order to prevent the confusion and evils that would arise from the different missions seeking their scholars, agents, and congregations from the same families, and thus "furnishing, as the natives in India express it, two bazaars," with resulting dissatisfaction and instability. The buildings of each mission should be in the division of the port city where its missionaries actually labor, and all such arrangements should be made by the missionaries on the spot in mutual consultation. Thirdly, no other common ground need be conceded, unless under very special circumstances indeed. Every missionary society should resolutely respect the territorial limits of each other's operations, no matter how strong the temptation might be to rush into a district where as the result of some pioneering effort there is now the prospect of the yield of an early harvest. Only a body of Christians which believes that the preaching of the gospel of salvation has been exclusively committed to it would be guilty of such an act.

> It will no doubt require strong principle to resist the temptation just mentioned; but it will be a great point gained in the work of missions, when the *territorial* limits of the districts occupied by each evangelical missionary society, are respected by the missionaries and members of all other missionary societies. And surely among missionary societies this may be done without a controversy, and even without a congress.

Fourth, all should accept the L.M.S. suggestion that "when any [large] section of the missionary field is occupied by one society, it shall be deemed suitable that another society contemplating operations in the same section, should in the first instance, communicate with the society already in the field."

This document written by Rufus Anderson had been committed by the Prudential Committee to a special committee of five. This committee brought in three resolutions which form the celebrated American Board policy statement on comity, unanimously adopted by the Annual Meeting of 1838:

> *Resolved,* That in the opinion of this Board the subject of non-interference in the plans and operations of different missionary societies among the heathen, demands a serious consideration by such societies with a view if possible, to a mutual and satisfactory understanding, and that this Board instruct its Prudential Committee to direct special attention to the subject and to correspond with such other societies as they may think proper, for the purpose of securing so desirable an object.
>
> *Resolved,* That this Board regard the principle centers of business and marts of commerce in the immediate neighborhood of great fields, which are receiving or demanding missionary labor, as common ground, for the missionaries of different societies; and would suggest the importance of mutual agreement, so far as it shall be possible, among missionaries residing in such places, with regard to the territorial bounds to their labors.
>
> *Resolved,* That this Board respectfully suggest and recommend, whenever a society has a mission already in a district or country where another society contemplates operations, that it be deemed suitable that the societies whose missionaries are already in the field, be appraized of the fact, and consulted, before such operations are commenced.

One member of the special committee which recommended the adoption of the resolutions was the Rev. David Abeel, who had served as a missionary of the American Bible Society and observer for the American Board on the China coast and in southeast Asia. In this same year, 1838, he published his exhortation to missionary zeal, a book entitled *The Missionary Convention*. This work recounted the course of an imaginary great convention of representatives of all heathen peoples and Christian proponents and opponents of missions. The missionary Christians are portrayed as either presenting the claims of the Great Commission and the needs of mankind or refuting the objections and misrepresentations of their opponents in the churches. The heathen ask embarrassing questions of the Christians and make strong claims upon the missionary societies to meet the needs of their respective nations. One of the protagonists for effective missionary action makes a plea for comity.[20] He asserts that there is one rule of action which if observed by all sects would sacrifice no party interest while also guaranteeing that the more important interests of the Redeemer's Kingdom be not sacrificed to sectarian agrandizement. Comity would prevent conflict and confusion, and would also divert the attention of societies and their missionaries from areas already occupied to those still unoccupied and destitute. Were this the case, then "how soon their dying fellowmen in every land would feel the quickening influence. The maddening shouts of superstition would soon cease; the groans of the self-tortured devotee would be heard no more; the errors and vices of heathendom would pass away, and the heavy curse of God be lifted from a rebellious world."

Meanwhile the American Board put its announced policy into effect immediately, and arranged a mutually satisfactory division of territory with the Protestant Episcopal Church at Cape Palmas in West Africa.[21] Thereafter the missionaries of the Board in various fields entered into numerous comity compacts,[22] and the policy and practice were so thoroughly

[20] Abeel, D., *The Missionary Convention*, pp. 95–96.

[21] A.B.C.F.M., *Annual Report, 1839*, p. 55.

[22] The American Board is a good example of the elusiveness of comity agreements. Miss Mary A. Walker, Librarian of the Board, reported the following agreements known from the *Annual Reports* and records at headquarters, but they are only a small part of the total: Angola, 1927, with the United Church of Canada; Mexico, the 1914 general comity agreement, and 1918, exchange of territory with Southern Methodists; China, 1901, division of Paotingfu with Presbyterian Church in the U.S.A., 1911 or 1912—exchange of outstations with L.M.S.; 1911—Kalgan turned over to Methodist Protestants; 1867–1907—successive delimitations of Pangchuang field with neigh-

accepted that it was not deemed necessary to mention it in the famous "Outline of Missionary Policy" of 1856. It is apparently covered in the avowal of the need of economy.[23] Nor does Rufus Anderson, the author of the policy statements of 1838 and 1856, lay stress on it in his book, *Foreign Missions, their Relations and Claims* (1869). Dr. N. G. Clark, in his *Discourse Commemorative of Rev. Rufus Anderson. D.D., LL.D.*, when eulogizing the statesmanship of the former secretary and stressing his effective leadership in the whole Protestant missionary enterprise, makes passing reference to the few exceptions which the Board has encountered in the observance of comity. When he states "that from the employees of certain societies bearing a Protestant name we may not invariably expect common Christian comity," that phrase *common Christian comity* reveals the general attitude and expectation.[24]

---

boring missions; 1857–66—division of Foochow area among C.M.S., Methodist Episcopal North, and American Board Missions; Micronesia, 1907—Truk and Ponape transferred to Liebenzeller Mission; 1910—Guam transferred to General Association of General Baptists; 1917—Gilbert Islands transferred to L.M.S.; India Marathi Mission; 1879—agreement with S.P.G.; 1892 and 1902—participation in comity rules of the Decennial Missionary Conference; 1902—revision of agreement with S.P.G.; 1907—agreement with Methodist Episcopal Mission; 1911—agreement with C.M.S., on division of territory north of Poona; 1912—agreement with Australian Christian Mission; 1914—revision of agreement with Methodist Episcopal Mission; 1914—agreement with American Presbyterian Mission on Satara district; 1923—another revision with Methodist Episcopal Mission; India Madura Mission, 1852–70—various divisions and exchanges with neighbors; Balkans, 1856–57—division of Bulgaria between Methodist Episcopal and American Board Missions; 1907—joint occupation of Sofia; 1921—Monastir in Jugoslavia turned over to Methodists, 1922—Serbia and Albania turned over to Methodists; Near East, 1870—Syrian and Nestorian Missions allocated to Presbyterian Church in the U.S.A.; 1910–11—unsuccessful attempts at agreements with Deutsches Hilfsbund and German Orient Mission; 1920—transfer of Mardin station to Presbyterians (returned in 1927); 1923–24—agreements with Presbyterians on Aleppo; and Philippines, participation in the home base agreement of 1898 and field comity agreement of 1901, the latter giving Mindanao to the Board.

[23] A.B.C.F.M., *Annual Report, 1856*, p. 51.

[24] Clark, N. G., *Discourse Commemorative of Rev. Rufus Anderson, D.D., LL.D.*, p. 26.

Dr. Clark restated the old arguments for comity in his pamphlets, *Missionary Comity* (1886) and *Economy in Missions* (1891).[25] He stresses the elimination of the waste and inefficiency which are products of overlapping and duplication, the confusion and embarrassment that are due to denominational differences in the same area, and the need for concentration and intensive development. He referred to the constant policy of the Board in these words:

> The American Board from the first, when almost the whole world was open to its choice, has studiously sought to carry out its own methods of work by taking countries or sections of countries not otherwise occupied. More than once it was withdrawn from fields originally selected, on the coming in of other agencies adequate to care for them, and sometimes at the sacrifice of no little time and effort.

He gives as illustrations the withdrawal from Canton and Shanghai in favor of the Presbyterian Church in the U.S.A., and the surrender of Amoy to the Reformed Church in America, when that body withdrew from the American Board and set up its own Board of Foreign Missions. He cites the giving up of whole fields, such as Persia, to the Presbyterians, when the New School and Old School General Assemblies united in 1870 and the former's constituency withdrew from participation in the American Board. A similar action in much later times was the handing over in 1927 of a large part of the Angola Mission in an agreement, including territorial delimitation, with the United Church of Canada after its formation.[26] Clark cited Japan, Mexico, and Spain as locations of later missions in districts selected because they were not occupied by others.

[25] Clark, N. G., *Missionary Comity—Methods and Means for Carrying Forward the Work in the Foreign Field* (1886) and *True and False Economy in Foreign Missions* (1896).
[26] Mimeographed document available from the Board.

The existing British societies in 1838 were already committed to the general observance of comity, as the officers of the L.M.S. had informed the American Board. It was not necessary then to say much more about it, only to practice it. Policy statements among the pioneer Protestant societies and boards are, therefore, rare, and it is somewhat unusual, but not surprising, to find the Wesleyan Methodist Missionary Society explicitly declaring its adherence to the principle in its "Statement of Policy" of April 29, 1914, where it is stated:

> In every district already occupied the Society is observing the recognized laws of comity with other Missions, so as to avoid overlapping of effort and waste of energy. In large city centers spheres of influence are determined by mutual agreement with other Missions; while in country districts larger areas have been marked off for occupation by the several missions. This rule will be closely followed in all natural expansion of the areas at present occupied. . . . A necessary proviso of the above rule is that where an area has been assigned to the Society it should be occupied adequately within a reasonable time; failing that, the right of sole occupation must be relinquished.[27]

Stock, in his *History of the Church Missionary Society*, affirms the staunch adherence of the C.M.S. and other major British societies to this policy and practice.[28] The various American agencies were apt to follow the lead of Rufus Anderson and the American Board and fell into line in this matter as in others. It was in India especially, where there was so largely set the general pattern of Protestant missionary work, and in the South Pacific that the actual practice of comity as delimitation of territory was early achieved and held up as the normal requirement of all Protestant agencies.

[27] Findlay G. G. and W. W. Holdsworth, *op. cit.*, vol. I, pp. 176–177.
[28] Stock, E., *History of the Church Missionary Society*, vol. III, p. 410.

The development in India will be treated in the following chapter.

The L.M.S. turned over areas in which it had pioneered in the South Pacific to other societies. Aneityum and Tanna in the New Hebrides were notable examples. Not only did it turn over the former to John Geddie of the Presbyterian Church of Nova Scotia in 1848, but provided him transportation and supplies through the services of the Society's ships. Three L.M.S. missionaries accompanied Geddie, and one, Thomas Powell, remained with him for a year.[29] Gradually, "on the principle of the division of labor," the L.M.S. gave over the remainder of its work in the New Hebrides to the Presbyterian Church.[30]

Bishop George Augustus Selwyn, the founder of the Melanesian Mission, set what was to be cited as a powerful precedent by Anglicans. He recognized the prior occupation of Aneityum by the Presbyterians, to whom he paid a friendly visit in 1849.[31] He proposed a division of territory between Anglicans and Presbyterians, which has remained the only formal comity agreement in the New Hebrides.[32] There are references to an "engagement" which he made with the L.M.S.[33] and to a general scheme of division of labor and responsibility among the societies at work in the South Pacific, which was tacitly accepted and followed.[34] The office of the Melanesian Mission has reported to the writer that, although generally accepted, no copy of a document embodying the agreement has ever been found. A later Bishop

[29] L.M.S., *Fifty-fifth Report, 1849*, p. 40; Lovett, R., *op. cit.*, pp. 406–7. J. W. Burton mentions that the agreement was made with the Presbyterians in 1848 (*op. cit.*, p. 87).
[30] Lovett, *op. cit.*, vol I, p. 460.
[31] *The Island Mission*, pp. 19–20.
[32] Dovey, J. W., *The Gospel in the South Pacific*, p. 15; Fox, C. E., *Lord of the Southern Isles*, p. 6.
[33] Pascoe, G. F., *Two Hundred Years of the S.P.G.*, vol. I, p. 446.
[34] *Pan-Anglican Congress, 1908*, vol. V, p. 165; *World Missionary Conference, 1910*, vol. VIII, p. 13.

of Melanesia said at the Pan-Anglican Congress of 1908 that Bishop Selwyn "wrote down the different islands and assigned them to   different societies, having regard to missionaries, already located, and claiming the Solomon Islands (where there was no mission) as the special field of the Anglican Church." This he said was an unwritten, tacit agreement which had then worked well for fifty years. Selwyn's original document ended with the words, "Let there be no strife, I pray thee, between my herdsmen and thy herdsmen." Preaching in England, Bishop Selwyn declared:

> We make a rule never to introduce controversy among native peoples. If the ground has been preoccupied by any other religious body, we forbear to enter. And I can speak from observation, ranging over nearly half the Southern Pacific Ocean, that wherever this law of religious unity is adopted, there the gospel has its full and unchecked power. Nature itself has so divided our mission field that each laborer may work without interference from his neighbor.[35]

During the discussion on comity at the Centenary Conference of Protestant Missions of the World at London in 1888, Bishop Suter of Nelson, New Zealand, stated that the Bishop John Selwyn of Melanesia was continuing the principle first set forth by his father of avoiding introducing Anglican missions in areas occupied by Wesleyans and Presbyterians.[36]

Only a limited number of agencies planted missions in the South Pacific, and the distances between the islands being so vast and the missionary staff so relatively small, despite the limited number of comity agreements little overlapping occurred. The Mormons were the only intruders reported in most places. In Papua, where the size of the land presented

[35] Curteis, G. A., *Bishop Selwyn of New Zealand and Litchfield*, p. 152; *Pan-Anglican Congress, 1908*, vol. V, p. 165, for preceding quotation.
[36] *Centenary Conference on the Protestant Missions of the World*, vol. II, p. 458.

a very different situation, Burton reported in 1930 that a friendly understanding and very little overlapping among societies prevailed. He observed, nevertheless:

> One can see, however, that unless the missionary societies at the home base maintain their comity, differences are bound to arise, for many of the lines of demarcation that have been drawn are either lines of latitude or longitude, or arbitrary divisions that have no relation whatever to the tribal life of the people, hence it may easily happen that, in any one country that has been thus portioned out, complications may arise.[37]

All these agreements were principally among British societies, since until a very late date the American Board of Commissioners for Foreign Missions was the only North American agency other than the Nova Scotia Presbyterians in the whole region, and the Société des Missions Évangéliques de Paris entered in order to take over British work that had become politically too difficult in French colonies. The Dutch missions in Indonesia were all Reformed, and seem to have adjusted to each other without much difficulty. Because of political pressures under German rule and the advent of German missionaries, the American Board handed over Truk and Ponape to the Liebenzeller Mission in 1907.[38] It also surrendered Guam to the Foreign Mission Society of the General Association of General Baptists in 1910 and the Gilbert Islands to the London Missionary Society (L.M.S.) in 1917, abrogating an earlier agreement by which the field of the L.M.S. was defined as the islands south of the equator with two exceptions and that of the American Board as the remainder of the islands.[39]

Perhaps no other incident more clearly shows the strength

[37] Burton, J. W., *op. cit.*, p. 31.
[38] A.B.C.F.M., *Annual Report, 1907*, p. 149.
[39] *Ibid., 1917;* Letter of Mary A. Walker, Boston, Jan. 8, 1954.

of the common conviction about the obligation to observe comity during the nineteenth century than the stand of the Church Missionary Society (C.M.S.) in the matter of the Madagascar bishopric. The L.M.S. established a mission in Madagascar in 1818 and founded a church which survived almost unprecedented persecution. A great revival occurred in 1861 and the new king invited the exiled L.M.S. missionaries to return. Anglicans in Great Britain and South Africa clamored for a mission there. Both the Society for the Propagation of the Gospel in Foreign Parts (S.P.G.) and the C.M.S. agreed that the L.M.S. must first be consulted. Accordingly a conference was held at the S.P.G. House in London in 1863. Dr. Tidman represented the L.M.S., and the Anglican representatives were the Archbishop of York, the Bishop of London (afterwards Archbishop of Canterbury), the Bishops of Oxford and Capetown, and the C.M.S. secretaries. There was acceptance of an agreement reached in the field by Dr. Ellis of the L.M.S. and Bishop Ryan of Maritius that an Anglican mission be begun on the coast and work up toward the capital, Antananarivo, and be visited occasionally by the Bishop of Maritius, who would have episcopal jurisdiction over it. The L.M.S. stated through Dr. Tidman that there was room for several societies to work on the island and that the Anglican missionaries would be most welcome, provided that existing churches be not disturbed by the introduction of different customs and practices and by the residence of an Anglican bishop at the capital city. The secretaries of the C.M.S. stated their agreement, but the S.P.G. bishops made no statement.[40] Both societies sent out missionaries in 1863, with all personnel to be subject to the Bishop of Maritius.

The question of a bishop for the island was soon raised

[40] The detailed statement given in the C.M.S. "Minute on the Projected Appointment of a Bishop to Madagascar," in *Church Missionary Record*, New Series, vol. I (1871), pp. 59–62; see also Stock, E., *op. cit.*, vol. II, pp. 477–478.

again, and in 1870 the directors and secretaries of the
C.M.S. were perturbed when confronted without prior consultation by the appointment of a bishop for Antananarivo
to whom their missionaries were expected to be subject. It
was thought necessary to consult again with the L.M.S.,
which reported on its mission in the island and reiterated its
belief that the presence of a bishop at the capital would be
detrimental to its established church life and work. The
C.M.S. then issued a Minute that declared: "These facts
speak for themselves, and forbid the attempt of any other
Society to interfere with a field of labor so well occupied."
It cited the policy of Bishop Selwyn and referred to "the
difficulties connected with the Bishopric of Honolulu" which
"afford a caution against sending a Bishop into the sphere of
a native church organized upon another system." And it protested: "It cannot be necessary at the present day to argue in
favor of the principle of non-interference between the missions of different Societies, which this Society has always
maintained in common with most other Societies." Since
"Her Majesty cannot confer jurisdiction beyond Her domains," the C.M.S. is expected voluntarily to subject its missionaries to the new bishop; but it cannot break its pledge to
the L.M.S., and, therefore, it would rather withdraw its mission entirely from Madagascar, if necessary. It, therefore,
suggested that if a bishop were sent, the C.M.S. areas be
excluded from his jurisdiction and these remain under the
Bishop of Mauritius. A storm of disapproval in Great Britain
backed up the position of the C.M.S., and the bishop-desig-
nate resigned. The C.M.S. restated its case and cited many
actions of the L.M.S. favorable to that Anglican Society.[41]
The London Society now changed its attitude and sent a
warm invitation to establish a mission at the capital. The

[41] *Church Missionary Intelligencer*, New Series, vol. VII (June, 1871), pp.
184–192.

Government disapproved the appointment of a bishop, but a bishop for the mission was consecrated by Scottish bishops.[42] The C.M.S. then withdrew its mission.

The Popular Conferences Promote Acceptance

Comity was, then, generally the accepted policy of the societies and boards and their field missions by the middle of the nineteenth century, but it was the great popular conferences which advertised and popularized it among the supporters of the societies.

The first great interdenominational missionary assembly, generally considered to be the spiritual ancestor of the modern ecumenical missionary conferences, was the Union Missionary Convention, held in New York in 1854 on the occasion of the visit of Dr. Alexander Duff of Calcutta. The fourth topic on the docket was phrased in these terms: "In view of the great extent of the Heathen world and the degree to which it is opened, is it expedient for different missionary boards to plant stations on the same ground?" After a very full discussion Dr. Duff offered the following resolution, which was unanimously adopted:

> *Resolved,* That considering the vast extent of the yet unevangelized world of Heathenism, and the limited means of evangelization at the disposal of the existing Evangelical Churches or Societies, it would be very desirable, that, with the exception of great centers, such as the capitals of powerful kingdoms, any efficient pre-occupancy of any particular portion of the Heathen field by any Evangelic Church or Society should be respected by others, and left in their undisturbed possession: At the same time acknowledging with

[42] Stock, E., *op. cit.,* vol. II, p. 480; see Thompson, H. P., *Into All Lands,* pp. 336–338, for S.P.G. viewpoint.

thankfulness to God, that heretofore there has been so little interference with each other's fields of labor.[43]

The London Conference of 1854 called for the practical expression of unity in cooperation, especially conferences, while the Liverpool Conference of 1860 only voiced its appreciation of this practical cooperation prevailing on the mission field.[44] The General Conference on Foreign Missions at Mildmay Park, London, in 1878 was so planned as to present a world-wide geographical survey, but at the preliminary meeting Dr. Mullins gave an address on "The Increased Co-operation of Missionary Agencies," in which he referred to the prevalence of comity agreements.[45] However, at the Centenary Conference of Protestant Missions of the World at London in 1888 the subject was formally placed on the agenda.

It was shortly before this Conference, in 1886, that the layman and industrialist Robert Arthington of Leeds called for a "World's Missionary Council" that would "apportion the world itself, a part or parts to each society, dividing the whole inhabited earth into missionary districts, spheres of evangelistic efforts." [46] He suggested a scheme of division of territory and assignment to societies that seemed practicable to him; and he gave full place to the American, Dutch, French, and German missionary organizations, as well as to the British. Robert Arthington found in foreign missions the great passion of his life, actively participated in their direc-

---

[43] *Union Missionary Convention, New York, 1854, Proceedings of* —, pp. 16–17.

[44] "The Missionary Conference, London": Report by T. R. Brooke in *Evangelical Christendom*, vol. VIII (1854), pp. 432–433; the paper on "A Plea for Mutual Sympathy and Practical Cooperation," by J. B. Masden, is in vol. IX (1855), pp. 1–6; *Conference on Missions Held in Liverpool, 1860*, p. 12.

[45] *General Conference on Foreign Missions, London, 1878, Proceedings of* —.

[46] *Missionary Review of the World*, vol. X, No. 1 (January 1887), pp. 18–19.

tion, and in his will left £1,000,000 for the work. This was the largest gift ever made directly to mission work by any donor in Great Britain, and is probably the largest single gift ever made to the cause by one person at any time or in any nation.[47]

It was this Centenary Conference which introduced the word *comity* into the vocabulary of foreign missions, or at least won general acceptance of the term. Previously the principle was usually expressed by the terms *territorial division* or *delimitation of territory,* or *non-interference.* The subject was ably presented in two papers by Professor Gustav Warneck of Germany, who was unable to present his address personally and for whom it had to be read, and Dr. A. C. Thompson of the American Board of Commissioners for Foreign Missions.[48] These papers marshalled the same arguments for comity that had earlier been raised on the mission fields and among the directors of the pioneer societies and boards: comity permitted the unity which Christ asked of His Church, at the same time allowing freedom and diversity; concord among brethren is the rule on the mission field; all have rights entitled to be respected by others; comity makes for economy in evangelism; priority of occupation establishes rights which should be recognized; and the agreements concerning the practices which accompany comity make for equity in administration.

Dr. Warneck's objective was spiritual unity, outwardly recognizable in practical relations between societies. He advised that if the separate societies were to institute and maintain comity, it is necessary for the missionaries and their supporters at home to become mutually acquainted, to bind themselves to avoid all overstepping of boundaries, and more constantly to hold out helping hands to each other. He gently

[47] Chirgwin, A. M., *Arthington's Million,* London: Livingstone Press, n. d.
[48] *Centenary Conference on Protestant Missions of the World,* London, 1888, vol. II, pp. 429–462.

chided Englishmen and Americans about their lack of knowledge of German missions, and he rebuked American and British missionary activity in Germany as a violation of comity at the home base. Professor Warneck asked all societies to avoid entering the fields of others, to make agreements for the division of territory, scrupulously to avoid proselytism, to receive members from other missions only after proper consultation, to refuse firmly to accept those under discipline by other churches, and to agree together on stipends for native workers. He warmly recommended regional missionary conferences, warned about the dangers in which European colonialism was involving missions, and called for greater cooperation generally. Specifically he called for the formation of "a Standing Central Committee of Protestant Missionary Agencies" with headquarters in London, composed of delegates from all societies, and with related missionary conferences in each Protestant nation. This scheme has close affinity with the plan later adopted for the International Missionary Council. One of its functions, as proposed by the German authority on missions, would be the arbitration of any differences which might arise with regard to boundaries of areas of occupation. Professor Warneck in conclusion pleaded that all look upon missions as a common cause.

Dr. Thompson, in the second paper, defined missionary comity as "the observance of equity and Christian courtesy in foreign evangelization." He made his plea for comity along the line mentioned above, and called for the same kind of mutual relations between missionaries as Professor Warneck had advocated. He added a new note to comity when he asserted that "intermarriage between missionaries of different Societies furnishes occasion for comity"! Equity demands that the expenses of outfit, travel, and support during the interrupted term be refunded to the mission transferring the newly wedded person. Thompson stated that comity pre-

vailed, but that there were, nevertheless, zealous denomina-
tionalists who violated it both in spirit and practice. Therefore, he proposed a Committee of Reference as an impartial
referee in cases of alleged violations, either a single international committee or one in each large country.

The ensuing discussion revealed that most of the older and
major missions staunchly adhered to comity, but that with
the sharp increase of denominationalism in the West and
with the rapid multiplication of societies and boards, there
were now some, perhaps even many, exceptions. Again and
again men spoke "out of bitter experience" of the need for
accepted rules for the guidance of all missionary agencies.
The exceptions then came so much into prominence that J.
Hudson Taylor, the renowned founder of the China Inland
Mission, exclaimed: "I hope this audience will not go away
with the idea that these discourtesies are the rule. Brotherly
love is the rule." [49] Fortunately, for every example of a violation of comity cited, the delegates could offer more examples
of mutual agreement on delimitation of territory and of violations or alleged infringements that had been righted by the
action of a field mission or the directors of a society.

Comity had been discussed under the topic "Mutual Relations." That it was now considered to be only the first stage
in proper and effective missionary relationships was indicated by the fact that still under the general heading of
"Missionary Comity" the conference moved on to the consideration of a more advanced stage, namely, "Cooperation."

The series of large, popular assemblies of an unofficial
character terminated in the Ecumenical Missionary Conference at New York in 1900. This meeting introduced the term
ecumenical into contemporary Protestant usage. The Conference gave full place on its agenda to the consideration of
comity in all types of missionary work. Once again free discussion of the subject demonstrated that quite generally sat-

[49] *Ibid.*, p. 456.

isfactory mutual relations, involving delimitation of territory and noninterference, prevailed both in spirit and in practice.

Actually the Interdenominational Conference of Foreign Missionary Boards of the United States and Canada had seen the possibility of using the 1900 Conference as a stimulus to further development of comity and cooperation and had taken steps to insure such a result. There was a discussion of comity in the course of the 1898 annual meeting, inspired by a resolution of an assembly of national evangelistic workers in Mexico.[50] W. H. Grant, who had initiated the discussion, defined the practice in these words: "Comity itself is very simple. It means simply division of the field and rules of employment and discipline." The context of the discussion was the challenge of the unoccupied fields and the elimination of waste by overlapping and competition so that men and money might be released for an evangelistic advance. This was the day when the watchword was "The evangelization of the world in this generation."

Dr. Grant offered this solution:

> *Resolved*, That a Committee on Comity and Unoccupied Fields be appointed to correspond with the Boards and Societies with the view to the most economic distribution of the missionary force now supported by our Churches, and with the general purpose of bringing about a great practical advance in cooperation and division of the field as one of the chief results of the Conference of 1900.[51]

The resolution was referred to the Business Committee, which deleted the words "and division of the field," for which it substituted "especially in higher education"; and it was adopted.[52]

[50] Interdenominational Conference of Foreign Missionary Boards of the United States and Canada, *Annual Report, 1898*, pp. 93–100.
[51] *Ibid.*, 1898, p. 95.
[52] *Ibid.*, 1898, p. 4.

Before this Committee could report to the next annual meeting, the Spanish-American War had been fought. The speedy action of a number of boards in dispatching missionaries to Puerto Rico, the Philippines, and, it was expected, to Cuba also, in accord with prior comity arrangements, had given great impetus to further interest and discussion. When the Committee made its report in 1899,[53] the text asserted that despite all the references to the perfect brotherhood and cooperation on the mission field it should be kept in mind and laid to heart that there were scores of pages in the reports of the missionary conferences recently held at Bombay, Shanghai, and London filled with agonized complaints about interference and rivalry. Some persons had said that something had better first be done at home about these things before trying to develop them further abroad where conditions were recognized as being so much better than in the sending churches. However, the Committee retorted:

> Cooperation and unity abroad will react to produce cooperation and unity at home. We in this Conference, moreover, and the missionaries whom we represent, can do very little to secure full comity at home; we can do everything to secure it abroad. That we cannot do the one, will not excuse us for failing to do the other, which is within our power.[54]

The report listed the following basic principles on which local agreement could be secured, if generally adopted or approved by the boards and societies as fundamental policy:

> 1. *Church Union.* The aim of the missionary movement should be the establishment of a common Christian Church in each land, and not the extension and perpetuation of western divisions which have little or no significance to the young churches.

[53] *Ibid.*, 1899, pp. 106–121.
[54] *Ibid.*, 1899, p. 107.

2. *Territorial Division.* If missionaries were all working for one national church, the sole purpose of such comity arrangements would be economy in the use of resources. The actual situation makes territorial delimitation necessary in order to avoid disagreement and rivalry.

3. *Comity in Discipline and Administration.* Every mission should respect the acts of discipline and the principles of administration of other missions. Converts or native workers should not be received nor employed without prior consultation with the mission which they have left.

4. *The Spirit of Comity in the Use of Mission Money.* There should be agreement between missions whose work is contiguous as to scales of wages of native workers.

5. *Education, Publishing, and Hospitals.* One hospital should suffice, as a rule, for any one station, no matter how many different missions might have been established there. Similarly, through division of labor duplication in literature work and in higher education should also be avoided.

6. *Questions of Comity Involved in Intermarriage of Missionaries.* There should be an equitable repayment by the husband's mission to the wife's mission for the expenses of travel, salary for the broken term, etc.

Therefore, the representatives of the North American boards were primed for the discussion of comity when the subject came before the Ecumenical Conference on Foreign Missions in New York in May, 1900.[55] There were some who, like the Brooklyn Congregationalist pastor, Dr. A. F. J. Behrends, denounced comity and such agreements as had just parceled out Puerto Rico for not going far enough. He declared: "I like not that word 'comity.' It is veneered selfishness. . . . Fusion is what we need; co-operation is what we must have." [56] However, the great majority of speakers lauded the spirit and practice of such mutual arrangements. The Chairman of the Executive Committee of the American Bap-

[55] *Ecumenical Missionary Conference, New York, 1900,* vol. I, pp. 233–277.
[56] *Ibid.,* p. 207.

tist Union, Dr. H. M. King, opened the discussion on that note. Comity, according to him, is

> the spirit of Christ manifesting itself in all the forms, and methods, and activities of foreign evangelization, and in all the intercourse and relations of those who are seeking to prosecute it. . . . It is the expression of that courtesy and thoughtful regard for the rights, and the feelings, and the convictions of others which should ever and everywhere characterize the intercourse of Christian gentlemen.[57]

Comity is born of the love of Christ and inculcated both by the great commandment and our Lord's sacerdotal prayer for the unity of his believers. It expresses the underlying unity among all Christians, but does not demand organic church union. This speaker who introduced the subject then proposed "a few practical applications and proper limitations to the spirit of missionary comity."[58] These include: a united mission by all branches of any one of the Protestant communions, so as to eliminate intra-confessional divisions among Baptists, Methodists, Presbyterians, and others; priority of occupancy by any agency should always be recognized by all others, excepting the great centers of population; amicable division of new territory in order to speed evangelization, to be the rule; the holding of intermission conferences, making proper provision for exchange of members and workers, always guarding against receiving those who change for unworthy motives, and the like. Underlying all is the basic idea that comity is intended to make possible speedy and economical evangelization. "Our motto as missionary bodies may often be: 'Divide that we may conquer, scatter that we may increase, separate that we may compass.'"

When a number of persons declared that comity ought to begin at home, this provided an opportunity for Dr. A.

[57] *Ibid.*, p. 233.
[58] *Ibid.*, pp. 234–235.

Schreiber, Director of the Rhenish Missionary Society, to
subscribe heartily to the view and ask that it be applied to
the whole Western sending base of missions. Certain American agencies were treating Germany as a heathen land and
sending missionaries there! This was not the spirit of comity.[59] Many had their say, and the report as printed gives an
especially large place to the remarks of persons from the
United Kingdom.[60] Comity was endorsed by the representatives of nondenominational faith missions, and especially by
Dr. J. Hudson Taylor. Territorial delimitation and assignment for the sake of effective evangelism was quite generally
taken for granted, and the discussion tended rather to consideration of forms of cooperation in functional services such
as printing, medical work, and higher education. Dr. Suther-
land, secretary of the Department of Missions of the Methodist Church in Canada summed up the many aspects of the
matter and offered a review of principles much like that with
which the discussion had begun, concluding with definite
instructions from the home boards to the missionaries to cultivate both comity and cooperation and with the proposal
that there be formed in each field a representative committee
of consultation and reference empowered to consider the
larger questions of practical comity.[61]

The North American boards omitted their annual meeting
in 1900 because of the Ecumenical Conference on Foreign
Missions. It had apparently been clear from the discussions
at the conference and from the responses of the American
agencies that there was such general agreement about comity that it was scarcely worth taking time for further deliber-
ations on the subject. The Committee on Comity reported to
the annual conference in 1901 that previous discussions,
notably in the Conference of 1900, "have placed the impor-

[59] *Ibid.*, pp. 237–238.
[60] *Ibid.*, pp. 233–277; scan the entire section to note participants.
[61] *Ibid.*, p. 277.

tance of comity in so clear and convincing a light that any further discussion of the general question seems unnecessary." There was a general consensus. As the conclusion of its services and as a summary of this consensus, the Committee recommended that the organization send a letter to all the boards setting forth the desirableness of comity and cooperation, and asking the concurrence of each board in issuing instructions to its missionaries to note that the board favored comity and cooperation and that they should work toward those ends on the field; to authorize or appoint a missionary in each field to serve on a joint committee on comity and cooperation; and to ask through such representatives that these joint field committees take practical action on the interchange of service of missionaries, on territorial division to eliminate duplication, on cooperation in printing, publishing, higher education, theological training (by churches of similar doctrine and polity), pay of native workers, and on organic union of native churches by missions holding similar systems of doctrine and polity.[62] The report, including these recommendations, was adopted by the conference, and that ended the service of the Committee.[63]

The Board of Foreign Missions of the Presbyterian Church in the U.S.A., had not waited for this action. Immediately after the Ecumenical Missionary Conference, at its meeting on May 15, 1900, the Board adopted a statement of policy which endorsed organic church union and, when that was not possible, called for territorial comity, for accompanying agreements on salaries, discipline, and functional cooperation.[64] The General Assembly's Standing Committee on Foreign Missions that same year hailed this statement "with

[62] Interdenominational Conference of Foreign Missionary Boards of the United States and Canada, *Annual Report, 1901*, pp. 16–17.

[63] *Ibid.*, p. 3.

[64] Presbyterian Church in the U.S.A., Board of Foreign Missions, *Annual Report, 1900*, pp. 5–6; Brown, Arthur J., *One Hundred Years*, pp. 88–89.

sincere gratitude and satisfaction," and the Assembly gave it unanimous approval.[65] Once again later, in 1916, that body voted: "That the Assembly reiterate its hearty approval of the Board's policy to promote comity, co-operation, and union in all parcticable ways, thus avoiding denominational overlapping and the undue multiplication of agencies in a given field, but using men and money to the best advantage."[66] This Board's attitude was typical, although perhaps more explicit, of the views and policy, written or unwritten, of the great majority of denominational boards and societies.

Not only the Interdenominational Conference of Foreign Missionary Boards of the United States and Canada was concerned with comity. The German Societies in 1885 created an informal committee to represent them jointly in relationships with their own and other colonial governments. This loose association became in 1897 the formally constituted *Ausschuss der deutschen evangelischen Missionagesellshaften* or Standing Committee of the German Evangelical Missionary Societies. It not only successfully negotiated with government agencies on behalf of all the German missions in the German colonies, but it served also as the advocate on behalf of non-German agencies. One of its most outstanding accomplishments was the defense of established principles of missionary comity, especially of the recognition of priority of occupation, when the German colonial authorities were threatening to exclude missionaries from other countries, as in the case of the American Board missionaries in the Marshall Islands.[67]

The high tide of discussion of comity and its general popularization came, then, about 1900, especially in the London and New York Conferences of 1888 and 1900. Thereafter, it

[65] Quoted by Brown, *One Hundred Years*, p. 89.

[66] *Ibid.*

[67] Hogg, W. R., *Ecumenical Foundations*, pp. 72–73; but this writer can find no evidence for Dr. Hogg's attributing to the Ausschuss the territorial division of German East Africa.

was generally and tacitly accepted by the church missions which were in the field and also by the older interdenominational or nondenominational faith missions. Africa and Latin America were lagging behind the other areas, however, and would need a push by the Edinburgh Conference of 1910. Comity had prepared the ground, and interest and discussion turned to more positive forms of cooperation. But the seeds of disintegration of the now commonly held policy and practice had already also been sown. The references to rivalry and competition that were rife in the conferences of the period indicate the appearance of new agencies which held themselves aloof from the older fellowship of foreign missions. They would become more and more numerous. Moreover, what was even more ominous was the repudiation of territorial agreements by the Anglican bishops in India.[68] Robert E. Speer called it to the attention of the North American mission boards as threatening the whole historical position of the missions in such matters and making the need for cooperation all the greater.[69]

The discussion of comity in international missionary conferences came to an end in the very first official conference based on actual representation of missionary agencies, namely the World Missionary Conference at Edinburgh in 1910.[70] Comity had long since come to be regarded as belonging to the natural order of Protestant missionary action, and concern was now focused on positive and effective means, systems, and institutions of cooperation and on movements towards organic union among the young churches. This assembly of foreign missionaries, administrative secretaries, board and society members—the policy-making per-

---

[68] *Church Missionary Intelligencer*, New Series, vol. XXV (1900), p. 275; *Pan-Anglican Congress, 1908*, vol. V, p. 162, and Appendix S.D. 4(e).

[69] Interdenominational Conference of Foreign Missionary Boards of the United States and Canada, *Annual Report, 1901*, p. 19.

[70] On the background, sessions, work, and results of this conference see Hogg, W. R., *op. cit.*, pp. 45ff.

sonnel of the Protestant missionary enterprise—became the fountainhead of the modern Ecumenical Movement, as is well known. Its concern for the strengthening of positive cooperation led to the creation of its own Continuation Committee and ultimately to the formation of the International Missionary Council. It also set in motion the forces which developed the Faith and Order Movement and stimulated the Life and Work Movement, which were eventually to merge into the World Council of Churches. And presently the International Missionary Council is being merged into the World Council of Churches, so that after half a century the total ecumenical vision and ministry which were the concern of the people at Edinburgh in 1910 has a single institutional symbol and organ of expression.

The Edinburgh Conference sought cooperation on the part of numerous sovereign denominational units in the carrying out of a single world mission which comprised them all and was more than the sum of their separate efforts. The reports of the Commission on Cooperation and the Promotion of Unity warned that: "Before, however, either such cooperation or unity can be looked for, that spirit of considerateness, fair dealing, Christian courtesy and brotherliness, which is called 'comity,' must be prevalent." [71] Comity was there considered to be only the *more negative aspect of cooperation*. Only one brief chapter in the whole of volume VIII on Cooperation and Unity was given to it. [72] This section demonstrates that efficiency and economy require comity arrangements. Furthermore, the avoidance of overlapping and of interference with the work of others is demanded by the spirit of Christian charity. It is asserted that comity agreements, and consequently positive cooperation, would be strengthened by the establishment in every field of an authoritative, representative organization. While there was a

[71] *World Missionary Conference, Edinburgh, 1910,* vol. VIII, p. 10.
[72] *Ibid.,* pp. 12–26.

consensus about the desirability of agreements on territorial assignments, it now had to be recognized that some bodies inherently exclusive, which might have accepted comity arrangements in a pioneer period, would now demand the right to go where they might wish. Also there had to be note taken that new nondenominational missionary agencies were arising in numbers, and that the "evangelistic free lances" among them would be unwilling to be restricted to any sphere of their own or to leave alone either the areas or the converts of others.[73]

John R. Mott, when listing comity as one of the forms of cooperation in a report to the Jerusalem Conference of 1928, stated that it was hardly necessary to call attention to it, since it was a rare instance when any agency failed to observe both the letter and the spirit of comity.[74] Comity was accepted by practically all the missions which considered themselves to be in the historic stream of Protestant missions, but the policy and practice were despite Mott's assurance still being undermined by the free lances and the exclusivists who were poles apart in their concept of the church. Yet despite the corrosion due to these two forces, a catalogue of the forms and organs of missionary cooperation made in 1935 could, nevertheless, be prefaced with the statement: "Comity and the principle of division of territory are taken for granted now by most boards and their missions."[75]

[73] *Ibid.*, p. 17.
[74] *Jerusalem Meeting of the International Missionary Council, 1928,* vol. VII, p. 7.
[75] Fahs, C. H. and H. E. Davis, *Conspectus of Cooperative Missionary Enterprises,* p. 2.

CHAPTER III

Delimitation of Territory and Noninterference: Comity in India

The Regional Conferences on Comity

INDIA led other major mission fields, apart from the Pacific islands, in the attainment of comity, and provided a model for other regions. Pioneer India missions took over some features of the American Indian missions, and then in turn set the pattern for the development of Protestant mission methods in other geographical areas. This was because the missions there were somewhat older than in many other areas and, until later developments in China, comprised the greatest variety of confessions, denominations, and nationalities. Discussion and action on comity can easily be followed in the records of the India missionary conferences, and these disclose how the idea grew in scope and content through the decades, beginning simply with the concept of noninterference and then coming finally to be regarded as mutual recognition and the essential basis for cooperation. A special reason existed for stimulating the missions in India to seek comity agreements and mutual understanding about relationships. Where two or more churches or missions overlapped each tended to be identified with a particular caste, and nearly all the missionaries were convinced that a caste church violates the very nature of membership in the body of Christ.[1]

The subject must of necessity have been raised in the local city missionary unions, but it first emerges clearly for the

---

[1] See for example, *Minutes of the Fourth Biennial Meeting of the Andrha Christian Council, 1929*, pp. 38–39, 10–11.

record at the first meeting of the South India Missionary Conference at Ootacamund in 1858, where extensive regulations were drawn up for recommendation to the missionary societies. Although this was numerically a small gathering, its concerns were vast and its vision broad. The Conference by formal resolution requested the Rev. G. V. Pope of the Society for the Propagation of the Gospel in Foreign Parts (S.P.G.) to bring in a paper on "the laws which should govern Missionary Societies in their relation with one another in their respective fields." [2]

Mr. Pope's report is worthy of a full summary. [3] Such a commonly agreed-upon set of laws or principles is essential and unavoidable, according to him. Missionary societies and all their agents ought to act in strict accord with them, especially when selecting a new station and when some missionary gives the appearance of interfering in the district of another society. There are four basic factors or principles which underlie missionary action in India. First, the vast field is beyond the powers of any one society or of them all together to evangelize at present. Secondly, Protestant missionaries agree sufficiently to regard each other as fellow workers, to rejoice in one another's success, and to regard each other's fields as brought under Christian teaching. The maintenance of friendly relations among the missions is so important, in the third place, that scarcely any consideration can make the disturbance of those relations expedient, and the introduction of controversy would result in nothing but evil. Fourthly, since missionaries are primarily evangelists and not pastors, and since their work is only preparatory, they must look forward to the day when there will arise a "Church of India" differing in many respects from any Christian community in Europe or America. If these principles are

[2] *South India Missionary Conference, Ootacamund, 1858, Proceedings of —*, p. 3.
[3] *Ibid.*, pp. 334–337.

admitted, then it should be easy to discern the laws which may be derived from them and which ought to be followed. Actually the only law is the law of love, but there are twelve regulations which may be set down as aids in obeying that great law.

The twelve laws for missionary societies and missionaries are these: (1) When one society is in possession of a field, no other should enter without its cordial consent. (2) There should be no proselyting. (3) Every missionary should be slow to encourage native Christians to change denominational affiliation. (4) When Christians do seek to change their church membership, the missionary to whom they apply should satisfy himself "by long, careful, and conscientious inquiry that there is no worldly incentive at work." (5) Be very sceptical about any native's professed desire to change his denominational affiliation on the grounds of doctrine and be thoroughly satisfied, for this is rarely genuine. (6) Since native Christian servants in the course of their service pass from one missionary to another across denominational lines, a master should never unduly use his influence to make proselytes of those he employs nor follow a former servant into the territory of another mission to seek converts among his family. (7) No missionary dare to constitute himself a court of appeal from the decision of another missionary; and (8) He should never enter into relationship or negotiation with anyone who has been excommunicated. (9) If he should be requested to receive into membership a Christian from another denomination, he should at once lay the matter before the pastor of the church to which that person has belonged, and take no step without his consent—"consent which in a really fitting case no honest man would withhold." (10) When there is a difference of opinion on the merits of a case, no time should be lost in referring the matter to arbitration by experienced missionaries on whom the principals involved agree. (11) No native catechist should be allowed to interfere in such a case. And finally, (12) "It would be well in all such cases for each missionary to ask himself whether in encouraging the applicant in question, the evils resulting may not on the whole far exceed the good to be expected."

The brethren attending the conference agreed with Mr. Pope, for his paper had set down in words the prevailing viewpoint and summarized prevailing practice. It is evident that there was nothing novel in the ideas here presented, except the fact that they had been formulated and well presented to a representative, although unofficial, body of missionaries related to half of India. The Ootacamund Conference, therefore, resolved:

> That the Conference highly approve the principles laid down and the rules founded upon them, for the guidance of Societies and their agents in this important matter, contained in the above able paper on this subject; and would most earnestly urge upon all concerned their faithful observance, believing them to be eminently calculated not only to preserve peace between Missionary brethren of different Societies labouring in the same or adjacent localities, but also to promote the true prosperity of the Native Churches.[4]

It is apparent that the members of this Conference were much in earnest, for they next passed a resolution in censure of one of the German missions for alleged interference with others, and drew up a letter of brotherly reproof and protest addressed to the directors of that society in Germany.[5] The Leipzig Mission was so lone an offender at this time that a reputation for "sheep stealing" and interference became fastened upon it that was hard to live down.[6] The offense

---

[4] *Ibid.*, p. 337.

[5] *Ibid.*, pp. 337–339.

[6] Even among Anglicans after some of them had begun to "follow up" converts; see Stock, E., *History of the Church Missionary Society,* vol. III, p. 496; vol. IV, pp. 164, 410.

condemned at this time was the reception by some missionaries of members of other denominations without sufficient inquiry. Also it was charged that caste distinctions had been condoned and permitted within the church. This action could not be legally binding, since the Conference had no administrative nor legislative authority, and no society could be forced to bow to its will, but the missionaries relied on the disciplinary force of a consensus among themselves.

The missionaries in North India had been meeting together in conference even longer than those of the South. However, it was not until the third meeting of the North India Missionary Conference at Lahore from December 26, 1862, to January 2, 1863, five years after the first meeting, that comity was discussed.[7] The Rev. J. Taylor of the Church of Scotland Mission presented a paper advocating the division of territory, noninterference, the observing of standard inter-mission discipline in reception of members and agents, and uniform standards of employment and pay for workers. Interestingly, while each mission is to honor the discipline of the others yet: "It shall not be binding upon any Mission, to respect the discipline of another, which rests upon any denominational tenet."

When the South India Conference met a second time at Bangalore in 1879, comity did not come up for discussion.[8] The third meeting of the series was convened at Madras in 1900. It broke new ground for the entire world-wide missionary enterprise by being composed of official delegates formally elected or appointed by the participating missions, and thus able to speak for them and to act on their behalf.[9]

[7] *Punjab Missionary Conference Held at Lahore, 1862–63, Report of the —*, pp. 292–299, esp. 298.
[8] *The Missionary Conference: South India and Ceylon, 1879.*
[9] On the significance of this precedent, see Hogg, *Ecumenical Foundations,* pp. 21–23, 106–107.

Since this was an official body, a more authoritative statement on comity could be adopted than that accepted by the first conference of the series forty-three years earlier. A Committee on Comity and Cooperation in Mission Work, appointed before the sessions were held, and indicating by its name that by this time comity was regarded as only the first step in cooperation, reported to the assembly. Official machinery was decades behind opinion and practice, because the jealously guarded sovereignty of denominations and societies at the home base inhibited the development of authoritative field organs, on the one hand, and also because in most matters a known consensus, on the other, made much machinery unnecessary as long as the agencies remained few. It was more often than not the arrival of later missions which had not shared in the earlier development or had not attained as yet the common ecumenical viewpoint which made organization and official procedure necessary or at least advisable. The report indicated that comity was widely observed, but that there had been some violations.[10] There was added a new charge to the old ones about invasion of territory, reception of persons under discipline, and the enticement of native workers by higher pay. This was the complaint of "the drawing away of pupils from contiguous colleges and schools by reduced fees and liberal scholarships." When the Conference accepted the report of the Committee, it affirmed its "cordial adherence to the principles of comity in regard to territorial division," urged all societies not yet observing the practice to adopt it, and expressed the hope that newly arriving societies would labor only in unoccupied fields. Moreover, the members of this body admonished the older missions not to make excessive claims to territory which they could not actually and effectively occupy.

This representative assembly adopted resolutions on the

[10] *South Indian Missionary Conference Held at Madras, 1900, Report of —,* pp. 70–71.

several matters intimately involved with the delimitation of territory and which guaranteed noninterference in one another's affairs. Those concerning the employment of native workers and the reception of members followed the usual earlier line. Every missionary or pastor was advised to issue a certificate of status to any member who might remove to a distant location, expecting that such a document would be honored as either a letter of commendation for Christian fellowship while at that place or as a letter of transfer of membership by the church or mission at the new place of residence. Schools were asked to avoid rivalry by coming to a mutual understanding about fees and scholarships. And the series of more or less usual resolutions was given genuine force by the addition of a final one of quite a different nature. The Conference appointed a committee of seven persons charged with devising a permanent method of arbitration of all disputes between missions in South India. It was also given the by no means inconsiderable task of gathering together a record of existing territorial comity agreements between the missionary societies. This special committee was instructed to report directly to all the missions represented at the Conference. Official machinery was to be provided, but it is important to note that the members still felt that: "The best guarantee for the observance of comity is the brotherliness created by cooperation in missionary work." [11] Comity had been earlier the stepping stone to genuine mutuality and fellowship, it had then become the guarantee of noninterference in one another's affairs, but now it was looked upon as the by-product of genuine cooperation. Actually it still remained the essential base for positive cooperation. Unity in South India had now advanced well beyond the rather negative stage of noninterference effected through the delimitation of territory to that of positive action in a cooperative enterprise.

[11] *Ibid.*, p. 74.

The National Decennial Conferences

It would appear to be a more or less general rule that each stage of development attained on a more restricted local level had to be won again on a regional level, and then finally on a national plane. National missionary conferences for the whole of India, including Burma and Ceylon, were held every ten years, beginning with the one convened at Allahabad from December 26, 1872, to January 1, 1873. The most that this assembly would do about the subject was to "put on record their sense of the grave importance of the principle of mutual non-interference of Missionary Societies." [12]

While the Second Decennial Missionary Conference at Calcutta over the Christmas-New Year holiday, 1882–1883, heard many of its members speak about unity and united action, no step was taken to deal with or to advance the cause of comity on a national scale.[13] But the matter was warmly debated at the Third Decennial Conference at Bombay in the winter of 1892–1893. It was at this Conference that the clash between Bishop James Mills Thoburn of the American Methodist Episcopal Church and his Anglican neighbor, Bishop Clifford of Lucknow, over comity led Anglicans to think of the two as the primary champions of opposite views. It would probably be a shock to many Methodists to learn that Anglicans thought them to be opposed to comity, although not "sheep stealers," and looked askance at them for advocating the right of a church to follow its members—a policy that was soon to become the official Anglican position to the disappointment and resentment of most other denominations.[14] Thoburn advocated dropping

[12] General Missionary Conference Held at Allahabad, 1872–1873, p. 485.
[13] Decennial Missionary Conference Held at Calcutta, 1882–83. Report of the Second —.
[14] Stock, E., History of the Church Missionary Society, vol. III, p. 495.

what he admitted was the "traditional doctrine" of territorial division and noninterference, but the members of that assembly firmly informed the Bishop that they considered certain recent actions by his mission to be encroachments on the well-established right of others. They expressed their conviction as to the necessity of continued support of the long-established policy. There were two papers presented to the Conference opposing one by Thoburn. The discussion on all three supported a proposal that a national committee on comity be established.[15] It should be noted that Bishop Thoburn did not advocate cutthroat competition, but wished to substitute for territorial division what he described as "working together in amity," cooperation, and the disciplining of unfraternal conduct by the societies if one of their agents gave offense. This assembly was far too large a body to accomplish detailed legislation, and the majority, surprised to learn that there was no constitution for the Decennial Conferences, was suddenly overcome with timidity and feared to put emphasis on resolutions. The result was anticlimactic. After all the intense and warm debate, and having arrived at a sure consensus, the Conference took no more formal action than to recommend that the societies neither employ native agents from other missions nor receive members under discipline without thorough consultation and prior approval by those missions.[16]

Fortunately, before another decade passed and the next Decennial Conference could be held, the South India Conference at Madras in 1900 had broken new ground, pioneered in a new type of cooperation, and leaped the old hurdle of jealousy over denominational sovereignty. Moreover, its work

[15] *Decennial Missionary Conference Held at Bombay, 1892–93, Report of the Third —,* vol. II, pp. 590–636. Thoburn's paper had first been prepared for the Calcutta Missionary Conference, and when a postponement prevented its being read before that body, it had been published in the *Harvest Field,* vol. X (February, 1890), pp. 281–291.
[16] *Ibid.,* p. 746.

had been so effective that its influence was potent. The principle of official representation by societies was adopted for the national Decennial Conference which came two years later. Although it was hedged about with limitations, the Fourth Decennial Missionary Conference at Madras in 1902 declared itself to be a testimony to the fact that comity existed between all missionary agencies working in India.[17] It adopted resolutions favoring delimitation of territory, the formation of provincial missionary associations, and cooperation in various types of functional work.[18] Moreover, it created the Board of Arbitration which had been requested ten years earlier.[19] The machinery was thus not set up until almost a century after the practice had been initiated in India.

The Board of Arbitration

This national Board of Arbitration was intended to act in any dispute which might arise between the several missions. The Conference appointed to it forty persons, each being a representative of a different society participating in the Conference. Such membership was not to continue in the case of a person whose mission did not subsequently formally commit itself to the principle of arbitration. Newly entering missions, or others not now in membership, would be eligible for representation if they would declare their adoption of the principle. Whenever two missions might find themselves involved in a dispute, they were asked first to attempt to settle it between themselves. Only if they could not agree

[17] *Fourth Decennial Missionary Conference Held in Madras, December 11–18, 1902, Report of —*, p. 156.
[18] *Ibid.*, pp. 159–160.
[19] *Ibid.*, pp. 160–164.

should they appeal to the Board. The Board was instructed to work out its own system of arbitration, but the Conference laid down several basic requirements. These fundamental requirements include: The Board may act only when a case is formally and officially referred to it by the officers of the missions concerned. It cannot initiate action. Should one party decline arbitration, the other may ask the Board to use its good offices to effect reconciliation. Any decision rendered by the Board or its duly appointed representatives is final. There is no appeal to the Conference. Whenever the Board should appoint representatives to investigate a case and make a decision, each of the missions involved would be permitted to choose an equal number of representatives from among the members of the Board, and the Board then name one additional member. A separate Board for Ceylon was recommended, but not appointed.

The Madras Conference further made the usual request for mutual consultation and clearance when national workers desired to change employment from one mission to another. Adjacent missions were asked to work out uniform standards of pay and status for their evangelists, teachers, and other workers. Similar consultation and approval were requested in transfer of members, with a special warning against acceptance of any persons under discipline before the removal of the ban or judgment by the church that had imposed the discipline. Moreover, out of a sense of evangelistic obligation, the Conference asked its new Board of Arbitration to go beyond matters pertaining strictly to comity and obtain detailed information about unoccupied areas. When this information had been assembled, the Board should place before the churches of Europe and America the evangelistic needs in those areas.

It is interesting to note that despite the repudiation of further comity agreements by the Provincial Synod of Anglican

Bishops in 1900,[20] Anglican missionaries representing both the Church Missionary Society (C.M.S.) and the Society for the Propagation of the Gospel (S.P.G.) were appointed to membership on the Board of Arbitration. However, since the Bishops had repudiated further territorial agreements, the societies apparently did not accept formal representation on the Board that was to enforce a policy and practice in the development of which they had formerly taken so leading a part. Other missionaries regretted that "another spirit has taken possession of a portion of the Church of England in India during the last few decades, a spirit contrary to the broad and more generous attitude it formerly held towards other Christians."[21] The Bishop of Travancore said that this was not a repudiation of the agreements already made, and Dr. Weitbrecht reported in 1908 that most Anglican missions were still keeping agreements.[22] The C.M.S. continued to abide by the old agreements and even enter into new ones, and so did the S.P.G., although now considered to be cold to comity in general. About 1910 the C.M.S. and United Free Church of Scotland found themselves in some confusion due to overlapping in a district in western India. The two agencies conferred, reached a decision most amicably, and drew up a geographical boundary between their two fields.[23] Similarly in 1911 the Marathi Mission of the American Board of Commissioners for Foreign Missions and the C.M.S. mission in the adjoining field drew a line of demarcation from Poona northeastward, awarding all territory west of that line to the C.M.S. and that east of it to the American mission; while the S.P.G. and the American Marathi Mission had

[20] *Church Missionary Intelligencer,* vol. LI [New Series, vol. XXV] (1900), p. 275.

[21] *Harvest Field,* Fourth Series, vol. XXII, No. 11 (November, 1901), p. 361.

[22] *Pan-Anglican Congress, 1908,* vol. V, p. 162; Appendix S. D. 4 (e), pp. 2–9.

[23] *Harvest Field,* vol. XLII, No. 1 (January, 1922), p. 16.

earlier in 1902 revised their mutual agreement.[24] Far to the north, the S.P.G. corresponded with the mission of the United Presbyterian Church of North America about opening work in Rawalpindi, and the former agreed to confine their activities to the Sadar area.[25] The S.P.C. also demonstrated adherence to the commonly accepted principles of comity when a case arose in 1913. That Society was about to refer the case to the National Missionary Conference, when representatives of the two missions met and settled the matter between themselves.[26]

Comity had come in India, and most places, to mean mutual recognition of each other as true and valid members in the body of Christ as well as noninterference. Noninterference really rested on such recognition and mutual respect. The prevailing attitude is illustrated by the reaction to the proposal by a missionary of the S.P.G. brought to the South India Missionary Association. He, in the name of comity, endeavored to persuade the Committee of that Association to pass a resolution which would require all mission schools to grant "liberty of conscience for agents (i.e., teachers) to whatever religious creed they may subscribe." This sounds like an application to teachers of the conscience clause applied to the protection of non-Christian children by some governments from time to time. However, what it really meant was that Anglican teachers who took posts in schools belonging to other missions should not be expected to participate in the school's worship. It put Christian denominational differences in the same category as differences between

[24] American Board of Commissioners for Foreign Missions, Marathi Mission, *Constitution and By-Laws, 1928*, p. 28; *Minutes, 1911*, Resolution 98; Letter of Mary A. Walker, Librarian of the A.B.C.F.M., Boston, January 8, 1954.

[25] Letter of Dr. Harris J. Stewart, General Sec., Sialkot Mission, United Presbyterian Church of N.A., to Dr. Glen P. Read, November 27, 1952.

[26] *Harvest Field*, vol. XXXIII, Nos. 10–12 (September–December, 1913), pp. 382–286, 361–362, 389–395, 457–462. There was a mistake in paging in one number.

faiths, such as between Christianity and Hinduism and Islam, and the average missionary would not countenance that. The proposal called forth a series of letters and editorials in *Harvest Field* during 1901. These comments not only repudiated the suggestion, but brought out clearly the general devotion to the spirit of mutual recognition that underlay the practice of comity. The editor of the magazine wrote, for example: "The great majority of Protestant missionaries act upon the belief that [comity] means more than cooperation in social and moral movements, more than the recognition of spheres of work and mutual consultation in interest of church discipline; it includes also the possibility of 'fellowship in worship. . . .' " [27]

A few years were required to establish the system of arbitration and to get it functioning. However, soon a Central Court of Arbitration with six associated Provincial Courts were to be found in operation. Thirty-six societies held formal membership in them at the beginning of 1909.[28] The system sought to combine simplicity of organization with an effective method of arbitration. Its aim was to "reduce to a minimum the evils of rivalry and competition, guard against the sin of wasting our Lord's money, give increased efficiency to existing agencies, spread the Gospel more swiftly in the regions beyond, and demonstrate before the world the essential oneness of Protestant Christianity." Hoping that the spirit of comity prevailed as strongly among the mission boards of the West as among their missionaries in the East, the authors of the scheme asked to be allowed to settle in the field such practical questions of comity as might arise from time to time. The plan was to be subject to modification as experience might prove necessary.[29]

[27] *Ibid.*, p. 362.
[28] *Ibid.*, New Series, vol. XX, No. 2 (February, 1909), p. 79.
[29] The appeal to the home boards and societies for liberty of action is interesting in view of the fact that so little attention to comity matters is to be noted in the annual reports and homebase records. It would seem that liberty of action on the field was the rule.

The Central Court consisted of eight members elected by the General Board plus the Convener of the Board, who was to serve *ex officio* as the honorary secretary of the Court. This body was charged with the preparation of a general statement of principles; and instructed to

> adjudicate on all matters of comity affecting the fields of labour; to secure information on unoccupied fields into which new missions might be invited; to keep records of decisions, to communicate them to the home boards and societies, and, if desirable, to publish them in the Indian press; and to fill any vacancies which might occur during any term of service.

Each Provincial Court was to consist of five persons, including an honorary secretary elected by the members of the national Board of Arbitration who represented the missions in that particular province. The duties of a Provincial Court were to be threefold: first, to adjudicate any local matter referred to it by the Central Court, expected to be mainly "such breaches of the recognized laws of comity as affect workers, members, or adherents, and possibly minor territorial difficulties"; second, to secure for the Central Court data on the occupation of areas and regions; and, third, to keep a proper record of its decisions, and to inform the Central Court of the disposal of each case.

The societies and boards represented through their missionaries on the Board of Arbitration were asked to make a very small contribution annually. The costs involved in the arbitration of a particular case were to be paid by the missions which had referred the matter to the Board. The sovereignty of the societies and boards was safeguarded by the statement that "the Home Boards will always have the power of deciding whether a matter is or is not to be referred to the Court of Arbitration."

The basic assumptions of comity on which the scheme was

to rest were set forth in a statement which gathered up the practical wisdom gained through the decades with respect to policy and practice. It includes the following points: [30] The Board of Arbitration would act only when a case had been officially referred to it for adjudication by the missions actually involved in it, although it might seek to use its good offices to find and effect a settlement if only one of the parties involved appealed to it. Decisions of the Court are final. The panel for adjudication of any case was to be composed as set forth in the enabling document of 1902. When new territory is to be entered, the mission that is best prepared for immediate, effective occupation shall be given the first opportunity. With respect to already occupied territory, any mission or missions which effectively occupy a field shall have the exclusive right to work it. However, cities with a population of over 100,000 are exempt from such limitation. "By effective occupation is meant an area, town, or village, so occupied that the religious needs of the people, in the view of the Court of Arbitration, have been effectively provided for." Continued neglect of any area invalidates supposed rights of occupation. With regard to the transfer of workers and members, local considerations should be of prime importance, and so no general rules are provided. Due regard shall always be given to liberty of conscience on the part of national Christians, who quite clearly have as much right to change denominational membership for valid reasons as their brethren in the West. In all such matters the principles laid down in Resolutions VIII and IX in the Comity Section of the *Report* of the previous Decennial Missionary Conference shall be taken as guides, namely, there shall be clearance with the other agency in the transfer of members or workers and refusal to accept into membership or employment any person under excommunication or other form of discipline.

[30] *Ibid.*, New Series, vol. XX, No. 2 (February, 1909), pp. 77–78.

India's system of arbitration was publicized at the Edinburgh Conference in 1910 and was held up as a model for missions in other areas of the world.[31] Then following that great assembly, its Continuation Committee under John R. Mott sponsored the important series of Continuation Committee Conferences in Asia. Mott held conferences at Colombo, Madras, Bombay, Jubbulpore, Allahabad, Lahore, and Calcutta, culminating in the India National Conference at Calcutta in December, 1912. This was locally accepted as the Decennial Conference due in that year.[32] This assembly established on the foundation of the old nationwide Decennial Conferences a new National Missionary Council of India and provided for the creation of affiliated representative Provincial Councils of Missions.[33] It was quite the logical consequence then, that after the new order had become established, the Board of Arbitration recommended that its functions be taken over by these permanent agencies. Accordingly a new "Statement on Comity among Missions in India" was drawn up for submission to the National Missionary Council at its first meeting in February, 1914.[34] This statement was but an elaboration of the earlier documents. General approval of the principles was given, and a committee was appointed, charged with fully perfecting the statement. The committee reported at the meeting of the Council in 1916. Its "Statement" was adopted, and it was ordered sent down to the Provincial Councils as a guide to any action which they might take. These area bodies were

[31] *World Missionary Conference, 1910*, vol. VIII, pp. 25, 149–150.
[32] *Findings of the National Conference Held in Calcutta, December 18–21, 1912, under the Presidency of Dr. John R. Mott; Continuation Committee Conferences in Asia*, pp. 119–153; *Harvest Field*, New Series, vol. XXIV (whole XXXIII), No. 1 (January, 1913), pp. 6–14.
[33] Hogg, W. R., *op. cit.*, p. 153.
[34] *National Missionary Council of India, 1915, Proceedings of the Second Meeting of —*, pp. 7–14 (The Continuation Committee meeting in 1912 is counted as the First); see also *National Christian Council Review*, vol. LXIX, No. 12 (December, 1949), p. 513.

permitted to make modifications, and then, after adoption of the document, they were to submit it to their constituent members for ratification.[35]

The editor of the national missionary magazine, *Harvest Field,* commented on the statement as it was sent to the daughter councils in this manner:

> This document has a considerable history, and a full record of it would show how strong is the desire to secure a series of recommendations couched in language acceptable to all. When so many persons at so many different times have taken upon themselves to frame such a code, one must not look for a nicely balanced piece of literature. One paragraph bears the impress of one personality, and a second reveals the inspiration of another. The whole, however, is marked by sanity and brotherliness. The document is of so great value that, though somewhat lengthy, we print it entire for the careful study of all who are eager for the evangelization of this land.

> This document is not a code of laws, but a code of ethics, and as such appeals to the moral judgment of every Christian worker. The statement is set forth with the approval of the National Council and with the earnest prayer that it may form a standard for the guidance of all who share in the evangelization of the people and the rule of the churches. . . . If all the Missions and Churches voluntarily accept this code of Comity as a guide to inter-mission and inter-church relationships, a very important step will have been taken to unite and compact the Churches of this land. No one must be coerced, save by the overwhelming compulsion of love to the great Head of the Church, Jesus Christ, Savior and Lord.[36]

The Provincial Councils immediately gave sympathetic

[35] *Harvest Field,* vol. XVII (XXXVI), No. 12 (December, 1916), pp. 471–476.
[36] *Ibid.,* pp. 442–443.

attention to the comity statement.[37] Some accepted the document almost exactly as received, while others made detailed recommendations for revision. The Madras Council, for example, in 1916 heard its special Committee on Comity and Cooperation report that the principles should be adopted, and that the document should be entitled "Statement on Comity among Missions and Churches in India" with an explanatory footnote indicating that the principles were indeed recommended to the churches as well as missions. It suggested, moreover, that the whole subject be treated more fully in a handbook. Preliminary investigation had disclosed that the national body was not interested in such a handbook, wishing only the brief statement. Therefore, such a handbook might be a project for South India.[38] The report was accepted at the annual meeting and the committee asked to prepare such a handbook.[39] The National Missionary Council did subsequently accept the suggestion regarding the title, and it added a footnote which read: "It is understood that Church Organizations which are in a position to take independent action should be regarded as Missions for the purpose of this statement." It also voted to publish a small handbook, but apparently this never appeared.

The Punjab Representative Council took up the recommendations in their earliest stage at the 1914 meeting in Lahore. A Committee headed by the Anglican Bishop of Lahore brought in detailed recommendations, spelling out carefully provisions for admission to membership, transfer of workers, treatment of persons under discipline, and the like. Its recommendation concerning the delimitation of territory shows the effect of the Anglican viewpoint and the chair-

[37] *National Missionary Council, Proceedings of the Fourth Meeting of the —, 1917*, p. 10.
[38] *Bulletin of the Madras Representative Council of Missions,* April 1916, pp. 13–15.
[39] *Ibid.,* pp. 2–4.

man's influence, and ran contrary to the spirit of the document proposed by the National Council.[40] It called the practice "only a temporary measure, fraught with serious and inevitable drawbacks." The Council, however, debated the proposals offered by the Committee and wrote its own "Standards of Comity." [41] It substituted for the Committee's statement on the division of territory this declaration: "That this Council recognizes that Territorial Delimitation while perhaps temporary, has been a most useful principle in the Missionary enterprise in the past, and should, as far as possible, be continued." It did recognize the right of members of a denomination living within the territory of another to invite a minister of their own church to visit them for pastoral care, provided that such visits did not become the occasion or basis for organized missionary propaganda. This Council also made very excellent proposals in its statement looking towards the more active promotion of comity and cooperation, including united evangelistic efforts, coordination of programs, and union projects. The Anglican Bishop at the next annual meeting reported criticism of the previous year's actions from two opposite points of view, from the Anglican Metropolitan and from the secretary of the National Missionary Council. All fifteen of the missions represented in the Council had sent in acknowledgment of their adherence to the rules as formulated. After animated discussion it was unanimously voted: "That this Council, recognizing that the very existence of the Representative Council rests on the basis of Comity Standards being observed by Missions represented in the Council, desires to reiterate its decision that the recognition of Comity Standards shall be a condition of admission in the P.R.C.M." [42] The same Council in 1917

[40] *Punjab Representative Council of Missions, Proceedings of the Second Annual Meeting of the —, 1914*, p. 2.
[41] *Ibid.*, pp. 4–7.
[42] *Ibid., Third Annual Meeting, 1915*, p. 3.

18475

combined the National Missionary Council's statement with its own "Standards of Comity." [43]

The Bengal and Assam Council in 1916 adopted as its own with slight modification the general statement submitted to it, and made a few more verbal changes in 1917.[44] Ten of the member missions had reported their adherence to the statement by the 1919 annual meeting.[45] The course of events in these three Provincial Councils may be taken as typical reactions on the part of the daughter councils.

Having received the reports of the affiliated bodies, the National Missionary Council made slight changes in the document in light of the suggestions and recommendations received. As then adopted it has remained, with very little change, the cornerstone of the cooperative edifice in India and the guide to basic inter-mission and interchurch relationships. The rise of mature Indian churches made a missionary council obsolete and removed comity matters and interchurch relationships from the hands of the missionaries. The National Missionary Council was, therefore, transformed into the National Christian Council of India. For many years both churches and missions were members of it, but eventually membership was restricted to churches. The same considerations made advisable slight changes in phrasing and teminology of the statement on comity. It was, therefore, slightly revised in 1938. It stands as the product of more than a century of experience and of eighty years of effort to formulate a satisfactory statement. In its slightly variable forms since 1902 it has ranked as the standard missionary statement of the principles and practice of comity. Other fields of the mission looked to it as a model. When next revised it would be no longer a document of missions, but of the national churches.

[43] *Ibid., Sixth Annual Meeting, 1918,* pp. 3–4, 16–20.
[44] *Bengal and Assam Representative Council of Missions, Proceedings of the Third Meeting of —, 1916,* pp. 26–30; *Fourth Meeting, 1917,* pp. 28–35.
[45] *Ibid., Fifth Meeting, 1919,* pp. 6–7.

STATEMENT ON COMITY AMONG MISSIONS AND CHURCHES
IN INDIA [46]

Introduction

The subject of comity is part of a wider subject. The primary task which lies before the Indian Church and the Foreign Missionary Societies at work in India is the evangelization of that land. For the accomplishment of this task the proper inter-relation of the forces and methods employed is scarcely less important than their adequacy and suitability. Such inter-relation has two principal branches:

(a) cooperative efforts

(b) hearty agreement and mutual considerateness with regard to separate efforts.

(a) Under cooperative efforts would be classed the union of ecclesiastical bodies, or steps taken towards such union, and cooperation between Missions in particular works or kinds of work, educational, medical, literary, etc.

With such efforts, important as they are, the present statement will deal only incidentally, but it is right always to bear in mind their close connection with the other side of inter-relation.

(b) The inter-relation of efforts which are made separately is the subject of this statement on comity. Comity may be defined as the spirit of considerateness and fair dealing which is the fruit of Christian courtesy and common sense. The object of this statement is to set forth the principles of comity and their application to Christian work in this country.

The rules given below are to be regarded as agreed statements adopted after a long period of consideration and not as standards to be imposed on missions and churches. Active

[46] Printed as a pamphlet by the National Missionary Council of India, n.d.; also in *National Christian Council Review,* vol. LXIX, No. 12 (December, 1949), pp. 536–541; vol. LXXII, No. 3 (March, 1952), pp. 116–126; Missionary Research Library, *Occasional Bulletin,* vol. VIII, No. 5 (April 30, 1952), pp. 8–12.

cooperation between Christian bodies in a given area in particular tasks and not merely their smooth working in isolation should be the purpose we have always to keep in view.

I. Arbitration and Conciliation

It is agreed:

1. That the principle of arbitration should be applied as widely as possible to all matters of dispute between missions or churches provided that the fundamental principles of the ecclesiastical bodies concerned be not thereby called in question.

2. That Provincial Christian Councils should be ready to act in the matter of arbitration and conciliation, and should make arrangements by which those matters can be dealt with between the sessions of the Council.

3. That in all cases of disagreement the mission or churches concerned should first attempt a settlement between themselves, and that reference should be made to a Provincial Christian Council only after such attempts have failed.

4. That a Provincial Christian Council should arbitrate only when any case is referred to it by the official representatives of both the bodies involved in any dispute. But in case one party declines arbitration, it shall still be open to the other party to appeal to the Council to use its friendly offices to bring about a settlement.

5. That the decision of a Provincial Christian Council or its appointed representatives will be advisory or final as shall be agreed by the parties concerned before the case is heard.

6. That for the settlement of any dispute, the appointed representatives should include an equal representation on behalf of the missions or churches directly concerned, chosen by themselves, preferably from the membership of the Provincial Christian Council, it being left to the Council to appoint an additional member or members, whether of its own body or not, having regard to the nature of the subject upon which arbitration is sought.

7. That a Provincial Christian Council may seek the aid of the National Christian Council in any matter affecting arbitration between missions or churches.

8. That any award or agreement arrived at after arbitration or conciliation should be reduced to writing.

II. Territorial Arrangements

(Cases in which two or three Missions are working or proposing to work in the same area)

The history of comity in past years has shown that there are some churches and missions which do not see their way to enter into any arrangement regarding territorial divisions, and there are other churches and missions which, while they have no such difficulty in regard to the delimitations to territory, insist upon certain restrictions with regard to the application of the principle. Experience has proved that even such difficulties are not always insuperable.

No attempt has been made to define what may be regarded as the 'effective occupation' of any sphere. Effective occupation depends upon the particular stage the work has reached. To make Christ known to all the people is the ideal in the early stages of evangelization. To equip the Indian Church for permanently dealing with that task constitutes the need of the later stage of development. In the earlier stage conditions differ so widely that neither the ratio of a geographical area, nor the numerical ratio of population to staff employed can be regarded as a satisfactory criterion. It must be left to the judgment of the Provincial Christian Council concerned to decide how far any area in any Province can be said to be effectively occupied.

It is agreed:

1. That in the event of any mission or church wishing to enter a new and unoccupied sphere in any Provincial area, consultation with the Provincial Christian Council for that sphere should precede any definite steps for occupation.

2. That wherever a mission or church is already working in

a district in which another mission, for any reason, contemplates operations, the former should be appraised of the fact and consulted before any steps are taken to begin work.

3. That any mission or church proposing to make any further advance in the opening up of new stations or substations in areas already partially occupied by other societies should consult with them before doing so.

4. That in areas in which different missions or churches are at work in close proximity to one another and under circumstances that are conducive to cooperative efforts, the different missions or churches should from time to time consult with one another as to the possibility of cooperation in institutional work (educational, medical, industrial, etc.), and no institutional work likely to affect the work of another mission or church should be initiated without consultation, and if possible agreement, with the other Christian organizations occupying the same area.

5. That in areas in which two or more similar institutions (educational, medical, industrial, etc.) now exist in such proximity to each other as to cause overlapping, it is desirable that negotiations be opened to see whether they could be united, or be utilized for different departments of the same work.

6. That agreements in regard to territorial arrangements already existing, or which may in future be arrived at in any way, should be reduced to writing, and carefully preserved.

7. That while the right of Christians to the ministrations of their own Communion is recognized, and while, congregations or small gatherings of Christians isolated from their own Communion should be expected to engage in evangelistic work on a voluntary basis, such ministrations and efforts should not be regarded as warranting isolated congregations in undertaking missionary operations that would in any way conflict with the work of the missions or churches occupying the field.

8. (a) That cities where the population (as in the Presidency cities and a few others) is of great extent and diversity, may be regarded as open to the effort of any Society. But a

Society desiring to enter, especially if it proposes to work amongst a special class or classes, should act on the principle laid down in Rule 1 above, with a view to the avoidance of overlapping.

If the question should arise as to whether a particular city belongs to this class, the Provincial Christian Council of the area should determine the question.

(b) That in smaller cities or towns, where the population is comparatively homogeneous and a mission or missions already have extensive work, any other mission or church contemplating entrance should act on the principle laid down in Rules 2 and 3 above.

(c) That when the mission or church so contemplating entrance into a city or town of this class is at work in the area of which that city or town is the recognized center, and desires a footing in the town for the sake of its work in the area, that consideration should be recognized as one of much weight.

III. Transfer of Mission or Church Workers

It is agreed:

That no worker or ex-worker of one mission or church should be employed by another mission or church without full preliminary consultation with the mission or church with which the worker is or was formerly connected. Consultation ought to include such matters as the personal character of the worker, and the question whether he is under any obligation to the mission or church with which he has been connected. In cases where such obligation is financial, as for instance, in the case of a worker who obtained his education on the definite understanding that he would serve the mission or church for a certain time, arrangements should be made in the event of a transfer taking place for a discharge of the obligation as may be mutually agreed upon.

The principle of this section shall apply also to the case of pupils in a mission or church school whom a representative of some other mission or church may propose to receive.

IV. Salaries of Mission or Church Workers

It is agreed:

1. That the adequate remuneration of all grades of workers in a Provincial area, and especially the need of revising salaries in view of changing economic conditions, are desirable subjects for the consideration of Provincial Christian Councils, and are deserving of their careful attention.

2. That while there seem to be great difficulties in standardizing the salaries of all Christian workers, educational, medical, and evangelistic, it is important that missions and churches should endeavor to cut off all occasions of jealousy and misunderstanding that may arise from inequalities in the remuneration of workers whose work and qualifications are similar.

V. Treatment of Workers Under Discipline

It is agreed:

1. That the disciplinary censure of one mission or church for clearly established fault in character and conduct should be respected by another.

2. That workers dismissed on such grounds by one mission or church should never be employed by another without previous consultation with the authority dismissing them. In case of disagreement reference should be made to the Secretary of the Provincial Christian Council, who may, if necessary, arrange for arbitration.

VI. Relation of Churches to Members of Other Churches

While it is agreed that it will conduce to the interest of the Kingdom of Christ in India that all churches which can unite without compromising their own principles should do so, and also that any churches which can enter into a federation without compromising their own principles should do so, the following three recommendations are offered to such churches as can, consistently with their own laws and principles, adopt

them, though they may not at the present time be able to
advance either to corporate union or to federation:

1. That churches should do their best to give spiritual
opportunities and assistance to members of other churches
who stand in need of them.

2. That church members from one area temporarily visiting
the sphere of another church organization should bring with
them certificates of membership, to be recognized for such
period only as the visit lasts.

3. That church members settling in the sphere of another
church organization should be given a certificate enabling
that church, if it see fit, to receive them into its fellowship.

VII. Baptism and Admission to Church Membership

It is agreed:

1. That it seems desirable for Provincial Christian Councils
to consider the possibility of a more uniform standard regarding baptism and the conditions of admission to church
membership.

2. That no church or mission should baptize or admit to
church membership, or accept as a candidate for baptism or
admission to church membership, any person who is already
receiving regular preparatory instruction, or is an admitted
catechumen in another church, without first consulting with
the officials of that church, but the final choice of the church
which he will join must rest with the candidate.

VIII. Treatment of Church Members under Discipline

It is agreed:

1. That different churches should mutually respect each
other's discipline.

2. That when no certificate is brought by the member of
one church applying for membership in another church,
enquiry should always be made into his conduct and standing
in the former.

3. That when a member of one church desires admission
into another, if on enquiry it proves that he is under dis-

cipline, or has rendered himself liable to discipline, for a grave fault against the moral law of Christ, his admission should not, as a general rule, be considered, until he has given evidence of repentance and reformation, and if discipline has been imposed, has completed the term of discipline in the church which has imposed it.

4. When a member of one church desires admission to another, and after enquiry from the former it appears that there has been no grave moral delinquency, but that the difference between him and his church is one of doctrinal or practical principle, on which the views of the two churches differ, the church approached may proceed to deal with the applicant according to its own laws, whether it be on his own initiative or in consequence of action taken against him by his church that the applicant came to desire to change his Communion.

Conclusion

In commending this statement on comity to the Christian organizations, the National Christian Council wish to add that all such rules of comity as those which it has drawn up will be kept easily and loyally in proportion as the missionaries and members of the different churches live on terms of Christian fellowship with one another. They should strive to meet not only when matters of difference arise, but in ordinary friendly intercourse and in consultation over the work of their lives, and thus to learn what each others' views and aspirations are. The Council rejoice that men and women of different missions and churches are increasingly meeting in conferences and councils and language schools. The Council would add that besides taking all opportunities for acquantance and consultation, the leaders and members of different churches should from time to time seek opportunities of joining in common worship in such ways as their laws and principles may permit, being well assured that nothing will be so full of blessing for the cause that churches and missions have at heart as the common offering of thanks and praise to the Author of all good, and the common seeking of light and guidance from the Author of all wisdom.

The editor of the *National Christian Council Review,* looking back in 1949 over the long development of the system of comity in India, could say:

> The historical development of these rules and principles shows clearly that they have not been imposed on Christian bodies, but have grown out of experience gained over several generations. Their authority exists only in the recognition of the necessity of Christian harmony and cooperation.[47]

[47] *National Christian Council Review,* vol. LXIX, No. 12 (December, 1949), p. 513.

CHAPTER IV

Comity as an Aid in Evangelization: Territorial Division in China

THE early Protestant missionary approach to China was characterized by Christian brotherhood and by a common concern that there should be enlisted evangelistic forces adequate to the enormous task of occupying a vast empire. Robert Morrison encouraged the American churches to send forth men. The Dutch Reformed pioneer, David Abeel, as the agent of the American Bible Society and the American Board of Commissioners for Foreign Missions, together with William J. Boone, the first missionary bishop of the Episcopal Church, traveled along the China coast seeking the best sites for missions. The celebrated German missionary, Karl A. Gützlaff, was frequently asked for advice. Scarcely any newcomer a generation later sought a location in central China without consulting Dr. Griffith John at Hankow.

China opened very slowly to missionary residence and work. The five treaty ports of Canton, Amoy, Foochow, Ningpo, and Shanghai were opened by the treaties of 1842–46. Treaties of 1858–60 forced open other ports, including Nanking, Chinkiang, Kiukiang, and Hankow on the Yangtze River in the heart of the country. They also granted the right of itineration in the interior, made possible the purchase of property, and, in effect, if not by their very letter, opened up the land to Christian occupation. When the first ports were opened, those societies which had been working among the Chinese in southeast Asia and Indonesia in preparation for this very opportunity rushed to occupy them. Newer agencies followed. Thus the precedent was set for joint occupation of a city or district by more than one

111

agency. When the interior was opened, there continued to be a tendency to seek out great cities.

This joint occupation of the cities had at one and the same time two opposite effects. First of all, just as in the provincial capitals or presidency cities in India, close proximity and mutual problems stimulated unity, cooperation, and local comity agreements. On the other hand, since too many missions sought the same cities, this practice made for overlapping, and perhaps delayed the development of over-all comity agreements. When a discussion of comity did arise outside local groups, the concern was not, as in India, with noninterference so much as with the stimulation of full and effective evangelistic occupation of the entire country. The India missionaries came to be concerned about that also, but in China it was the major consideration from the outset.

Comity agreements began with the partitioning of the port cities between the societies present there when missionaries were confined within their walls. When the work could be extended inland from them, further agreements were made. The process was frequently repeated as the interior regions were occupied. Thus, for example, the Church Missionary Society (C.M.S.), the American Board of Commissioners for Foreign Missions, and the Methodist Episcopal Mission divided the province of Fukien among them in the second decade after Foochow was opened.[1] The Scottish and Irish Presbyterians, drawn to Manchuria by the appeal of the English Presbyterian pioneer, William C. Burns, divided that great northeastern region between them by drawing a north-south line, the former taking the east, the latter the west.[2] The Wesleyan Methodist missionary, J. Cox, lived for a time with Dr. Griffith John in Hankow. When property could be secured for Cox, the two missions divided the city, the Wesleyans taking the upper city along the Han River, the

[1] MacGillivray, D., ed., *A Century of Protestant Missions in China*, p. 255.
[2] *Ibid.*, p. 223; see also p. 176.

London Missionary Society (L.M.S.) occupying the lower regions along the Yangtze.[3] They made a similar division of Wuchang a few years later.[4] These examples might be multiplied.

A most remarkable instance of comity and unity was demonstrated at Amoy. This city was originally a station of the American Board, staffed in part by missionaries of the Reformed Church in America. When that church withdrew from cooperation in the American Board in 1857, Amoy was handed over to its Board of Foreign Missions. American Presbyterian missionaries also came there in the earliest days, but after several years went elsewhere, handing over their work to the Reformed Mission. The L.M.S. entered in 1844, and the English Presbyterians in 1850. The three missions then divided the Amoy region into separate spheres of operation and proceeded to develop all phases of the work in close cooperation. Moreover, the Reformed and Presbyterian missions, sharing a common doctrine and polity, united in establishing a single indigenous church, independent of either the American or British parent, the first union church in China.[5]

Another unusual development in China was the denominational diversity and adjustment worked out by the China Inland Mission in its earlier period. This pioneer and model of all the later faith missions under the inspiration and leadership of J. Hudson Taylor set out to carry the gospel to all the far reaches of the interior then untouched by the denominational missions. Nondenominational in organization, Taylor and his followers thought of the China Inland Mission (C.I.M.) as truly interdenominational, providing an instrument in which any of the existing church orders might be established in China, so long as their representatives would

[3] *Ibid.*, p. 189.
[4] *Ibid.*, p. 92.
[5] *Ibid.*, pp. 367–368.

work within the fellowship of the organization, be subject to its administration, and accept its methods. D. E. Hoste, Director General of the Mission, wrote in 1918:

> . . . different parts of the field occupied by the Mission have been allocated to Anglicans, Presbyterians, Methodists, Baptists, and so on; it being clearly understood that, so long as certain lines of doctrine and missionary methods are adhered to, as laid down in the Constitution of the Mission, the Executive of the Mission does not exercise official ecclesiastical jurisdiction over the various churches. In each district the Mission has its own arrangements for the maintenance of the missionaries and their work, and of mission property. This, however, is distinct from the ecclesiastical government of the churches.[6]

In accord with this policy Anglicans were assigned to the mission district in Szechuan, and that mission was combined with the C.M.S. unit in the province to form a single diocese. Similarly Baptist churches were established in southern Shansi and related to those planted by the English Baptist Missionary Society. Three Presbyterian districts were created in different parts of the country. Most of the continental European societies affiliated with the C.I.M. were Lutheran in background. However, with these exceptions the C.I.M. became in effect another denomination. Nevertheless, J. Hudson Taylor, D. E. Hoste, and many of their colleagues were strong advocates of comity, and their utterances in its support are recorded in the records of numerous conferences.

There was no general meeting of Protestant missionaries in China until 1877. It was in that year that there assembled in Shanghai the General Conference of the Protestant Missionaries of China. Both church union and cooperation in occupation were in the agenda. Dr. Carstairs Douglass of

[6] China Continuation Committee, M. T. Stauffer, ed., *The Christian Occupation of China,* p. 332.

Amoy on this occasion called for a division of territory as
had been done in South India.[7] He regarded this as necessary
to the evangelism of the vast interior. There was at the time
only one missionary to 2,000,000 people in the most vast mission field on the globe. The root principle required, he
declared, is brotherly love, stemming from love of Christ.
The practical application of this principle is systematic cooperation by mutual assistance and division of labor. There
must be cooperation in works of a general character, such as
literature production. In working the fields already occupied
there should be mutual recognition of each other's discipline,
union projects, and division of the countryside around the
cities. In occupying the vast regions yet untouched they
should be carefully divided and the evangelistic responsibility for them should be assigned specifically.

The Conference appointed a Committee on the Division
of the Field, and this brought in a report.[8] The several missions at work in any area were requested to work in different
localities, while new missions were asked to seek unoccupied
territory. Cooperation in functional work was recommended
One recommendation of more than usual interest reads:
"That in the case of sickness or absence, or on other occasions calling for assistance, missionaries should supply each
other's need, and thus by mutual help seek to vindicate the
great truth that they are brethren in Christ Jesus and fellow
workers in the same great undertaking." [9]

Thirteen years later the Second General Conference of
Missionaries was held in Shanghai, the favorite location for
meetings of a national scope. The subject, "Division of the
Field," was on the agenda. The Rev. J. W. Stevenson in
introducing the topic stated that with rare exceptions a good
understanding with regard to separate fields prevailed among

[7] *General Conference of the Protestant Missionaries of China*, Shanghai,
1877, *Records of the —*, p. 443.
[8] *Ibid.*, 1877, pp. 15, 471–472.
[9] *Ibid.*, 1877, p. 471, third recommendation.

the China missionaries.[10] The Rev. John McCarthy of the
C.I.M. presented an essay on cooperation which called for
church union, and in it he deplored the occupation of the
same city by a number of agencies, while whole regions were
still untouched.[11] Some conference members were not prepared to follow him. The founder of the C.I.M. regarded division of the field as a help to rapid evangelization of the
country. The Rev. J. Hudson Taylor remarked:

> With regard to the division of the field, if we could come to
> some definite arrangement by which certain societies or indi-
> viduals would definitely undertake to extend in certain direc-
> tion so that we could divide up the whole of China into large
> parishes, the rapid evangelization of China would soon be
> accomplished.[12]

The resolutions which were adopted after the discussion read
like similar ones in India, recommending that large cities
in contrast to small ones be regarded as open ground for
common occupation, that new missions go to unoccupied
ground, that disagreements over occupation be settled by
arbitration, that care be taken not to receive persons who
are candidates for baptism in another church in the same
place, that acts of discipline by church bodies be mutually
recognized, and that no agents be transferred from one mission to another without proper consultation.[13] The resolution
went farther than the Indian actions of the same time in
explicitly recognizing the inherent right of every church
member to transfer his membership to another denomination.
The Committee on Comity stated that "in view of the spirit
of unity and brotherly love prevailing among us" it was not
necessary to propose more than these simple resolutions,

[10] *Ibid.*, 1890, p. 592.
[11] *Ibid.*, 1890, pp. 594–600.
[12] *Ibid.*, 1890, p. 602.
[13] *Ibid.*, 1890, xlix–1.

"which embody some of the ordinary rules of procedure long in use in many of our missions." [14]

The prevalence of this spirit of good will was attested by the Rev. G. T. Caudlin of the Methodist New Connexion Mission in an article in the *Chinese Recorder* in 1893.[15] He agreed that there had been the lowest minimum of friction possible under the circumstances. However, he deplored the extent of wasteful overlapping and strongly advocated not just comity, but union. He reported that seven agencies worked in Peking, four in Tientsin, eight in Shanghai, and still more in Canton. An English Baptist missionary, R. C. Forsyth, also called for denominational federation and provincial missionary unions, and the Rev. John Stevens of Shanghai seconded his proposals.[16] Dr. Griffith John of the L.M.S. in central China spoke for many of his brethren in another article in the same journal when he advocated comity on a territorial basis, warned against selfish claims to occupation of areas too large to be worked adequately, and suggested means for promoting unity where several missions were present in the same locality.[17] The L.M.S. followed his advice by turning over its Hunan field to the Reformed Church in the United States and to the Presbyterian Church in the U.S.A.

Such sentiments found expression in concrete terms in Szechuan, Yünnan, and Kweichow, three large and populous provinces in western China. The agencies involved were the American Baptist Missionary Union, the China Inland Mission, Church Missionary Society, Friends Foreign Missionary Association, London Missionary Society, Bible Christian Mission, Methodist Episcopal Mission, Canadian Methodist Mission, National Bible Society of Scotland, and the Ameri-

[14] *Ibid., 1890*, p. xlix.
[15] *Chinese Recorder*, vol. XXIV, No. 12 (December, 1893), pp. 553–567.
[16] *Ibid.*, vol. XXVI, No. 7 (July 1895), pp. 315–318; No. 10 (October 1895), pp. 383–485.
[17] *Ibid.*, vol. XXIX, No. 10 (October, 1898), pp. 467–471.

can Bible Society. The last two were not, of course, engaged in operating evangelistic and Christian institutional work, but in assisting all the others through their specialized activities. A comprehensive plan of regional cooperation was adopted in 1899.[18]

The plan was based on the sure ground of mutual intercession. The residents of every mission station and every missionary who happened to be away from his station and alone was requested to pray for the entire Christian work in western China and for one another each week on Wednesday morning. A monthly bulletin of information was to be published so that all might be informed about each other. It was agreed that the several societies would mutually recognize and receive each other's members and that every church member removing from one station to another would receive a letter of commendation. Pulpit exchange was recommended, as well as united services and meetings in places where two or more missions were present. Full inter-mission consultation was to precede any transfer of native workers. The Chungking Committee was asked to set up a union training school for evangelists. An Advisory Board of Reference and Cooperation was created. When any matter could not be settled satisfactorily by the missions concerned, it should be referred to that board. Principles for a division of territory were laid down, and any new mission desiring to enter western China was requested to consult with the Advisory Board. The actual delimitation of territory was apparently made by the missions in direct consultation with each other. The aim sought by these was a spirit of harmony and cooperation which would speed the complete occupation of the field. The effect was so beneficial that in 1908 an attempt was made by the Conference to form a single united church for western China. Eleven years later a very favorable report of the work

[18] West China Missionary Conference at Chungking, 1899, Records of the —, pp. 7–9.

and influence of this Advisory Board was given to the Edinburgh Conference.[19]

Regional conferences were formed in other parts of China, such as the Peking, Wu-Han, Shanghai, and Canton districts.[20] Soon after the end of the Boxer troubles the missions in the capital province of Chihli or Hopeh undertook to arrange to delimit their fields.[21] Before beginning reconstruction in Paotingfu, the mission of the Presbyterian Church in the U.S.A. and that of the American Board divided the city, the former taking the northern half, the latter the southern portion.[22] The American Board also by successive agreements with other missions completed the delimitation of its Pangchwang Station on the northern border of Shantung.[23] The missions at work in the province of Hunan, one of the last to open to Protestant missions, held a conference in Changsha June 19–20, 1903, and assigned spheres of occupation.[24]

It was at this time also that the Peking missionaries led by Dr. Thomas Cochrane undertook a movement to create a nation-wide federation of the churches and missionary forces. Dr. Cochrane initiated the movement by reading a paper on "Some Problems in Mission Work" before the Peking Missionary Conference in November, 1902, in which he emphasized the importance of exhibiting to the Chinese the essential unity of the various Protestant branches of the Christian Church. The Conference was so moved that it appointed a Committee on Union to consider the subject with a view to practical action. On February 27, 1903, this committee sent a circular to every known missionary in

[19] *World Missionary Conference, 1910,* vol. VIII, pp. 24, 33–34.
[20] *Conference on Federation Held at Peking, 1905, The Records of a —,* p. 86.
[21] *Ibid.,* p. 115.
[22] MacGillivray, D., ed., *op. cit.,* p. 201.
[23] *Ibid.,* p. 282.
[24] *Ibid.,* p. 38.

China asking each individual's opinion on four questions: (1) the preparation of a union hymn book; (2) the adoption of a common designation for churches and chapels; (3) the adoption of common terms for God and Holy Spirit; and (4) the federation of all the Protestant churches in China. The response was so favorable that in April the committee issued a call for a Conference of North China Missionaries at Peitaho, the summer resort on the Gulf of Pei-Chihli, on August 24, 1904. The conference met as called and after three days of discussion unanimously endorsed Dr. Cochrane's four proposals. The Peking Union Committee was made the committee of the Conference and was empowered to proceed with calling a general conference on federation. The Union Committee undertook to request each mission in China to name one representative to a General Committee, called to meet in Peking. Thus it was that the Conference on Federation was held at Peking from September 28 to October 1, 1905.[25]

The replies to the four questions sent out by the Peking Committee were overwhelmingly favorable, and enthusiasm at the Conference ran high, but in the end ecclesiastical considerations and caution prevailed. The Conference decided that it was not sufficiently authoritative to take responsibility for establishing the federation and referred the matter to those planning for the Centenary Missionary Conference, which would be held in 1907, the centennial anniversary of the arrival of Robert Morrison in China.[26] The "Outline of Tentative Scheme of Federation" included within the work of the proposed organization initiative in arranging for mutual division of territory to avoid overlapping, free interchange of members, and occupation of vacant fields.[27]

The subject of comity and federation, as might then be

[25] *Conference on Federation Held at Peking, 1905, The Records of a —,* pp. 3–4; Dr. Cochrane reviews the history of the movement.
[26] *Ibid.,* p. 115.
[27] *Ibid.,* p. 79.

expected, had a large place in the program of the Centenary Missionary Conference at Shanghai from April 25 to May 8, 1907. The Peking Committee's formula was not offered, but resolutions were adopted calling for the formation of a federal union under the title, "The Christian Federation of China." [28] The purpose was stated as: "to foster and encourage the sentiment and practice of union, to organize union effort whenever and wherever possible, and in general to seek through all such effort to hasten the establishment of the Kingdom of God in China." Provincial councils on a representative basis were to be formed, and the National Representative Council was to consist of delegates from each of these. Comity was not mentioned specifically in the document adopted, but the responsibility of the Federation for it was there by inference. The formation of provincial councils and associations was accelerated,[29] but the national organization was long delayed and was finally provided by the creation of the China Continuation Committee in 1913.

Instances of territorial division and elimination of overlapping were not lacking during the next few years,[30] but as late as 1910 Dr. P. F. Price could lament that: "Many large cities have from three to ten central mission stations, while other populous centers have only one, or none at all. Some small places have two or three outstations of different denominations, while other extensive areas have none at all." [31] However, by the time that the Edinburgh Conference Continuation Committee held a series of conferences in China in 1913, Shantung could report,

[28] *China Centenary Missionary Conference Records*, pp. 719–721; see pp. 689–721 for the entire discussion.
[29] Latourette, K. S., *A History of Christian Missions in China*, p. 668. Mention is made of councils or conferences in Chekiang, Kiangsu, Kwangtung, Kwangsi, Manchuria, Chihli, Shantung, Honan, Kiangsi, Anhui, Hupeh, Hunan, North Fukien, and South Fukien.
[30] *Ibid.* p. 664.
[31] Price, P. F., "What Is Effective Occupation?" in *Chinese Recorder*, vol. XLI, No. 6 (June, 1910), p. 395.

> . . . The principle of comity is generally observed in the Province of Shantung. We have division of territory; transference of churches from one Mission to another where geographical conditions seem to make it advisable; transference of members by letter from one Church to another; and inquiries have been made with a view to securing more uniformity in the scale of salaries.[32]

The Peking Conference called for provincial councils, which would be responsible for effecting the division of territory, and requested a Board of Arbitration for all China.[33] Dr. Thomas Cochrane, who was the foremost instigator of the federation movement brought out his *Survey of the Missionary Occupation of China* in 1913 at the time of the Continuation Committee Conferences. He bore witness to the harmony that prevailed, and declared: "Delimitation of territory and union in education and evangelistic work in the large centers are more and more in evidence year by year, and all that is now needed to complete the exhibition of Mission Comity is mutual planning on a large scale." [34]

The China national Conference concluding the series sponsored by the Continuation Committee was concerned with furthering all forms of cooperation and with effective occupation of the country.[35] It provided for a China Continuation Committee to carry on the work of the conference and to consolidate the earlier gains in cooperation. The new national organ made rapid progress under the leadership of an able secretariat, including E. C. Lobenstine, Ch'en Ching-yi, and A. L. Warnshuis.

The existence of a continuing national organ of cooperation with a competent staff made possible the attainment of many things long advocated but never before achieved. At

---

[32] *The Continuation Committee Conferences in Asia, 1912–1913*, p. 259.
[33] *Ibid.*, pp. 286–287.
[34] Cochrane, T., *Survey of the Missionary Occupation of China*, p. 371.
[35] *Continuation Committee Conferences in Asia 1912–1913*, pp. 231–367.

the Fourth Annual Meeting of the China Continuation Committee in 1916, the attention of the delegates was so favorably directed to the statement on comity recently adopted by the National Missionary Council of India that a Special Committee on Comity was appointed and assigned the task of collecting information from comity committees in China and abroad and of preparing a report for the next meeting.[36] D. E. Hoste of C.I.M. was made chairman. This committee was also charged by the Executive Committee with making a careful study of the extent to which breaches of comity exist. To this the committee replied at the next annual meeting that there had been a number of protests received from different parts of China against the actions of a small number of societies which were seeking to establish themselves by proselyting methods.[37] It was hoped that the adoption of a common statement on comity by churches and societies would prevent the recurrence of such troubles. The India Statement, revised in phrasing and terminology to meet the situation in China, was proposed by the committee and adopted by the assembly.[38]

The statement was commended to the churches and missions for their consideration and adoption, with the request that a report on action by these bodies be made at the next annual meeting. The Executive Committee of the China Continuation Committee was made the organ for arbitration and was charged with continuing the work of the Committee on Comity. The foreign secretary reported later in the year that there had been only a few cases of misunderstanding between missions referred to the Executive body.[39] By the time of the next annual meeting 68 replies had been received

[36] *China Continuation Committee, Proceedings of the Fourth Annual Meeting of the —, 1916,* pp. 21–22, 29.

[37] *Ibid., Fifth Annual Meeting,* 1917, pp. 120–121; see also *China Mission Yearbook, 1917,* p. 475.

[38] *Ibid.,* pp. 20, 120–124; *Chinese Recorder,* vol. XLVI, No. 6 (June, 1917), pp. 348–358; *Christian Occupation of China,* pp. lxxxv–lxxxvi.

[39] *China Mission Yearbook, 1917,* p. 475.

from church and mission authorities, 34 having given formal approval, and the 34 others having promised to bring the statement before the next official meeting of their organization.[40] At the 1919 meeting the secretaries were able to report that 108 mission bodies with 4,456 missionaries had approved the Statement; approval was pending in the case of 19 bodies with 785 missionaries; no reply had been received from 17 with 278 missionaries; and they had not yet been able to present the Statement to 29 bodies with 393 missionaries.[41] A year later it could be said that 57 per cent of the societies with 70 per cent of the missionaries had accepted the Statement, and that no agency had voted to disapprove it..[42] By 1922, when the great survey volume was completed, 115 missions (including each separate unit of major societies) had signified their acceptance.[43]

The "Survey": The Missionary Occupation of China

Since the question of comity was linked with effective occupation of the country in the minds of so many missionaries, a factual survey was urgently needed for the sake of intelligent discussion and action. Requests for a survey were made repeatedly but the lack of a continuing, active national body thwarted their fulfillment. Dr. Thomas Cochrane attempted to provide this desirable tool with his useful book on the missionary occupation of China, but the task was be-

[40] *Chinese Recorder,* vol. XLIX, No. 6 (June, 1918), p. 303; *China Continuation Committee, Proceedings of the Sixth Annual Meeting of the —,* 1918, p. 25.

[41] *Ibid., Seventh Annual Meeting, 1919,* pp. 86–89. The Seventh Day Adventists were not able to accept territorial limitations, but filed a statement indicating their intention to follow certain procedures in the spirit of comity, pp. 89–90.

[42] *Chinese Recorder,* vol. L, No. 6 (June, 1919), p. 373.

[43] *Christian Occupation of China,* p. lxxxvii.

yond the ability of one man to perform unaided by a central authority and large financial resources.[44] The National Conference of 1913 called by the Continuation Committee of the Edinburgh Conference laid responsibility for a survey upon its own Continuation Committee, but it was not until 1916 that active preparation for the project was begun. After two more years the survey actually got under way when an active committee, chaired by Dr. E. C. Lobenstine, was given a secretary, Reverend Milton T. Stauffer, with an adequate staff and office facilities. A prodigious feat was performed in the next three years, and in 1922 there was published the monumental volume entitled *The Christian Occupation of China*, the most comprehensive quantitative survey ever made of a major mission field.[45]

A quotation from Robert E. Speer opposite page 1 gives a definition of what constitutes adequate missionary occupation. (It has been quoted on page 17 of the Introduction.) If not the standard of measure applied by the Survey Committee, it was at least the ideal. The first sentence of the Preface states: "The main purpose of this Survey has been the speedier and more effective evangelization of China."

The book revealed clearly the tremendous increase in missionary forces since 1900, taking the Boxer year as a divide "between the China that was and the China that will be." [46] During the first twenty years of the twentieth century as many new stations and residential areas were established as in all the ninety-three years of the nineteenth century. Yet this expansion was accompanied by that concentration of workers and institutions about which some persons had been

[44] *Survey of the Missionary Occupation of China.*
[45] China Continuation Committee, Stauffer, Milton T., ed., *The Christian Occupation of China: A General Survey of the Numerical Strength and Geographical Distribution of the Christian Forces in China Made by the Special Committee on Survey and Occupation, China Continuation Committee, 1918–21.* Shanghai, 1922.
[46] *Ibid.,* pp. 32–39.

complaining since the opening of the century. New workers from the West went largely into old stations, since the number of residential centers increased only 24 per cent over against an increase of 55 per cent in the number of missionaries. Of the missionaries 66 per cent were living in cities of over 50,000 inhabitants, while Chinese workers were scattered more widely. The concentration was greater on the part of American than British agencies. Extension was, then, becoming more and more the responsibility of the Chinese staff. With respect to missionary societies, in 1900 there had been 61 at work in China; now there were 130, plus about 36 affiliated or independent Chinese agencies. However, the opening of new residential stations was not so much due to the activities of these new, relatively smaller societies, but of those of the older agencies. The newer ones went largely to the cities where the old societies were already working and where they frequently made a place for the newcomers.

The *Survey*, as the book was usually called, seems to understand comity to mean unity expressed chiefly through cooperative enterprises and various degrees of union, with territorial division being only incidental to this. It reported that there had been a steady growth in comity and understanding between denominations. It seems to credit this to the common occupation of the large cities where missionaries of various societies came into intimate relationship. On the other hand, it observed that 83 per cent of the missionaries were in stations held by a single mission and, therefore, isolated and hampered in learning to think and work with others. Progress in union had been most significant in educational work, and most notable in theological education, where it might have been least expected. Eight denominations were working together in the Canton Union Theological Seminary, for example. Could there be any clearer indication of the degree to which unity prevailed? General education followed, and then medical work. Church union had so far been along lines of denominational consolidation. Anglicans, Lutherans, and Presbyterians had each created national church bodies. The centralized service to the Christian community was being provided by such organs as the China Continuation Committee, the China Christian Educational Association, and the China Medical Missionary Association. Although a united church for China had not come into existence, there had been a deepening of emphasis on unity, and it was evident that the Christian Church in China "had "entered upon the period of its corporate life." [47]

Seven provinces no longer had any territory unclaimed by some agency, but nevertheless there was still so much unclaimed country in the far western provinces and part of Manchuria that nearly one fourth of China proper still remained unoccupied. In addition an area as large as China proper was still unentered and unclaimed in Mongolia, Sinkiang, Kokonor, Chuanpien, and Tibet. Moreover, 46 per cent of the total area of the nineteen provinces of China proper was beyond ten li (three and one third miles) from any evangelistic center. Shantung had the most adequate coverage with only 4 per cent of its area being more than ten li from a church or preaching place. Unclaimed and relatively unoccupied areas were carefully located and described, so that old agencies able to expand or new ones just arriving might know where to locate.

An invaluable series of maps for each province and for all of China was carefully drawn by experts on the basis of the comprehensive data so diligently assembled. The general maps of Protestant Mission Fields (p. 330) shows that, with the exception of the great cities, there had come about a far greater degree of denominationalism by geography than might have been expected. Overlapping was greatest along the eastern seaboard and the lower half of the Yangtze Valley, where the missionary enterprise had entered in the

[47] *Ibid.*, p. 308.

earlier period. Throughout the country were to be found vast expanses where the Christians all belonged to one major branch of the church.

Part III on "The Christian Occupation of the Provinces" reports on comity agreements in each of the nineteen provinces. In Anhwei[48] the fields of six missions overlapped around Wuhu, and three of the ten missions in the province were without any field delimitations. The Presbyterian Church in the U.S.A. alone had definite comity agreements with neighboring missions. The China Inland Mission (C.I.M.) had bilateral understandings with both the American Episcopalians and the Methodist Episcopal Mission. In all other cases agreements as to territory were tacit and not formal.

Since Ningpo was one of the original five treaty ports opened to residence by foreigners, the province of Chekiang was early claimed by many agencies. Fourteen societies were present, and excepting in the western part of the province there was much overlapping. Nevertheless, all the larger missions reported either written or oral agreements.[49] Only two societies had no agreements with others. The C.M.S. reported a definite understanding in each of its stations regarding the delimitation of the field, and there existed printed agreements between it and the C.I.M. with respect to the areas around Taichow, Tientai, Hwangyen, and Taiping. The same mission had an agreement with the Presbyterian Church in the U.S.A. about the Iwu district. The United Methodist Church, the C.I.M., and the Presbyterians had each agreed not to establish preaching places within five li (about two miles) of those maintained by either of the other two, with the exception of Wenchow. The Presbyterians and Methodists had made a compact not to open new work within ten li of a station belonging to the other party, or within twenty li with-

[48] *Ibid.*, p. 42.
[49] *Ibid.*, p. 50.

out prior consultation. Other missions had only general agreements or understandings.

Szechuan, as the result of the agreement of 1899, was an example of complete partition by mutual agreement.[50] The only important instance of overlapping occurred in an area east of Chengtu where the Friends and the Methodist Episcopal Mission were both at work. Neighboring Kweichow was an example of a province where there was much unoccupied territory, little overlapping, and only one comity agreement, and that one a family affair, between the C.I.M. and its affiliate, the Friedenshort Deaconess Mission.[51]

These examples will be sufficient to illustrate the types of situations to be found in the different sections of the country.

The Survey had one effect certainly not foreseen by those who so devotedly and laboriously prepared it. Students discovered in it a plot to subvert the nation and seize control of the government. These students had led the popular demonstration against Japanese aggression in 1919. They held the center of the stage in nationalist agitation during the next few years. They were highly skeptical of religion, and in them the traditional agnosticism of the Chinese literati had been re-enforced by materialistic skepticism about spiritual and ethical values, scientism, and Communism, all of which had been imported from the West. The Burton Commission Report, *Christian Education in China*, chanced to be published simultaneously with the *Christian Occupation of China*. The nationalist students, suspicious of religion to begin with, saw in these clear evidence of the imperialist purpose of the missions. The detailed demographic and economic studies, the statistical tables and charts, and above all the minutely detailed maps showing the division and assignment of every last acre of the country had only one meaning to them. Then in the Burton Report they and their teachers became aware

[50] *Ibid.*, pp. 222–223.
[51] *Ibid.*, p. 179.

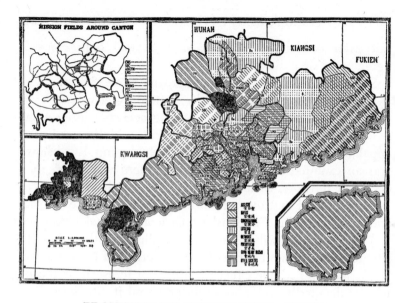

PROVINCE OF KWANGTUNG, CHINA

An example of serious overlapping of mission agencies in the neighborhood of a major port city, Canton, with later division of territory by comity agreements in the hinterland.

Missions: ABCFM—American Board of Commissioners for Foreign Missions; ABF—American Baptist Foreign Mission Society; B—Basel Mission; Bn—Berlin Mission; CIM—China Inland Mission; CMS—Church Missionary Society; CNTM—China New Testament Mission; EPM—English Presbyterian Mission; Ev M—Evangel Mission; KCM—Kieler Mission; LMS—London Missionary Society; PN—Presbyterian Church in the U.S.A.; PCC—Presbyterian Church in Canada; PCNZ—Presbyterian Church of New Zealand; RM—Rhenish Mission; RPC—Reformed Presbyterian Mission; SBC—Southern Baptist Convention; SCHM—South China Holiness Mission; SEFC—Swedish Evangelical Free Church (U.S.A.); UB—United Brethren in Christ; WMMS—Wesleyan Methodist Missionary Society. From *The Christian Occupation of China*, p. 159.

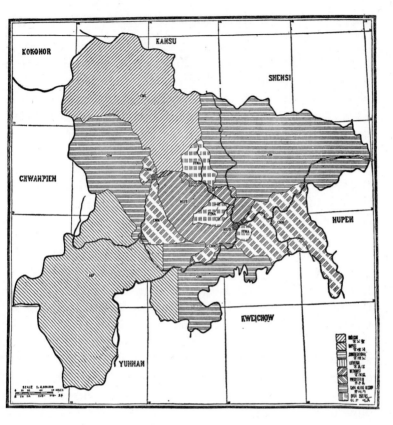

PROVINCE OF SZECHUAN, CHINA

A typical example of total division of territory by comity agreements without overlapping.

Missions: ABF—American Baptist Foreign Mission Society; CIM—China Inland Mission; CMS—Church Missionary Society; FFMA—Friends Foreign Mission Association; CMM—Canadian Methodist Mission; MEFB—Board of Foreign Missions, Methodist Episcopal Church. From *The Christian Occupation of China*, p. 222.

for the first time of the magnitude of the Protestant educational enterprise in China. This seemed to them, not the pioneer model that it had really been, but a dangerous rival system to that which the government was slowly building. They charged that the Christian schools were denationalizing the students. There was a demand for either nationalization or registration and control of the schools, and registration was soon imposed.

The Christian Occupation of China was published just on the eve of the National Christian Conference of 1922 and furnished most of the grist for its mill. This assembly, called by the China Continuation Committee, brought into being the National Christian Council. Its report, entitled *The Chinese Church As Revealed in the National Christian Conference, 1922*, is indicative of its nature.[52] More than half of the thousand delegates were Chinese and the Church in China, not the foreign missionary enterprise in China, was at the center. A new period in the history of Christianity had arrived. The data in the survey dealing with comity and cooperation were reviewed by the Conference, but apparently nothing special was done about it and no action was taken.[53] Nothing about comity and arbitration was written into the statement on the functions of the Council, although it might be assumed to be involved in the phrase "to foster and express the fellowship and unity of the Christian Church in China." [54] Perhaps this avoidance of the subject was due to the fundamentalist controversy then raging in the land.[55] The evidence of essential unity demonstrated by the data in the survey should have been a rebuke to those partisans who so violently endeavored to destroy the unity of the fellowship.

[52] *The Chinese Church as Revealed in the National Christian Conference, Held in Shanghai, Tuesday, May 2, to Thursday, May 11, 1922;* Shanghai: Oriental Press [1922].

[53] *Ibid.*, pp. 127–131.

[54] *Ibid.*, p. 694.

[55] Latourette, K. S., *A History of Christian Missions in China,* pp. 795–796.

Apparently the missionaries and the Chinese church officers believed that the action on comity under the China Continuation Committee fully disposed of the matter. The responsibility for the promotion and safeguarding of comity was never specifically recognized by the National Christian Council. The memorandum on "Functions of the National Christian Council" presented at the annual meeting in 1923 disclaimed any concern for promoting organic church union but affirmed "a strong sense of responsibility to do everything it can to promote the fullest harmony and practical cooperation," and offered the guidance of the headquarter's staff to those agencies desiring to expand or new ones desiring to enter China.[56] It was to endeavor to keep the goal of complete occupation of the land before the churches. The Survey Committee endeavored to secure serious consideration of the data by regional conferences, Chinese home missionary societies, and missions.[57] No mention of comity appears in the annual reports during the decade following the establishment of the Council. The entrance of some new agencies which disregarded established work must have caused some uneasiness, but there are no references to it. At the end of that period the financial depression had set in and retrenchment lessened the pressure from such agencies.

At the 1935 meeting the effectiveness of the old Comity Agreement was recalled and it was suggested that something similar might now be worked out with respect to the use of the radio by Christian agencies.[58] It is rather odd that the Administrative or Executive Committees of the Council were not formally charged with serving as a Board of Arbitration as had been the case with the Executive Committee of the China Continuation Committee.

[56] National Christian Council of China, *Annual Report, 1922–1923*, pp. 66–67.
[57] *Ibid., Annual Report, 1923–1924*, pp. 106–107.
[58] *Ibid., Biennial Report, 1933–1935*, p. 46.

CHAPTER V

Comity through Advance Planning

Puerto Rico and the Philippines

THE missionary literature of the nineteenth and early twentieth centuries is filled with pleas for comity agreements for the purpose of fixing responsibility for, and then speeding evangelization in regions not yet occupied. Comity in most of the mission fields was developed by local initiative carrying out the accepted policy of the mission boards and societies. There are a few regions, notably Latin America, where the policy and practice were advanced through area-wide planning. There are also a few countries where, when they were newly opened, there was advance planning, including the division of territory. Puerto Rico and the Philippines fall into this category. Cuba was at the same time expected to form a third member of this trio, but that effort failed. Korea is also a good example of the rectification of early confusion by planning on the part of the majority.

"Manifest destiny," a powerful sentimental factor in the expansion of the United States to its present boundaries and then in both the acquiring of overseas territories and the exertion of influence in international affairs, was one motive in the enormous growth of American foreign missionary endeavor during the last half of the nineteenth century. Many Protestants believed that God had raised up the new nation to play a decisive role in the winning of the world for Christ. Quite naturally, when, as the result of the Spanish-American War, there were opened up to evangelical missions for the first time the new American possessions of Puerto Rico and

134

the Philippines along with the newly independent ally, Cuba, the Protestant mission boards of the United States regarded the opportunity as the special gift of providence requiring an urgent response on their part.

Arthur Judson Brown, on behalf of the Board of Foreign Missions of the Presbyterian Church in the U.S.A., of which he was a secretary, invited to a conference on July 13, 1898, representatives of all the boards known to be contemplating such new mission projects.[1] Seven boards were looking to Cuba, four to Puerto Rico, and three to the Philippine Islands. This conference met under a profound sense of moral and religious responsibility "that the Christian people of America should immediately and prayerfully consider the duty of entering the doors which God in His providence is thus opening." The members recorded the sentiment: "We believe that this feeling represents the deep and solemn Christian patriotism of the country, and that support will be given to the boards for this purpose." After this preamble resolutions were made that sought to implement the common concern.[2] Since the American Board of Commissioners had long been at work in the Caroline Islands and adequately cared for them, this should be recognized as the field of that board. Since no other board was interested in the Ladrone Islands, and the American Board was already in the Carolines, that board was asked to consider entering the Ladrones. Three joint committees were set up, one for each of the countries. Each interested board was requested to appoint two representatives, and these teams of two would combine to form the area committees. Thus if a certain board were interested in all three countries, its two men would serve on all three committees. Each committee was charged with studying the situation, sharing such information as might be received by

[1] Foreign Missions Conference of North America, *Annual Report, 1899,* p. 117; Brown, A. J., *One Hundred Years,* pp. 862–863.
[2] *Op. cit., 1899,* pp. 118–119.

each of the boards, and then to make an "amicable and economic distribution" of the territory among the boards.

The effort with regard to Cuba failed, but the other two were eminently successful.

The Committee on Puerto Rico was comprised of representatives of the American Baptist, Methodist Episcopal, Presbyterian U.S.A., and Congregational Boards. After it made its initial division several other boards adjusted to it.[3] The Congregationalists held the eastern end of the island; the Presbyterians, the western; while the Baptists, Methodists, and Disciples of Christ were located toward the center in adjoining areas. The Christian and Missionary Alliance was at Manaté in the north, and the United Brethren in Christ held several towns on the south coast. The agencies in the capital city, San Juan, were the Protestant Episcopal Church, Baptists, Lutherans, Presbyterians, Methodists, and the Y.M.C.A. The other large town, Ponce, was shared by the Disciples, United Brethren, Baptists, Christian Church, and the Episcopalians. Reporting this distribution in 1916, the Regional Conference at San Juan stated: "While this adjustment of evangelical forces might hardly be called ideal, it was an application of Christian statesmanship very greatly in advance of any scheme actually carried into effect elsewhere in Latin America." [4] At the Panama Conference earlier that year it was reported that some missions had come in without agreement as to territory, but had worked in complete harmony with the original group of missions, that there were thirteen societies on the island, and that from the beginning the plan had fostered a spirit of federation.[5] The good example in Puerto Rico was constantly held up to the missionaries in other parts of Latin America.

Two or three of the boards which had expected to move

[3] *Regional Conferences in Latin America*, pp. 344–345.
[4] *Ibid.*, p. 345.
[5] *Christian Work in Latin America*, vol. III, p. 27. (Panama Congress, 1916).

into the Philippines at once were forced to delay, but the
others proceeded with the common plan. When the missionaries arrived on the field they immediately set up the
Evangelical Union of the Philippine Islands in accord with
the consensus among the boards. Representatives of the
Methodists, Presbyterians, United Brethren, British and Foreign Bible Society, American Bible Society, and the Christian and Missionary Alliance met in Manila on April 24–26,
1901, and constituted the Evangelical Union.[6] One of its
initial actions was the carrying out of the mandate of the
boards on the division of the field. It is worth the space to
quote this unique document dividing an entire country among
the missions.[7]

WHEREAS several Evangelical Missionary Societies are
entering upon their work in the Philippine Islands; and
WHEREAS the evangelization of these people will be more
speedily accomplished by a division of the territory, thus
avoiding the waste of labor, time, and money arising from the
occupation of the same districts by more than one society,
which has marred the work in other and older fields,
THEREFORE BE IT RESOLVED, that each Mission now represented on the field accept the responsibility for the evangelization of certain well defined areas, to be mutually agreed
upon, such agreement to be open to revision at the end of
three years by the Evangelical Union at its regular meeting.
BE IT RESOLVED, that on the Island of Luzon, the Methodists
shall become responsible for the work in the Provinces of
Bulacan, Pampanga, Tarlac, Nueva Ecija, Pangasinan,
Bataan, and Zambales; the Presbyterians for the work in the
Provinces of Morong, Laguna, Batangas, Cavite, Tayabas,
and North and South Camarines, and Albay; the United

---

[6] [Philippine Federation of Christian Churches], *The Evangelical Church
in the Philippines: A Factual Statement*, pp. 4–5; Brown, A. J., *op. cit.*,
p. 867.
[7] [Philippine Federation of Christian Churches], *Pertinent Facts Regarding Comity Agreement*, p. 1.

Brethren for the work in the Provinces of La Union, Ilocos del Norte and Ilocos del Sur; also

BE IT RESOLVED, that no work be begun in the City or Province of Manila, except by mutual understanding between the Superintendents of the Missions whose interests are involved, and in case of disagreement the decision to rest with the Executive Committee of the Evangelical Union.

BE IT RESOLVED, that we recommend that the Baptists and Presbyterians will become responsible for the work in the Islands of Panay and Negros, they mutually deciding upon the portions of the Islands for which they will be individually responsible.

The following January this amendment to the agreement was adopted by the Executive Committee: [8]

RESOLVED that the provinces of the Cagayan Valley, i.e., of Isabela, Nueva Vizcaya and Cagayan be added to the territory of the Methodist Mission, (they agreeing not to enter the Visayas during the present term of three years of the original resolution). That the provinces of Brontoc, Abra, and Lepanto be added to the territory of the United Brethren Mission, and that the province of Benquet be considered common territory for the said missions.

That the islands of Cebu, Bohol, Leyte, Samar, Romblon, and Masbate be considered as part of the field of the Baptist and Presbyterian Missions. That the question of the field of the Christian Mission be left in abeyance until such time as they may be ready to decide as to their own wishes in the matter.

The Disciples of Christ and the United Brethren entered in 1901 and the American Board of Commissioners for Foreign Missions in 1902; and after that the final division of territory became: [9]

[8] *Ibid.*, pp. 1–2.
[9] *Ibid.*, p. 2.

Methodists: The provinces of Rizal, Bulacan, Pampanga, Tarlac, Nueva Ecija, Nueva Vizcaya, Pangasinan, Bataan, Zambales, Cagayan, Isabela, and Ilocos Sur, all on the island of Luzon.

Presbyterians: The provinces of Cavite, Laguna, Tayabas, Batangas, Camarines Norte, Camarines Sur, Albay, and Sorsogon on the island of Luzon; the island of Cebu; and Negros Oriental.

United Brethren: La Union and Mountain Provinces on Luzon.

Disciples of Christ: Ilocos Norte, Abra, Ilocos Sur north of Vigan, on Luzon: northern Mindoro; and designated places near Manila by agreement with the Presbyterians.

Congregationalists: Mindanao, excepting western end.

Baptists: The islands of Panay, southern Mindoro, Romblon, and Negros Occidental.

Christian and Missionary Alliance: Western Mindanao and the Sulu Archipelago.

This assignment of territory was faithfully adhered to until after liberation of the Philippines from the Japanese invaders toward the end of World War II, when the situation changed rapidly. The Evangelical Union became the National Christian Council in 1929, and that in turn gave way to the Philippine Federation of Evangelical Churches in 1934, which was reconstituted as the Philippine Federation of Christian Churches in 1947. The responsibility for comity matters passed from the original Executive Committee to a Comity Committee. The Philippine representatives at the Bangkok Conference in 1949 declared in their statement:

One of the factors in the large success attained by evangelical Christianity in the Philippines has been this territorial division under the supervision of the Evangelical Union. Compared with other mission fields the world over, it is probably safe to say that no other has shown such a large success and rapid progress, considering the short period of time, the limited number of missionaries, and the limited resources in money.[10]

The Protestant Episcopal Church alone refused to join the Evangelical Union and to participate in the comity agreement, thus taking a line quite contrary to its early practices. Because of "High Church" views of some of its leading figures, it regarded most of the Philippines as Christian country not open to missionary activity, and directed its ministry to the aborigines, the Chinese, and the English-speaking Americans and other foreigners. This attitude was quite different from that Church's earlier views in beginning work in Latin America.

Latin America

Comity was late in being introduced into Latin America as a whole. British and Continental European churches provided churches and pastoral care for their own colonial officers and staff, the military, commercial agents, and settlers in the Caribbean islands and coastal areas held in possession by their nations. Their associated missionary societies introducted missions to the natives in these places, the descendants of the Indians and of the Negro slaves, along with the later East Indian immigrants. These efforts largely overlapped. Protestant missions were excluded from the Spanish islands until Cuba received independence and Puerto Rico passed under the control of the United States, as has been shown. Mexico, the Central American lands, and the whole of South America excepting the European colonies, even after independence from Spain and Portugal, remained under the control of a ruling class either Spanish or Portuguese in culture

[10] [Philippine Federation of Christian Churches], *The Evangelical Church in the Philippines,* p. 6.

and either zealously or nominally Roman Catholic. Both the active intervention of the Roman Catholic Church with the governments and the suspicion of North American Protestants by the ruling class made the entrance of Protestant missions difficult, and until the twentieth century the evangelical churches grew slowly. Anglicans regarded this vast region as already Catholic Christian, having little real knowledge of the true spiritual state of the Indian and mixed population, and frowned upon missionary work excepting to pagans clearly known to be such. The American Episcopalians, however, departed from the British policy. The South American Missionary Society was the only agency related to the Church of England which carried on work for native peoples outside the British colonies. A few nondenominational societies based in the United Kingdom, Canada, and Australia were attracted there, including the Evangelical Union of South America and the Bolivian Indian Mission. The churches and nondenominational societies of the United States were the agencies principally interested in the region, and in the case of the former it was sometimes the Home Mission Board rather than the Foreign Board that was responsible. Nevertheless, until well into the twentieth century, when the situation changed with the rise of numerous faith missions, Latin America formed only a minor portion of the North American missionary enterprise. Latin America was excluded from consideration at the Edinburgh Missionary Conference of 1910 for various reasons.[11] Americans who attended that assembly held an extra, unofficial meeting on the work in that area; and, stimulated by the neglect at Edinburgh, the Foreign Missions Conference of North America called a conference on mission work in Latin America in March, 1913, at New York.[12] This conference set up a con-

---

[11] Hogg, W. R., *Ecumenical Foundations*, pp. 120–121, 131–132.
[12] *Conference on Missions in Latin America* (March, 1913), p. 9; Hogg, *Ecumenical Foundations*, p. 132.

tinuing Committee on Cooperation in Latin America, charged with the surveying of the needs of the huge unevangelized population of the region and with the coordinating of Protestant efforts towards meeting those needs.[13]

It became immediately evident, and this was fully documented in the material prepared for the Panama Conference of 1916, that there was a very thin and inadequate line of evangelical missionary occupation all the way from the Mexican-United States border to Cape Horn. There might be overlapping and competition at a few spots, but the general picture was one of vast spaces either unoccupied or inadequately occupied. There appeared to be urgent need for survey, common planning, enlistment of resources, and responsible occupation. Comity would be a first step toward effective evangelization.

Except for Puerto Rico, the greatest concentration of agencies and missionaries was in Mexico, and it was in that country that the new vision and emphasis first bore fruit. Representatives of eleven evangelical missionary agencies had met as early as 1888 in Mexico City in an effort to apportion the larger cities among the boards.[14] Apparently the missionaries, who had all too little knowledge of what happened in the missions in Asia and Africa, believed that they had limited power to act in such matters. Apparently some consensus was reached with respect to cities, it is to be inferred from the material in the report of the Panama Conference, but in the hope of achieving a complete nationwide division of responsibility they addressed the following resolution to the mission boards in the United States:

The Evangelical workers, gathered in their second general assembly in the City of Mexico, respectfully, but at the same time with great earnestness, beg of all missionary societies at

[13] Annual reports and minutes of the Committee on Cooperation in Latin America make their first appearance in 1917.

[14] *Christian Work in Latin America*, vol. III, Appendix D, p. 25.

work in this country that they come to an agreement as soon as possible concerning the adoption of the means best adapted to the securing of an equitable and economic distribution of territory among the respective missions, in order that the Gospel of our Lord Jesus Christ may the sooner be preached to the entire nation.[15]

All denominations did not carry out the consensus of that meeting, but a generation later it was affirmed that: "So far as cooperative plans have been carried out, their success has been in proportion to the observance of the resolutions of 1888, which recommended a division of territory." [16] The new Committee on Cooperation in Latin America as its first major action convened a conference of Missionaries and Missionary Boards Working in Mexico at Cincinnati in the summer of 1914.[17] Maps and statistics relating to all the missions had been prepared in advance. The Committee on Territorial Occupation brought in a report that was subsequently known as the "Cincinnati Plan," and it was adopted by the Conference. Preliminary to the assignment of territory and in explanation of it, the report stressed the facts that in all of Mexico there was but one missionary, including wives, to every 75,000 of the population, that fifteen states were without a single resident missionary, that resources were very unevenly divided across the land, that concentration by each mission in contiguous territory was highly desirable, and that there ought to be a 50 per cent increase in the missionary staff to supplement adequately the Mexican ministers.

While recognizing that neither the Committee nor the Con-

[15] Interdenominational Conference of Foreign Mission Boards of the United States and Canada, *Annual Report, 1898*, p. 27.

[16] *Christian Work in Latin America*, vol. III, p. 25.

[17] *Conference of Missionaries and Missionary Boards Working in Mexico, Cincinnati, Ohio, June 30–July 1, 1914*. This report is now very rare in the original pamphlet edition, but it was reprinted in the report of the Panama Congress in 1916: *Christian Work in Latin America*, Appendix D, vol. III, pp. 111–120.

ference actually had authority to assign territory and to request some missions to withdraw from places where they were already established, and acknowledging that some organizations would never enter a comity agreement, the report addressed itself to those boards which it was believed would cooperate in the scheme. As adopted, the recommended division of territory, by states as far as possible, was as follows: [18]

Congregationalists: Chihuahua, Sinaloa as far south as the Sinaloa River, Sonora, and Lower California

Baptists: Coahuila, Nueva Leon, Zacetecas, Durango, Mexico Federal District, and Aguas Calientes

Disciples of Christ: Coahuila, south from Piedras Negras along the International Railway to Monterey and to Torreón, thence north to Jiménez, including Mojada; and Nueva Leon

Friends and Southern Presbyterians: San Luis Potosí, Tamaulipas, and Nueva Leon

Methodists: San Luis Potosí, Guanajuato, Jalisco, Colima, Mexico Federal District, Hidalgo, Pueblo, Queretaro, Tlaxcala, Michoacan, Tepic, and Sinaloa north to the Sinaloa River

Associate Reformed Presbyterians: Tamaulipas, Vera Cruz, and eastern San Luis Potosí

Presbyterians U.S.A.: Mexico Federal District, Morelos, Vera Cruz, Campeche, Guerrero, Oaxaca, Chiapas, Tabasco, and Yucatán

The states of Nuevo Leon and Tamaulipas required special attention, and it was recommended that the state of Nuevo Leon be allotted to the Northern Baptists (present American Baptist Convention) with the exceptions that the Southern Presbyterians retain their holdings in the state and the Disciples theirs in the city of Monterey. It was asked that by mutual agreement among the agencies working in the state

[18] *Ibid.*, p. 116.

of Tamaulipas all but one board withdraw from towns of 10,000 or less, preference being given to priority of occupation, and that all but two withdraw from cities of 20,000. Blocks of new territory should each be assigned to a single board ready to undertake evangelization there.[19]

The General Committee of the Conference recommended that the Permanent Field Committee which was to be established include arbitration of differences among its functions.[20]

The Protestant Episcopal Church was not included in this division of territory because its representative stated that his Board could not participate in a comity agreement.

It was recognized that at this stage of the history of the evangelical churches in Mexico it was necessary to have the approval of the ministers and lay leaders of the churches for such a scheme. Two years later, at the Panama Conference, considerable national sentiment for the plan was reported.[21] Some of the boards were already moving to fulfill their responsibilities under the plan.

The first all-Latin America Conference was convened in Panama in February, 1916. Comity occupied a very important place in the discussions and actions because it was regarded as basic both to all other forms of cooperation and to effective evangelistic and pastoral occupation of the vast region under survey. "Cooperation based on a division of territory is its lowest form. . . . The getting-out-of-each-other's-way policy is better than getting into each other's way. In the evolution of effective cooperation it is an important initial step." [22] Careful surveys of the Latin lands and the evangelical missions therein revealed the inadequacy of the enterprise and seemed to make it clear that the delimitation of territory was highly desirable as the first step toward a

[19] A map showing the division of territory will be found in Camargo and Grubb, *Religion in the Republic of Mexico*, between pp. 88–89.
[20] *Christian Work in Latin America*, vol. III, p. 119.
[21] *Ibid.*, vol. III, pp. 24–26.
[22] *Ibid.*, vol. III, p. 21.

thoroughly reliable advance effort.[23] There was actually little overlapping, but where it occurred in some places the results were unfortunate and it wasted men and money that might be used in some untouched area. There had been by this date no comity agreements in Argentina, the countries of Central America, Chile (where providentially the societies had not overlapped), Cuba (with the exception that the Northern and Southern Baptists had agreed between themselves to take respectively the eastern and western parts of the island, and where the Southern Methodists were in the country by agreement with the Methodist Episcopal Church in Puerto Rico), and Peru; and in many other countries, although there had been no agreement, only one board or society was at work at a task that might be too great for it. Puerto Rico was the one outstanding exception to the rule and a fine example of the effectiveness of comity. In Brazil the Methodist Episcopal Church had in 1898 turned over a flourishing field in south Brazil to the Methodist Episcopal Church, South, in order to eliminate overlapping.[24] The various missions which together more or less nominally covered the country had frequently discussed the delimitation of territory, but had never acted effectively to achieve it. An Evangelical Alliance had been organized in Peru. It was planning to set up an Administrative and Arbitration Committee, which, among other things, would arbitrate disputes about territory and give advice to boards about unevangelized territories.[25]

An interesting "Definition of Occupation" was put before the Conference. It reads:

Each successive generation of Christians lives under the supremely important obligation to place the knowledge and privileges of the gospel within reach of the whole world of mankind. Accordingly, one or more Societies, foreign or in-

[23] *Ibid.*, vol. III, pp. 152–189.
[24] *Ibid.*, vol. III, pp. 21–26.
[25] *Ibid.*, vol. III, p. 27.

digenous, assuming or asking responsibility for the evangelization and Christian nurture of a given population, will undertake those high tasks with the implicit guarantee to fulfill them within the lifetime of the present generation. In the case of failure or of inability to employ means that give reasonable promise of attaining, under Divine Blessing, the ends as stated, they may not justifiably expect other Societies to refrain from entering and undertaking to serve the unreached people of the territory. On identical grounds, it is believed that any Society which accepts the principle of division of territory or functions will not best be advancing the whole cause by duplications of effort within the recognized field of another Society so long as related territory of its own is being ministered to on a scale below the standard calculated to reach the generation now living. The reality and vitality of the growing churches as shown in evangelistic zeal and self-denying service must be considered as among the criteria of effectiveness of occupation on the part of any Christian body. The judgment of the Commission is recorded that the application of the foregoing principles points to the wisdom of negotiations at this stage between several of the bodies at work in Latin America, looking to the interchange of territory where paralleling either already exists or is likely to appear as soon as vigorous expansion takes place. If the suggested exchange is brought about the effect would be to reduce the number of societies occupying some of the fields, to reduce the hopelessly large areas over which the efforts of some bodies are now diffused, to leave defined the regions clearly inviting new agencies to enter, and thus to afford a prospect that something like adequate attention can be bestowed upon such conspicuously neglected sections at Santo Domingo, Haiti, Central America, Colombia, Ecuador, Paraguay, interior and northern Brazil, Venezuela, and the Indians of Mexico, Peru, and Bolivia.

Since this was the general situation and most of the correspondents who had been consulted knew of no common planning, it appeared that a comprehensive plan for Latin

America was a necessity.[26] For, it was asserted: "A society usually proceeds as if it were the only mission in Latin America." All agencies could profit by falling into line with procedures practiced in most other parts of the world mission. There ought to be adequate mapping of territory, and a series of regional planning conferences ought to be held. Fortunately the majority of boards were found to be favorably inclined toward such planning. It was confidently affirmed that:

> There is found a general disposition throughout the mission field to accept those principles of comity which happily have now become the heritage of a large part of the Christian Church. There is little evidence of desire on the part of any Communion to make gains in any field out of the weakness or inefficiency of another. Both at home and abroad there is less of a purpose to serve merely denominational ends. The way is thus clear for a more statesmanlike view of missionary responsibility; for the considering of the entire field is the supreme interest of the Kingdom of Christ.[27]

There was an eagerness to make it clear that delimitation of territory and general planning be not regarded as merely an effort to hold the present line but rather as the first step in a major advance. The fixing of responsibility on the part of all agencies that would cooperate in the common task was the aim.

> Cooperative advance in winning the world for Christ must be along positive rather than negative lines. Allotments of responsibility are inclusive rather than exclusive. In our age of freedom no wall can be built, or ought to be built, for the purpose of shutting anybody out of any field of usefulness where duty calls. At the same time no portion of the human

[26] *Ibid.*, vol. I, pp. 186–187.
[27] *Ibid.*, vol. I, p. 187.

race should be left outside of the field of explicit responsibility on the part of someone. Cooperative arrangements recommended by this Congress are not for the purpose of limiting activities but on the contrary for the purpose of increasing and intensifying activities.[28]

Comity, therefore, was seen as an imperative. Everyone should recognize that the purpose was the enabling of a great advance movement. So, in the suggestions for positive measures of cooperation, division of territory was repeatedly proposed, in Brazil,[29] Central America,[30] Chile,[31] Cuba,[32] and Peru.[33] But always division of territory was advocated as but one type of necessary cooperation, and it is joined with such proposals as a common name for all evangelical churches, national councils or committees, union theological schools, and union literature production. Commission VIII on Cooperation and Promotion of Unity, therefore, brought to the Congress as its "findings" the proposal that ten types of cooperation be brought into effect wherever practicable.[34] The first was division of territory. "It is clearly an opportune time for mission boards to consider the division of territory in new fields and its adjustment in old fields. It is hoped that the British and American Bible Societies may divide Latin America between them and arrange for the interchange of their publications at cost price." This is certainly a weak "finding" in light of the strong arguments put forth in the various reports of commisions and well supported by the discussions! Listed sixth in the series was the formulation of rules of comity. "The study of already approved and accepted

[28] *Ibid.,* vol. III, p. 97.
[29] *Ibid.,* vol. III, p. 80.
[30] *Ibid.,* vol. III, p. 80.
[31] *Ibid.,* vol. III, p. 81.
[32] *Ibid.,* vol. III, p. 84.
[33] *Ibid.,* vol. III, p. 86.
[34] *Ibid.,* vol. III, pp. 102–103.

rules of comity under which some Boards are working at home and abroad, with reference to such matters as salaries, exchange of members, and discipline, and the adoption of similar policies by the missionary Societies operating in Latin America seems advisable." The other eight were: cooperation in literature, a publicity bureau, a joint educational survey, annual inter-mission conferences, cooperative evangelism, campaigns among the educated classes, fraternal relations or the cultivation of the spirit of brotherhood among all Christian groups striving for the uplift of the people, and the cooperative training of missionary candidates. This all seems so exceedingly inadequate in view of the reports and discussions. Individuals and committees had profited by acquaintance with the affairs and means of missions elsewhere in the world; they had together seen urgent needs and been challenged; they had individually and collectively urged united action absolutely drastic in repudiation of the old individualistic order; but this was a pioneer congress on cooperation in Latin America and there was apparently fear to accept resolutions which would sound as if limitations were being put upon the boards and missions in their sovereignty and freedom of policy and program. Perhaps it was thought that for the present it was enough to paint the realistic picture and voice the challenge and that the boards and missions would respond positively, especially as there were to be follow-up regional conferences. The reports and findings of each Commission were received and discussed, but never voted upon separately. A brief series of resolutions adopted by the whole Congress was intended to give acceptance of all the sectional findings. These resolutions recognized that British and European representation in the Congress had been too meager for such societies soon to implement the findings of the Commissions, but it laid upon the American section of the Committee on Cooperation in Latin America responsibility for taking steps promptly to give effect to those findings so far as the cooperation of Canadian and United States boards was concerned.[35]

The Panama Congress was followed immediately by seven regional conferences during the same year, 1916, at Lima, Santiago, Buenos Aires, Rio de Janeiro, Baranquilla, Havana, and San Juan.[36] These were too soon after the Panama Congress to have achieved action on comity, but they tended to reinforce the demand for progress. The Conference at Lima stressed the need for unity and even union. It recommended a common name for all the churches in Peru; asked for united plans for the occupation of unworked territory, including invitations to new missions; and declared a duplication of efforts, excepting in the capital city, to be undesirable.[37] The Santiago Conference reported that already the Presbyterian Mission had sent to the Board's offices in New York a scheme for the delimitation of territory between itself and the mission of the Methodist Episcopal Church, and that this proposal was before the comity committee of both missions. The report advised adjustment between the territories of the Methodist and Christian and Missionary Alliance missions also.[38] No official action was taken. The Buenos Aires Conference clearly laid out the needs and challenges in the three River Plate countries, and called for united action and union institutions of various types. Its findings affirmed the future need of a single united evangelical church, and it recommended as practical preliminary steps the delimitation of territory, a common name for all the churches, a union hymnbook and common use of a single version of the Bible, and a common form of church letter for transfer of membership.[39]

[35] Ibid., vol. III, p. 449.
[36] The reports were published in one volume: *Regional Conferences in Latin America, Reports of a Series of Seven Conferences . . . 1916;* N. Y.: pub. for the Committee on Cooperation in Latin America by the Missionary Education Movement, [1917].
[37] Ibid., pp. 63–64.
[38] Ibid., p. 124.
[39] Ibid., p. 215.

The Rio de Janeiro Conference simply adopted the findings of the Conference at Buenos Aires. The Baranquilla Conference found too little responsible missionary activity even to raise the question of comity. At the Havana meeting it was said that there was little or no denominational "overcrowding" while the field could be more than occupied by a slight readjustment.[40] The findings merely called for a thorough survey so that there might be more complete occupation of the island.[41]

Nine years later the Committee on Cooperation in Latin America held a second assembly, but limited to South America. This was the Congress on Christian work in South America convened at Montevideo in April, 1925, the documents of which are published in a volume entitled *Christian Work in South America*. The members of this Congress were informed that while "the ideal of an adequate, completely cooperative Christian program for all of Latin America is yet far from realization," reports received from both national churches and mission boards and societies indicated that there had been increasing recognition of the principle of divided responsibility in a united enterprise in each of the South American republics. Moreover, distinct progress had been made in the interval since the Panama Congress "in the actual delimitation of territory and the acceptance, by various Evangelical agencies, of definite, single or joint, responsibility for assigned areas."[42] The various areas were scrutinized. The Presbyterian Church in the U.S.A. was still the only organized mission in Colombia, and the task was too large for a single agency. A regional committee had been organized in Venezuela in March, 1923, a survey made, a conference held, and a division of territory adopted by six societies and boards.[43] Four small societies and some independent groups

[40] *Ibid.*, p. 329.
[41] *Ibid.*, p. 339.
[42] *Christian Work in South America*, vol. I, p. 66.
[43] *Ibid.*, pp. 69–71.

refused cooperation, but three fourths of the total missionary forces were cooperating in the scheme. The states of Sucre and Monagas were assigned to the Orinoco River Mission. Miranda went to the Presbyterian Mission along with an equal share in the Federal District with the English Branch of the Christian Missions in Many Lands or Plymouth Brethren, which was also to have the eastern and south-western portion of Guarico. The American branch of this mission was assigned a strip of territory north and south of the Orinoco River, from the Monagas-Amacuro boundary on the east westward to San Fernando de Apure, including parts of the states of Anzoateguia, Bolivar, Guarico, and Apure. The Canadian branch of the Plymouth Brethren was to hold the states of Carabobo, Yaracuy, and Lara excepting the southeastern corner, which was left to a group of independents. The Swedish Evangelical Free Church was assigned the states of Aragua and Falcon along with north-western Guarico. The Scandinavian Alliance Mission received the states of Zulia, Tachira, Merida, Trujillo, Zamora, and most of Apure.

No delimitation had been undertaken among the three societies working in Ecuador, but in Peru an agreement had been reached through the Peruvian Committee on Cooperation.[44] It took into account the three natural divisions of the country—natural geographically and strategically because of the development of communications within them. These are the central, southern, and northern areas. The region of the Ferrocarril Central (the Central Railway) went to the Methodist Episcopal Church, including the departments of Lima, Junin, and the province of Callao, with presumed responsibility for future occupancy of the departments of Ancachas, Huanuco, Ica, and Huancavelica. However, Lima was to be a common base for all boards and societies at work in the country. Also the Evangelical Union of South America

44 *Ibid.*, pp. 71–72.

was permitted to operate in certain towns of the central highlands where groups of its church members from Lima had located. The whole southern region, "the region of the Southern Railway," including Arequipa, Puno, and southern part of Cuzco was assigned to the Evangelical Union of South America. The northern area comprised principally the departments of Libertad and Cajamarca. This was recognized as the domain of the Free Church of Scotland. However, that mission entered into a later territorial agreement with the Church of the Nazarene and the Holiness Church for the division of the northern region among them. This was further enlarged to include the department of Lambayeque and a part of Piura. Throughout the country accessibility through communications was the guide rather than strict following of departmental boundaries. And, it was stated: "This arrangement was adopted as a distribution of territorial *responsibility*, but not of exclusive territorial privilege." Not all agencies in the country agreed to cooperate, and between 1920 and 1925 two large missions entered without reference to comity.

Chile also had seen progress in comity agreements.[45] The Presbyterian-Methodist proposal reported at the Santiago Conference had been effected in 1916, defining alternating rather than contiguous coastal areas and occupied districts from Tacna on the Peruvian border to Traiguen, Malleco, in the south. The Presbyterians and Christian and Missionary Alliance reached understanding with respect to the provinces of Concepcion and Chloe, and also with the South American Missionary Society, which worked among the Araucanian Indians between the Cautin River and Lake Llanquihue. These agreements left only the Seventh Day Adventists and the Southern Baptists outside of comity arrangements.

The Methodist Episcopal Church and the Disciples of

[45] *Ibid.*, p. 72.

Christ entered into agreement for territorial responsibility in the River Plate area.[46] The Methodists withdrew from Asunción and a strip along the Uruguay River. It was said that among the thirty denominational, nondenominational, and independent missions in the three River Plate countries no other formal division of territory existed, but that there was then an increasing awareness of the need of a comity agreement and of closer cooperation in occupancy and expansion. Some of the missions had adopted a policy of not opening stations in places where another mission was established, and the Mennonites, entering Argentina, had set a good example by locating in an area where no other agency was at work.

Brazil, which in the past had been saved from much duplication and friction largely by the immensity of the country, had known some instances of comity in early days.[47] Thus the Presbyterian Church in the U.S.A. had transferred their area and churches in Rio Grande do Sul to the Protestant Episcopal Church, and the Southern Methodists and Southern Presbyterians had adjusted their territorial responsibilities in Minas Geraes. After 1916 some other agreements were reached: between the Southern Presbyterians and the Christian and Missionary Alliance in the lower Amazon Valley; between the Methodists and two Presbyterian bodies leaving the states of Santa Catharina and Parana to the latter, and then between the Northern and Southern Presbyterian missions dividing that region; and between the Congregationalists and the Evangelical Union of South America in Pernambuco. The Bible societies had also agreed on territorial responsibilities. The actual state of affairs, after these various negotiations, was that without a general countrywide comity agreement there was a distribution of evangelical forces in distinct spheres of labor without much overlapping,

[46] *Ibid.*, pp. 73–75.
[47] *Ibid.*, p. 76.

but this occupation related to three well-defined coastal regions and not to the vast interior.

The Congress was informed that there was no territorial division in British Guiana but that societies tended to limit their efforts to different racial groups, as the African Methodist Mission to the Negroes; Anglican, Wesleyan, and Canadian Presbyterian societies to the East Indians; the Plymouth Brethren and the Society for the Propagation of the Gospel to the aboriginal Indians and Chinese. Such a racial "division of labor" might produce the equivalent of the "caste churches" which comity in India tried to avoid.

The Report of Commission I on Unoccupied Fields stated:

> While the present interdenominational and intersociety agreements are regarded as binding, the general distribution of areas is necessarily provisional rather than final. Further adjustments will be inevitable as the work advances. Growth and shifting of population will be a factor of necessary changes in some sections. There is always the expectation of the expansion and ascending leadership of the National churches with new plans of diffusion and occupation discerned by native insight into new situations which may arise. And not too distant on the horizon is the hope of a united Christian Church in South America, by which both denominational and national boundaries will be transcended.[48]

It stated further that there was practically unanimous approval of delimitation and assignment of the great territories still unoccupied, but that there was difference of opinion about further division and assignment of territory already allocated. Sentiment in Brazil was against further delimitation except in the hinterland, the societies in Chile believed themselves adequate to take care of the whole country without the entrance of additional agencies, while those in Peru saw need of surrendering some of the assigned territory to

[48] *Ibid.*, p. 79.

agencies that would effectively occupy it. Ecuador was without a plan of adequate occupation, and no effort should be
spared to assure for the country a wise partition of territory
and responsibility.[49] Specific suggestions were offered. In
Colombia and Bolivia division awaited the entrance of additional missions, which were much needed. The interior of
the continent was still largely unreached, and so were the
cultured classes and the students in the already occupied
areas.[50] Other special classes or elements also challenged.
Comity agreements could speed the advance into the interior, while common planning and cooperative efforts could
help in the other cases. Unentered areas were specifically
pointed out. The findings of the Commission urged that
agencies occupying a field should minister to the entire
population, not to any class or group; asserted that occupation of an area involved acceptance of responsibility for the
full development of work in the area, and when a society
found itself unable to occupy the region fully within a
reasonable time, it should invite others to cooperate there;
and called attention to the neglected interior.[51] Thus it is
evident that the Montevideo Congress marked a decided
advance over the situation prevailing at the time of the
Panama Congress, but that there was great need for the
further development of territorial assignments and comity
agreements in order to speed evangelization of untouched
areas and as the basis for more active cooperation in the
total ministry of the churches. At the same time it was quite
clear that more and more agencies were entering the South
American countries which did not respect prior occupancy,
had no desire to take part in a cooperative advance, and
were aggressive in asserting their right to plant churches and
institutions anywhere they might desire. Yet almost more

[49] *Ibid.*, pp. 80–99.
[50] *Ibid.*, pp. 89–99.
[51] *Ibid.*, pp. 141–142.

than in any other area of the missionary enterprise there was at this time in Latin America remarkable cooperation and mutuality between denominational church missions and non-denominational or interdenominational missions, exceeded perhaps only by the societies in the Congo.

Some assessment of the developments which followed after the Panama and Montevideo conferences may be made by an examination of the various Latin America volumes in the series of regional survey studies which the World Dominion Press published in the late 1920's and early 1930's, although few of them make specific references to comity agreements.

The "Cincinnati Plan" for Mexico had had a definitely mixed reception. It had been ratified at a conference in Mexico City in 1919. Living so much to themselves and being a combination of "foreign" and "home" mission boards (the latter without the broader knowledge and experience of the foreign agencies), the missionaries and the administrators for the Latin fields may not have realized that the moment was too late in the history of missions, even in that area, for unilateral action by the missionary element. It is the judgment of Dr. Gonzalo Baez Camargo and Sir Kenneth Grubb that the denominations which adopted the Cincinnati Plan and adhered to its provisions profited by it, but that it failed to accomplish all that was expected of it because of inherent defects, the opposition of some of the national leaders, and its interruption of the spontaneous development of cooperation.[52] Some of the national leaders regarded it as a foreign imposition, since it was an agreement adopted by mission boards before it had won the sympathy of some of the key nationals. Too much prominence had been given to the economic basis of the plan—its purpose to save men and money and use resources efficiently, rather than to its truly

[52] Camargo, G. B. and K. G. Grubb, *Religion in the Republic of Mexico*, pp. 104–105.

fundamental intention of effective evangelization of the country. Also North American practicality and common sense were not congenial to the Mexican mind, and it was pushed to completion too quickly. Dr. Arthur Judson Brown also makes some of these same judgments.[53] He illustrates the adverse national reaction by reference to the action of ministers and churches in an area in northern Mexico from which the Presbyterian Church in the U.S.A. withdrew. Rather than transfer allegiance to the denomination which was to occupy the area, these churches joined with others which had been established by the Southern Presbyterians and formed an independent, self-supporting presbytery.

Nevertheless, a deputation of the Board of Foreign Missions of the Presbyterian Church in the U.S.A. after visiting Mexico in 1922, were convinced that the Plan had worked so well that they ventured to make the statement that "Mexico, as no other country in the world, represents the triumph of co-operative Christian work over the old-time sectarian programme, and the whole Church gains thereby." [54]

Elsewhere in Latin America, the area descriptions and the tables show relatively little overlapping, although new agencies had entered many countries. Mr. Ritchie reported that in Chile the Presbyterians and Methodists had carefully defined their territory, eliminated overlapping and had entered into various forms of functional cooperations.[55]

Korea

After Korea was opened to intercourse with the Western nations, there was a rush of missionaries into the land from the China ports. Nine missions entered that land between

[53] Brown, A. J., *op. cit.*, p. 821.
[54] *Ibid.*, p. 824.
[55] Browning, W. E., *et al.*, *The West Coast Republics of South America*, p. 31.

1884 and 1897. However, some small missions withdrew, and eventually denominational differences became numerically few. Moreover, the Presbyterians put their stamp so much on all church life that only the Anglicans manifested characteristics very distinct from the others. Four Presbyterian missions established a single national church. Two Methodist missions also joined in fostering the growth of a single church, which became the second in size. The Oriental Missionary Society, which entered much later, produced congregations that coalesced into the Holiness Church, third numerically. The Anglican Church remained quite small, and a few others were almost infinitesimal. Yet at the beginning there was confusion, but common planning by the major missions introduced order and effective occupation of the land.

The Presbyterians formed a central organ for cooperation from the very outset, and it facilitated adjustments and even union. The Presbyterian Church in the U.S.A. entered the country in 1884. Five years later, in 1889, the first missionary of the Australian Presbyterian Church arrived. Then there was set up the United Council of the American and Victorian Churches, which became the Council of Missions Holding the Presbyterian Form of Government in 1893, following the arrival of the missionaries of the Presbyterian Church in the U.S. (Southern) the previous year.[56] The Canadian Presbyterians joined this body upon entrance in 1898. The object of the Council was "the organization of but one Presbyterian Church."[57] That hoped for church was established in 1907. With such an object in view, it is not surprising that the four Presbyterian missions speedily came to comity agreements and to forms of functional cooperation among themselves. A field agreement of 1892 assigning

[56] Paik, L. G., The History of Protestant Missions in Korea, 1832–1910, p. 188; Rhodes, H. A., ed., History of the Korea Mission, Presbyterian Church U.S.A., p. 450.

[57] Paik, L. G., op. cit., p. 189; Rhodes, H. A., op. cit., p. 450.

Chula Province (and at first Choong-chung) in the south to the Presbyterian Church in the U.S., was accepted by a joint conference of representatives of the two Boards of Foreign Missions in New York.[58] The Canadians upon arrival were assigned by agreement with the Northern Presbyterian Mission the two east coast Ham Kyung provinces. Fusan was turned over to the Australians in 1910, followed by the whole of South Kyungsang Province in 1913.[59] The Mission of the Presbyterian Church in the U.S.A. retained the other areas where it had been at work, with the approval of the three other Presbyterian bodies.

Comity agreements between the Presbyterians and the Methodists began early. Both the Presbyterian U.S.A. and the Methodist Episcopal Missions had located in Seoul simultaneously in 1885, and then began reaching out in all directions from that capital city. The Methodist Episcopal Church, South, went into Seoul also in 1896. It, too, expanded in all directions excepting southward. There was naturally some confusion due to this overlapping of three organizations, not counting the Anglicans, who were also present. But even before the last of these three American missions had been started, the Northern Methodists and Northern Presbyterians had effected their first territorial agreement on June 11, 1892. This was followed the next year by adoption of a set of rules for implementing that agreement.[60] Towns of five thousand or more populations were to be open to both missions; occupation of any town was defined as a minimum of four visits (including two by missionaries) in each year; further expansion was to be into unoccupied areas; each should receive members of the other only if they brought letters of transfer; there should be mutual respect of each other's discipline; workers might be transferred for employ-

[58] Rhodes, H. A., *op. cit.*, p. 440; Paik, *op. cit.*, p. 189.
[59] Rhodes, H. A., *op. cit.*, p. 441.
[60] *Ibid.*; Paik, *op. cit.*, p. 190; and The Agreement, pp. 433–434.

ment only by consent; and books should be sold, and not given away gratis. However, the Methodist Bishop, Dr. Foster, refused his assent to these rules; but, nevertheless, they were observed by the missionaries on both sides until the general agreement of 1909 was effected. Other adjustments between Presbyterians and Methodists included the division of North Pyengyang Province in 1905, when the Methodists also withdrew from Anju, and the demarcation of the boundaries between the same missions in South Pyengyang Province in 1906.[61]

The Southern Methodists and Northern Presbyterians also made agreements. Agreements in 1907 and 1908 about the region centering in Seoul gave to the Methodists two thirds of Kang-won Province and all Presbyterian churches and work north of Seoul; while the Presbyterians in turn received the southern one third of Kang-won and the Methodist converts and work east and west of Seoul.[62] Seoul was to be held jointly. The Canadians and Southern Methodists also made an agreement in 1908, with some exchange of territory.[63]

However, Methodists and Presbyterians came to feel the need of a more careful and thoroughgoing division of territory than that achieved by piecemeal actions. There were consultations between representatives of the various boards in New York in 1908, and a meeting in Seoul on February 20, 1909, but the proposals put forth by each party proved to be mutually unacceptable. After further conferences in August and September agreement was reached. It was a radical action involving the actual transfer of about four thousand church members on each side![64] For example, more than two thousand Prebyterians in the Chairyang field became Methodists. Seoul and Pyengyang were to be common ground. After the assignment of territory to the Canadians by the Northern Presbyterians in 1909, the final divi-

[61] Rhodes, H. A., op. cit., pp. 441–442; Paik, op. cit., p. 190.
[62] Rhodes, H. A., op. cit., p. 442; Paik, op. cit., pp. 190, 369–370.
[63] Paik, L. G., op. cit., p. 370.
[64] Ibid.; Rhodes, op. cit., pp. 442–443.

sion of the country between the four Presbyterian and two Methodist (four Methodist, if the separate Woman's Boards, which themselves sent missionaries, are counted) missions was, as described by Dr. George L. Paik:

> . . . the Southern Methodists [held] a solid block from Seoul to Songdo and Wonsan, . . . the Canadians the rest of the two Ham Kyeng provinces. In the south, the Northern Presbyterians, Northern Methodists, and Southern Presbyterians entered into an agreement which gave North Chung Chyong province to the Northern Presbyterians, South Chung Chyong province to the Northern Methodists, and the two Chun-la provinces to the Southern Presbyterians. In the southeast, the Northern Presbyterian Mission held the entire two Kyeng Song provinces except strips of territory southeast and southwest of the South Kyeng Song province which were given to the Australian mission.[65]

And in the north the lines of the 1892 and 1905–06 agreements separated Northern Presbyterians and Northern Methodists. Later the Australian Presbyterians got all of their province.

The other missions did not enter into this nation-wide comity compact, but they were small in comparison to the Methodist and Presbyterian forces, and so, although there was still some overlapping, a country-wide strategic distribution of the major forces had been achieved. This agreement generally remained in effect until the Communist invasion and the division of the country into separate North and South regimes. Then millions of refugees went south and settled where they might, regardless of whether it were Presbyterian or Methodist territory. The aggressive evangelistic zeal of the laity and a mass movement into the churches further complicated matters, and schisms within the Presbyterian household of faith brought further confusion. The comity agreements thus became obsolete, but were never repudiated.

[65] Paik, L. G., op. cit., p. 370.

CHAPTER VI

Japan and Congo: Contrasts

A Field without Delimitation of Territory

JAPAN is the one major mission field in which comity did not develop to any appreciable degree despite occupation by societies and boards that were cooperative in spirit and which followed a policy of territorial delimitation and non-interference elsewhere. The root of the matter lies in the confinement of Christianity to a small middle class in the cities with almost no penetration of the rural population. Congo presents a complete contrast. There in a large land with a completely rural population, led by a few cooperative denominations, both church societies and nondenominational faith missions, without planning in the early stages, managed to achieve division of the land and its complete coverage. Congo well illustrates the natural bent of all Protestant missionaries toward mutual recognition, adjustment, and cooperation. Japan reveals how in a crowded, restricted urban environment, without room for expansion in early stages, that natural tendency toward unity and cooperation could not find the normal expression. Yet both situations produced a drive toward church union.

Protestant missionaries first entered Japan in 1859, Korea in 1884, the Philippines in 1900, the Congo in 1878; and in some other parts of Africa their first generation of converts is still living. The same group of church boards and societies form the central core of the Protestant missionary enterprise in all these lands. One would assume, therefore, that all the missionaries of such societies who entered the

164

late-opening lands would have benefited from the earlier
experience of their societies and that the common policy
about comity would have been part of their original equip-
ment. The first two missionaries who arrived in Japan had
served in China. The first two English bishops in that country
formerly had served in South Africa and India. The usual
spirit of interdenominational fellowship was evident among
the missionaries who first arrived on the scene. The usual
pattern of mission methods prevailing elsewhere was repro-
duced in Japan, with the important exceptions that there
were few rural stations and outstations and medical work
was a very minor part of the program. The Japanese government early adopted Western medicine and introduced a
public health program. But by far the most unusual exception was the absence of territorial division of responsibility
and consequently of denominationalism by geography. The
denominations rubbed shoulders in Japan as they did no-
where else.

Just as in China, the missionaries in Japan were long confined to a limited number of port cities, and joint occupation of these was inevitable. Moreover, until 1873 Christianity remained proscribed in Japan; and even at that date
toleration was only tacitly and not explicitly granted. During
the first decade only four American missions were present,
and their small staff did not encounter any real conflict of
interests.[1] There was room for them all and they worked
together harmoniously.

It was not until 1899 that extraterritoriality was abolished
and foreigners, including missionaries, were permitted to
reside in the interior. Even then, unlike China, the missionaries were never able to break away from the cities. Social
and religious barriers in rural society were more insurmount-
able than the earlier legal ones. Thus it happened that the

[1] On this period see Thomas, Winburn T., *Protestant Beginnings in
Japan.*

agents of the missionary societies who arrived during the first four decades were all limited to the major cities, and those who came afterward kept to these and other towns, except as they reached out from them through Japanese evangelists or by short trips themselves. By that time Japanese Protestantism had taken on the character which it has preserved until the present. It had become a middle-class, urban movement. It was rooted among intellectuals, principally the samurai who had been displaced in the social and political revolution, and then in succeeding generations in a new class of Westernized intellectuals, products of the schools—minor government officials, lesser business men, and city people of education and moderate income. This distinct urban stamp was in sharp contrast to the young churches in other parts of Asia and in Africa. The strategy of occupation sought to lay hold very concretely upon every city and town, and consequently it was not much concerned with delimiting whole counties or prefectures for evangelistic responsibility by particular missions.

Furthermore, this urban Protestant community was far more fluid and mobile than the church members in other Asian countries. Members moved from city to city, hunting jobs. This was especially true of those in government service. Organic union along denominational lines or the presence almost everywhere of denominations belonging to the same general communion created nation-wide churches in contrast to most other mission fields, where denominationalism by geography resulted from comity agreements. Presbyterians and Reformed, Baptists, Anglicans, and Methodists seldom had to face the possibility of transfer of membership to another denomination upon removal to another city, no matter how many changes of residence they might make in a lifetime. This permitted the clannishness or group loyalty, said to be a characteristic of the Japanese, to be associated with denominationalism. This was a powerful obstruction to the delimitation of territory among the missions. Moreover, the Japanese themselves, especially in the Congregational and Presbyterian-Reformed Churches, took control of the machinery of church government at an early date. They left the institutions largely to the missionaries. They did take over the denominational spirit from the missionaries, despite the trend toward unity, and church life and thought were more a copy of Western patterns than elsewhere. Missions entered Japan at a time when denominationalism in America and Great Britain was more strongly felt than half a century earlier. There was no young church under missionary tutelage and restraint, and consequently the missionaries were not as free to initiate change as in most other places. Naturally the Japanese denominational leaders did not have the world-wide perspective and the knowledge about experience in other lands that missionaries shared with their brethren in other fields.

The tendency towards nation-wide denominational expansion and consciousness was described by Dr. William Imbrie in a paper prepared for Commission VIII of the Edinburgh Conference in 1910.[2] He wrote:

> For many years the Missions of the Presbyterian and Reformed Churches have occupied all the most important centers in the Empire; and the same thing, to a greater or less degree, is true of the other older and stronger Missions. There never was any 'common understanding' as to a 'delimitation of the field,' though for a time the region about Kobe, Osaka, and Kyoto, was regarded by some as especially the field of the American Board Mission. But in the course of time, Congregational Churches were established in Tokyo and other places; and the American Board Mission was practically constrained to extend its field to other parts of Japan. The Missions to the Presbyterian and Reformed Churches were located in Tokyo and Yokohama, in the north, in the south,

[2] *World Missionary Conference*, 1910, vol. VIII, pp. 18–19.

and on the west coast; and it was essential to the future of the one Church with which they were all connected that its parts should not be separated from each other by the great wedge of Central Japan. No doubt similar causes were operative in the case of other Missions also, and the development now described could hardly have been prevented even if an attempt to do so had been made. Now that strong Churches have been established, it would be impossible to change the policy. . . . Perhaps it is worth while to say in passing that in many respects the conditions in Japan resemble the conditions at home much more closely than is the case in some other fields.

Yet the tendency toward denominational exclusiveness was less strong than the early drive toward unity. There is great significance in the fact that the very first Japanese congregation organized, in Yokohama on March 10, 1872, was an independent congregation which refused to be ecclesiastically bound to any mission, and called itself The Church of Christ in Japan.[3] From that moment the ideal of a single union Protestant church for the whole of Japan was never lost. The story of the attempts to achieve such organic union does not belong to this present study.

It is not at all surprising, therefore, that when that staunch advocate of comity, Dr. Robert E. Speer, secretary of the Board of Foreign Missions of the Presbyterian Church in the U.S.A., visited Japan in 1897, he had to report that there had been no general apportionment of the country among the societies. Moreover, he had to conclude regretfully that a redistribution of territory was impossible.[4] That the Japan missions were not lacking in the spirit usually expressed in comity agreements was apparent, however, despite the lack

[3] Imbrie, William, *Church Unity in Japan*, p. 2; Iglehart, C. W., *A Century of Protestant Christianity in Japan*, pp. 56–57; Thomas, Winburn T., *Protestant Beginnings in Japan*, p. 89.

[4] Speer, Robert E., *Report on the Japan Missions of the Presbyterian Board of Foreign Missions*, p. 65.

of such territorial divisions. The missionaries had by-passed that initial stage and had attempted to begin at the level of mutually accepted standards of procedure and even at that of limited cooperation.

The very first General Convention of Protestant Missionaries in Japan was held in the dispensary chapel of Dr. James C. Hepburn in Yokohama from September 20 to 25, 1872, when there was but a handful of missionaries in the country. The elder of that first Church of Christ in Japan and the elders of union churches in Tokyo and Yokohama were included with the missionaries, which was a great advance over the first missionary conferences in other countries. The purpose of the meeting was to arrange for the production of a common version of the Scriptures, to discuss methods of work, and to consider the question of church organization.[5] That meeting may well be taken as the actual beginning of the church union movement in Japan. The work of Bible translation went forward from that day.

The earliest plea for a division of territory of which there is record was made by Rev. Charles F. Warren of the Church Missionary Society at the second General Conference of Protestant Missionaries at Osaka in 1883.[6] The missions by this time had increased to nineteen, and there were eighty-nine men, mostly with wives, and fifty-six single women missionaries—an unusual proportion of the latter at that period. Since these people were all confined as yet to the treaty ports, it is easy to get the impression that there was a super-abundance of missionaries. However, once extraterritoriality was abolished, the situation would change radically. Many agencies were small and weak. Mr. Warren thought the larger ones, attempting to cover the whole country without

[5] Imbrie, William, *Church Unity in Japan*, pp. 2–4.
[6] Warren, Charles F., "Should the Number of Foreign Missionaries Be Increased?", in *Proceedings of the General Conference of the Protestant Missionaries of Japan, Osaka, 1883*, pp. 420–431.

regard to one another's work and the total task, had too
many missionaries widely scattered in isolation. They would
profit by concentration in strong centers, to which smaller
outstations with more limited programs might be related. It
may be desirable for the major branches of the church to be
represented in every port, Mr. Warren continued, but the
presence of three denominations of any one of the several
communions was unwarranted. A redistribution of forces
could be very helpful. Nevertheless, the Conference passed
a resolution calling upon the churches in Europe and America to strengthen the missions in Japan, but had nothing to
say about division of territory and redistribution of the missionary staff.[7]

An action taken by the Missionary Association of Central
Japan in 1890, following a report on comity, is probably typical of the understanding which tacitly existed among many
of the missions. It was resolved:

> That where work is carried on side by side, no attempts
> should be made directly or indirectly to induce Christians or
> Christian workers connected with one body to join another, or
> to influence catechumens under instruction in connection
> with one Church or mission to receive baptism in another;
> and that the greatest care should be taken not to receive from
> another Church members in good standing without the usual
> commendatory letter, or a certificate of Christian character,
> or to recognize those under discipline in another Church
> without the fullest investigation, nor until after direct com-
> munication with the pastor or other responsible parties
> concerned.[8]

The editor of the missionary magazine, *The Japan Evangelist,* in the spring of 1900 expressed the hope that the

[7] *General Conference of the Protestant Missionaries of Japan, Osaka, 1883,*
p. 435.
[8] Quoted by Robert E. Speer in *Report on the Japan Missions,* p. 64.

forthcoming General Conference would establish a "Board of Comity," meaning by that term a federation of the missions.[9]

The discussion of issues related to cooperation and unity took up much of the time of that General Conference in Tokyo in 1900. Sentiment was crystalized in a resolution which affirmed unity, exhorted to labor for the full realization of corporate oneness, deplored the hindrance to effective evangelism caused by competition in the smaller fields and by the duplication of machinery and effort, and set up a committee to plan and promote a "Standing Committee of the Missions." [10]

The Constitution of the Standing Committee of the Cooperating Christian Missions of Japan, presented by that Committee, stated that the function of the new organization was "to serve as a general medium of reference, communication, and effort for the cooperating missions in matters of common interest and cooperative enterprises." [11] Upon the application of interested parties, or on its own initiative in matters of urgent importance, the Standing Committee might counsel with regard to the distribution of forces for evangelistic, educational, and philanthropic work, especially where expansion was contemplated; with regard to plans for cooperation in any kind of work; and with respect to the prevention of misunderstanding and the active promotion of harmony of spirit and uniformity of method. The last phrase could cover much ground. The Cooperating Missions, then, were to foster the spirit of comity with some slight attention to advice on occupation, but to go beyond that in promoting active cooperation on functional lines.

This Standing Committee of Cooperating Missions met in

[9] *Japan Evangelist,* vol. VII, No. 5 (May, 1900), p. 136.
[10] *General Conference of Protestant Missionaries in Japan, Tokyo, 1900,* p. 42.
[11] *Ibid.,* p. 960.

its first annual meeting in Tokyo in 1902 and continued to meet every year thereafter. It undertook to collect and tabulate statistics. It published a variety of Christian literature, including the annual *The Christian Movement in Japan,* which after some changes of title became eventually the *Japan Christian Yearbook.*[12] The first issue of this mission annual contained an article by Rev. E. H. Van Dyke calling attention to the serious problem of absentees on the rolls of the churches. It advocated a general agreement intended to encourage transfers, or at least active fellowship, when members removed from one place to another. This article influenced the editor to ask for a greater degree of interdenominational comity.[13] He states that some persons were asking for a geographical division, but the movement of the population rendered that impracticable. He rejoiced that there were so few cases of friction and hoped that any difficulties which might arise could be settled by the Standing Committee.

That the Standing Committee did deal with intermission conflicts is made evident by a reference in the report of the 1904 meeting to the referral by two missions of a matter of controversy between them.[14] The minutes of the following year's sessions include a statement that the matter had been satisfactorily adjusted.[15] There were no referrals in 1906. There were practiced, then, some of the usual accompaniments to territorial division, including arbitration of conflicts of interest between missions; but comity meant to the Japan missionaries, not delimitation of territory, but the maintenance of brotherly relations and even of active cooperation. Indeed, cooperation went so far that the name of the

[12] *The Christian Movement in Japan, 1903–1931,* with various titles slightly changed from time to time, and after 1932 continuing to the present as *The Japan Christian Yearbook.*
[13] *Ibid.,* 1903, pp. 40–42, 61–65.
[14] *Ibid.,* 1904, p. 58.
[15] *Ibid.,* 1905, p. 49.

Standing Committee was changed to The Federated Missions.[16]

A movement for a national church federation simultaneously ran parallel to the development of federation among the missions. It had its origin in early days in a general conference of Japanese Christians for mutual encouragement known as the Dai Shimbokukwai.[17] Later it was organized on the basis of the articles of the Evangelical Alliance, and was, indeed, known as the Evangelical Alliance of Japan. This body was transformed on December 19, 1911, into the Federation of Churches. That organ of cooperation was in turn merged with the National Christian Council of Japan, when it was established in 1923.[18]

Tokyo was a natural selection as the site of one of Dr. John R. Mott's Continuation Committee conferences. In fact he held a series, rather than a single conference, from April 3 to 11, 1913. These were, in order, a Conference of Missionaries, a Conference of Japanese Christian Leaders, and a Japan National Conference. The last of these put on record "its profound gratitude to God for the very large measure of Christian fellowship and of the observance of the principles of comity and cooperation on the part of Churches and Missions in Japan." [19] Recommendations called for the further extension of cooperation in education and literature work by the use of the same means as in evangelistic campaigns and theological education. The Conference of Missionaries had earlier recorded its gratitude for the same blessing. But it is baffling, indeed beyond understanding in view of all the earlier evidence, that the Conference declared

[16] *Standing Committee of Cooperating Christian Missions in Japan, Ninth Annual Meeting of the —, 1910,* reported in *Christian Movement in Japan,* 1910, p. 582.

[17] Imbrie, *Church Unity in Japan,* pp. 40–41.

[18] *The Christian Movement in Japan,* 1923, pp. 302–312; *Ibid.,* 1924, pp. 269–276; Hogg, *Ecumenical Foundations,* p. 213.

[19] *Continuation Committee Conferences in Asia, 1912–1913,* p. 459.

that "investigation has shown that in this work there is very little overlapping or even overcrowding." [20] This must at least mean that cooperation in united projects and scrupulous regard for the proprieties on the part of most missionaries had relieved the tension which might have resulted from joint occupation of the same cities and towns.

There was also established in Japan, as in other countries which Dr. Mott visited after the Edinburgh Conference, a Japan Continuation Committee, composed of representatives of the Federation of Churches and the Federated Missions.[21] However, since both of those bodies were very lively organizations, its role was not a very important one.[22] Its chief claim to fame is the calling of the National Christian Conference of 1922, which brought into being the National Christian Council.[23] That cooperative agency began functioning on November 13, 1923. A few years later the Federated Missions turned over to it the responsibilities of five of its committees, but, divested of most of its functions, it continued in existence until 1936 when it became the Fellowship of Christian Missionaries.[24]

The Federated Missions, the Federation of Churches, the Japan Continuation Committee, and the (American) Inter-Church World Movement were all interested in the making of surveys, including missionary occupation. These activities and concerns did result in a measure of support of a proposal to apportion unoccupied territory—which would, of course, be rural areas. The Federated Missions accordingly in its annual conference of 1911 created a Committee on Distribution of Forces to study thoroughly the question of a desirable increase in the missionary body in Japan. This committee

[20] *Ibid.*, p. 422.
[21] *Ibid.*, pp. 459–460.
[22] Hogg, *op. cit.*, p. 212.
[23] *Ibid.*, pp. 212–213.
[24] Iglehart, C. W., *A Century of Protestant Christianity in Japan*, pp. 210–211.

was charged with seeing what steps might be taken to coordinate evangelistic work more effectively, especially in relation to an advance, and to consider the possibility of assigning responsibility for specific districts to individual missions. The committee membership was appointed by the Executive Committee the following February, and Dr. G. W. Fulton was made chairman.[25]

This committee sought the cooperation and active interest of the entire missionary force in Japan by setting up twelve regional conferences. The call for these consultations cited the action of the Edinburgh Conference of 1910. The assemblies were asked among other things to state whether or not there was unnecessary and wasteful overlapping which might be remedied by a better adjustment of the forces and whether a delimitation of fields involving definite evangelistic responsibility might be made. The aid of the Federation of Churches was sought. Reports of the findings were made in 1912 and 1913.[26] Summarizing its findings in 1914, the committee stated that there was little overlapping of missionary and church forces in their respective fields. This stand was apparently made on the ground that there was room for all the agencies despite the number of missions in any one place. However, it was stated that the rural districts, which had about 80 per cent of the total population of the nation, were virtually untouched.[27] The report further stated: "The missionary bodies in the main were prepared to enter into arrangements distributing the unoccupied field, and to undertake responsibility for the evangelization of the assigned fields as soon as workers and resources should be increased so as to enable them to do so." It recorded with appreciation the help of the Federation of Churches and the Continuation Committee, and endorsed the latter's plea for

[25] *Christian Movement in Japan, 1912*, p. 191.
[26] *Ibid.*, pp. 197–238; *1913*, p. 191.
[27] *Conference of Federated Missions, 1914*, p. 12.

a long-term, forward-looking, comprehensive policy for co-ordinating the process of occupation and securing resources for it.

The regional situations are interesting. It was reported that in the southern island of Kyushu an earnest effort had been made through the years by the missions to stay out of each other's fields. The Chugoku conference made recommendations for the division of the kens of Hiroshima, Okayama, Tottori, and Yamaguchi. The other conferences made similar recommendations for their areas. It was made clear that delimitation of territory was not intended to give warrant for proselytizing but rather to assign responsibility for new evangelization. Inability or failure to accomplish the work within a reasonable period would cancel any mission's claim to the assigned area. The committee had done its job well, and the missions had the best of intentions. Something rather minor was achieved in the way of an advance, but on the whole there was very little real penetration of the countryside. Soon the comity agreements were apparently forgotten. Dr. Charles W. Iglehart commented in 1934:

> . . . in some instances at least the proposals did have an effect on the guidance of missionary advance in funds and personnel which followed during the five or ten years succeeding. So far as the writer's observation goes, however, they have by this time been utterly forgotten. Furthermore, they never had any appreciable effect on policies that owed their initiative to the Japanese Church leaders.[28]

This paper by Dr. Iglehart had been prepared for the Conference of the North American Mission Boards in Japan held in New York under the sponsorship of the Foreign Mis-

[28] Iglehart, C. W., "Comity and Cooperation in Japanese Christianity," a paper prepared for the Conference of the North American Missionary Boards in Japan, New York City, 1934.

sions Conference of North America in 1934. His report revealed that there was little or no delimitation of territory among the denominations; that there was, on the contrary, much paralleling of denominational churches and programs, but that there was little duplication in outlying villages. Moreover, he stated that the denominations had shown almost no variation as to type, emphasis, or function in society, and that no assignment of particular tasks had been attempted among them. He bore witness to the steady movement toward unity on the part of the Japanese churches. Initiative now rested with those churches, and not with the missions.

There was no marked change in the situation down to World War II. The creation of the single united Church of Christ in Japan (Kyodan) through government pressure, but in line with old aspirations and efforts, transformed the problem of comity between missions into a matter of internal adjustments within a nation-wide church. The withdrawal of certain of the denominational groups from that union after the war did not create any special new problems of overlapping or competition. Such problems did arise, however, when a host of new missionaries arrived, not connected with the older missions related to cooperative work and having little regard for the existing churches or their supporting missions.

The Development of Comity in Congo

Congo was the extreme opposite of Japan in every way. Here was not an ancient nation with a proud tradition and high culture, and with densely populated great cities and towns, but a vast, unexplored tropical wilderness of the Congo River basin, inhabited by numerous tribes of primitive people, speaking a variety of tongues. Stanley had no more than traced the great river from its headwaters to its mouth when the missionaries began to preach the gospel along its course. There was soon established a far-flung, widely separated line of mission stations along the river, penetrating into the interior, intended to be linked with the mission forces in East Africa and thus present a barrier to the southward expansion of Islam.

Until the railroad was opened in 1878 all newly arriving missionaries had by force of circumstances to walk for four days through lower Congo from the coast to Stanley Pool. The missionaries residing in the stations along the route gladly gave hospitality to the newcomers, and consultations about location were natural and unavoidable. This led to a practical comity in up-river locations without any formal means for delimitation of territory being provided.

There had been some friendly adjustments even in the earliest years. The Livingstone Inland Mission in 1884 surrendered down-river stations to the American Baptists and the Swedish Mission Covenant in order to free its resources for a further penetration into the interior; and the Baptists, in turn, in 1896 gave Bolenge to the Disciples of Christ as their initial location (occupied in 1899). Yet with the whole country before them, the missions soon became somewhat congested in the lower Congo. The exasperating feeling of being crowded there, jostling one another, and having no room for expansion, while most of the upper Congo was unoccupied, led to the inclusion of a paper on comity at the second Congo Missionary Conference at Leopoldville in 1904.

The first Conference had been held at the same place in 1902. At that time a permanent Committee on Arrangements for continuing Conferences had been created. There had been a discussion on possible union activity, namely, transport activities on the upper river for missionaries and goods.[29] One missionary also suggested printing as a field of union endeavor.

A young American Baptist missionary, Rev. Thomas Moody, presented the paper on comity in 1904.[30] He said that he could not add to what had been said at the Ecumenical Missionary Conference in New York in 1900. He proposed that either the whole Conference or a committee which it might appoint should be the arbiter on new locations, and that any society desiring to begin a mission in the Congo should consult it as to choice. Any society "holding and preaching the evangelical faith" ought to be allowed to work the territory in which it has priority of occupation without encroachment by others. Each mission should acknowledge the Christians of the others, and give and receive letters of dismissal. There ought to be a uniform salary scale for all native workers, and the time had come for a union training school to which the best men from all the missions in the lower Congo would be sent. Transportation, translation, and publishing ought to be undertaken cooperatively. Members, preachers, and teachers of one mission should be received by another only after careful inquiry. No missionary should leave his mission in order to join another until the end of his term of service, and then he had better wait until he was on furlough and see how things looked after he had had some rest. There was a consensus, but no action was taken. Behind the paper and the discussion was the fact that the missions in the lower Congo were "hedged in" while in the upper Congo there were forty tribes still without the gospel. Two years later the Conference of 1906 adopted a statement on the uniform reception of church members and set up a committee to prepare for a Federation of the Congo Missions.[31]

[29] *United Missionary Conference on the Congo, The First, 1902,* pp. 65–69.
[30] *Ibid., The Second, 1904,* pp. 32–34.
[31] *Ibid., The Third, 1906,* pp. 18–24, 106, 115.

The problem of overlapping territory was given much more attention at the 1907 Conference.[32] There was said to be unity among the missionaries, but overlapping was impairing fellowship and there was some rivalry. It was especially difficult where two missions had different rules about polygamy and temperance. There were now five societies in the lower Congo with twenty-two stations, hedged in and unable to expand farther, while there were but seventeen stations in all of the upper Congo. It was suggested that missions should not work across the boundaries between the Free State, the French areas, or the Portuguese territory, but confine themselves to one colonial government area only. Similarly it is best to remain within one single language area as well as to stay within natural boundaries. An English Baptist missionary proposed a resolution asking the home societies to set up a "Committee of Arbitration" for the Congo that would settle questions of delimitation of territory. The discussion was favorable, but the brethren could not come to any solution that seemed practical, and the matter was left open. However, the matter came up again in a paper by an American Baptist missionary and in the subsequent discussion on cooperation.[33] Sentiment was for avoiding crowding each other through adoption of a mutual plan, for a united training school and orphanages, for similar action in literary work, industrial training, and transportation. Above all it was required in evangelistic expansion, and a "Boundaries Committee" was requested. The up-river brethren were free of delimitation discussions, it was said, just because they were not crowded. The lower Congo was quite different, and some day there would have to be a United Church of the Lower Congo. In fact, the "Boundaries Committee" ought to become a "Missions Bureau," which would deal with boundaries, acquire information about mis-

[32] *Ibid., The Fourth, 1907*, pp. 51–56.
[33] *Ibid., The Fourth, 1907*, pp. 145–160.

sionary occupation in all of central Africa, gather information on the unoccupied fields, and secure the entrance of Protestant missions into these ahead of the Roman Catholics. Action, however, was limited to setting up an Inter-Mission Prayer Union and the drafting of a resolution on orphanages.

Then once again comity came up. Mr. Frederick Beale of the Congo Balolo Mission introduced the subject: "Would it be right to leave towns unevangelized merely because they are accounted as in the district of another mission?"[34] Mr. Beale demonstrated both his knowledge of the subject of comity, quoting from the Allahabad, Shanghai, and Punjab Conferences, and his stout adherence to such a policy. Most societies regarded big cities as open ground, but there were none that big in Congo. But what should be done if two or more societies agreed about spheres of work and then one of them neglected part of its field? A definition of "unevangelized" was needed. There was one up-river missionary "who considered a district 'evangelized' when he had once passed hurriedly through it." Mr. Beale suggested that if a town were totally neglected, one should first communicate with the mission responsible for it, and enter only if it is persisted in that neglect. "The question is really one of comity, by the observance of which the problem will in almost every case be solved and the difficulty will vanish." In fact: "It is the contempt of comity that causes what the late Dr. A. C. Thompson called 'Evangelistic Anarchy. It affects not unbelievers but Christians! It is an utterly needless waste of forces, and it imperils the welfare of the Church as a whole.'" Still no definite action was taken.

The refusal of the colonial government to grant Protestant missions the rights guaranteed them by the international treaties relating to the Congo for a time hampered further expansion and the entrance of new societies.[35] However, the

[34] *Ibid., The Fourth, 1907*, pp. 164–169.
[35] *Ibid., The Fifth, 1909*, p. 12.

vast unoccupied areas challenged the missionaries, and at the Sixth Conference at Bolenge in 1911 watchwords were "Forward! What steps can we take to reach unoccupied parts of North Congoland?" and "Africa and Congo for Christ in this generation." [36] Some adjustment of territory had apparently been taking place. For example, the American Baptists proposed an exchange of territory north of the Congo for a Swedish mission's Mukimbungu area, but that particular agreement was not carried through until about 1935. The years of discussion finally crystalized in a resolution establishing a commission of two members from each mission to consider the reconstruction of the present fields and to arrange those to be opened in the future. A further resolution established the Commission at once, the full membership of each mission later to ratify the election of representatives chosen by their brethren then present. This Commission was requested to draw up a resolution showing the needs of the North Bank and urging the attention of this pressing need upon the home churches. However, for some reason that is not clear the Commission never functioned, but the Committee on Arrangements was now replaced by a permanently functioning Continuation Committee. The societies and boards were requested to send each a deputation to the next 1913 meeting.[37]

It is not clear how far this development went. The projected 1913 meeting was postponed because of difficulties in arrangements,[38] and the outbreak of World War I prevented the holding of the conference set for September, 1914. No further meetings could be held until 1918. Apparently the Commission provided by the resolution of the 1911 Conference did not function and its responsibility devolved partly upon the Continuation Committee, since one

[36] *Ibid., The Sixth, 1911*, pp. 22–39.
[37] *Ibid., The Sixth, 1911*, pp. 107–108.
[38] *Congo Mission News*, No. 5 (November, 1913), pp. 15–16.

item that was placed on the agenda for 1913 was: "Should the Continuation Committee be empowered to deal with cases of overlapping?" Added was the note that at present it might only confer with those that asked its aid in matters of adjustment.[39] There was at least some consultation of the Committee by newcomers, for it reported in 1916 that the Swedish Baptists had asked for a possible field of operation.[40] When the seventh General Conference met at Luebo, Kasai, in 1918, it was reported that there were now fourteen missionary societies in the land, nine of which were represented there.[41] The map inside the back cover of the November, 1919, issue of the *Congo Mission News,* showing mission spheres, indicated no apparent overlapping in the north, although the map is not very detailed.

In the seventy-fifth anniversary book, *Highways for God in Congo,* Dr. George W. Carpenter states:

> During the two decades between the wars, 1919–39, the number of Protestant missions in Congo more than doubled, and it would become both tedious and confusing to describe each new venture in chronological order. However, a spirit of comity has always ruled inter-mission relationships in Congo, so new missions nearly always sought fields not already effectively occupied by others. Hence the younger missions can be grouped in relation to the areas which were still unoccupied at the close of World War I.[42]

"The Congo Mission Field: Its Complete Occupation" was the major theme of the 1918 Conference at Luebo.[43] The four preparatory papers surveyed the untouched tribes, the

[39] *Ibid.,* No. 1 (November, 1912), p. 12.
[40] *Ibid.,* No. 17 (November, 1916), p. 6.
[41] *United Missionary Conference on The Congo, The Seventh, 1918;* see list of the missions.
[42] Carpenter, George W., *Highways for God in Congo,* p. 26.
[43] *United Missionary Conference on The Congo, The Seventh, 1918.* The four papers on the theme were also printed separately as a pamphlet, 24 pp.

ground occupied since 1911, the extent to which the societies were willing to commit themselves to an advance, and a general plea for an advance. It is clear from the report of the Continuation Committee that in comity matters its only action had been the location of the one new Swedish field, but that this was regarded as a future field of responsibility. The few new missions had apparently made location on the basis of their own observations, but in the spirit of comity. Neglect of the growing cities and concern for them first appears at this meeting. The papers and discussion on co-operation and the Continuation Committee at the 1921 Conference took up the slack created by the long break in continuity since 1911.[44] The momentum gained here gathered force through the next three years, and at the ninth Conference at Leopoldville in 1924, that missionary body resolved itself into the Conseil Protestant du Congo, and voted itself out of existence when that council would become effective upon the election of counsellors by at least five missions.[45] The constitution of the Conseil Protestant provided for a Standing Committee on Comity, but its functions and rules of procedure were not defined.[46] Because of distances the Standing Committees rarely met, and the secretary of that Committee was largely responsible for getting its work done. The Conseil after its organization, was very active in comity matters without such affairs becoming matter of record. There were hardly any formal agreements committed to writing. Representatives of societies reached a consensus after consultation with the secretary of the Conseil. Further, there were a considerable number of appeals about comity infringements made to the Conseil, and in most instances the secretary resolved them by using his good offices through

[44] *Ibid., The Eighth, 1921*, pp. 234-40, 55-67, 146-155.
[45] *Ibid., The Ninth, 1945*, p. 145.
[46] *Ibid., The Ninth, 1945*, p. 145.

informal conversations and correspondence, according to Dr. George W. Carpenter and other experienced Congo missionaries.

The fact that the Congo missions managed to get along for almost half a century without an official organ for comity relations and still occupied the country with very little interference with each other reveals the spirit of unity that motivated them and bound them together in a common task. This was still largely the case in the period that followed the establishment of the Conseil, although more and more missions came into the country. The Comity Committee reported to the Conseil at the 1932 meeting: "Fortunately, in these latter years in Congo, this is the least worked of all the Council's committees. In 1931 there were no matters whatever referred to it." [47] Occasionally approval of admission to membership in the Conseil was deferred until the applicant had made satisfactory comity arrangements with its neighbors.[48] The Comity Committee is not mentioned in the revisions of the Constitutions in 1935, 1944, and 1955, but it was still functioning in 1948. The revised Constitution of 1955 provides for investigation of applicants, and the neighbors of such an applying agency must approve it "particularly with respect to mission and personal relationships and questions of comity." [49] Unfortunately, even the best situation is not perfect. There were some societies which entered the country and made location without consultations with the Conseil or anyone else. Their selection might be resented by the unconsulted missions, especially their nearest neighbors, without there being such a thing as a factual violation of comity.

[47] *Congo Mission News*, April, 1932, p. 11.
[48] An example: *Conseil Protestant du Congo, Minutes of Meeting, 1941,* Minute 512; *ibid., Meeting No. 21, 1948,* Minute 591.
[49] *Conseil Protestant du Congo, Constitution,* revised and ratified, 1955, Art. 13, Sec. 2 (p. 6).

There were forty-five separate missions in the Congo at the time of the seventy-fifth anniversary in 1953. The saturation point had been reached even before this date. The Conseil moved in 1935 to discourage any new agencies from entering the country and thus endeavored to prevent possible comity complications. It voted:

The Council, having taken cognizance of the existence of forty-three distinct Protestant missionary organizations in Congo Belge, with over two hundred stations distributed throughout the Colony, consider that there is no further call for the establishment of new missions in this area.

They consider that the cause of Evangelical missions would be much better served by the strengthening of existing organizations, both in personnel and funds, and by the unification of related bodies so as to reduce administrative costs and improve efficiency of work, rather than by the establishment of additional agencies.

The members of the Council have had occasion to observe the heavy costs and unnecessary hardships involved in the coming of inexperienced missionaries without the guidance and backing of an established society. Such costs and hardships were inescapable in the early days of Congo Missions, but are largely avoidable today.

The task of missions is so great and so urgent that any waste of resources in one direction curtails necessary work elsewhere. Moreover, every new organization is confronted with the necessity of securing civil rights in the Colony and of acquiring lands; and the Government, with reason, regards unfavorably the further multiplication of missionary organizations.

Therefore the Council strongly recommends to all interested parties that support be given to agencies already at work in the Congo, rather than directed to the creation of new ones.[50]

[50] *Conseil Protestant du Congo, Minutes of Meeting No. 13, 1935,* p. 13, Minute 354.

Further pressure from missions seeking entrance led the Conseil to reiterate this statement in 1945.[51]

Church missions and nondenominational faith missions alike had manifested this remarkable spirit of unity. Official machinery for comity arrangements and arbitration came late and was little used. It was the practical expression of the inner spirit and self-policing that led to the effective occupation of the Congo with very little overlapping and interference. The large area for expansion helped, to be sure, but in the latter years this was less and less a factor. The spirit of unity also exhibited itself more and more, beginning with united transport activities, literature work, and the Training Institute at Kimpesi. After the formation of the Conseil Protestant in 1924 cooperative work speedily increased, including such institutions as the United Mission House and the Librairie Évangélique au Congo. An idea so often proposed in other areas was actually accepted in the Congo; all the cooperating churches took the common name of the Church of Christ in Congo and accepted a common, transferable membership. The missions were very slow in allowing a national organ for this incipient church, but they theoretically accepted the ideal. Procrastination had lost the missions a great opportunity when independence came suddenly. Probably no field demonstrates better than Congo that comity in spirit and in practice has been a fundamental part of the Protestant mission system and that it is the basis on which active cooperation developed.

[51] *Ibid., Meeting No. 23, 1945,* p. 21, Minute 717.

CHAPTER VII

The Influence of Governments

The Effect of Geography

TERRITORIAL adjustments, both in form of delimited spheres of occupation and later changes in boundaries, were ordinarily due to the spirit of unity that prevailed among the missionaries and to their desire to fix responsibility for the speediest possible evangelization of a region. Sometimes, however, separation into distinct fields of operations was due to extraneous forces, such as the effect of topography or the policy of some colonial government.

Angola appears to be a country where geography separated the missions quite as effectively as territorial agreements might have done. There the hostility of the colonial government toward Protestants also inhibited the entrance of numerous societies and consequently forestalled competition for the same territories. Inter-mission rivalry could not easily develop in such circumstances. The well-known authority on Protestant missions in Angola, John T. Tucker, wrote: "Angola, for missionary purposes, may be considered as divided into zones each having its port of entry, its own trade routes into the interior, and its own variety of *Bantu* speech. In the past these zones were almost like water-tight compartments. There was very little cross-country communication." [1] There was consequently practically no overlapping, and agreements were scarcely needed between the few missions at work in the country. The one notable instance is the

---

[1] Tucker, John T., *Angola, The Land of the Blacksmith Prince*, p. 61; see the map between pages 10 and 11 and the tables on p. 138.

agreement of 1927 by which the American Board of Commissioners for Foreign Missions divided its field and turned over a portion of it to the Board of Foreign Missions of the United Church of Canada in 1927.[2] This included provision for a joint annual conference of the two missions and united operation of the central schools and the press at Dondi.

The geography of a land in relation to the initial penetration sometimes played an important role in determining location. The first missions which entered Congo located so close together in the bottleneck of lower Congo that they soon felt crowded, while those which came later fanned out into the vast region up-river beyond Stanley Pool.

Colonial Policy on Missions

More often it was the policy of some colonial or national government that imposed a specific location on a mission. The confining of all foreigners to residence in specific treaty ports for many years was responsible for the duplication and lack of comity in Japan. It was the cause of the first locations of the older missions in China and determined the areas into which they would expand from the cities when the restrictions were lifted. The old missions were all tied to the treaty ports on the sea and the Yangtze River when permission to travel and reside in the provinces was given, and, tied to those spots by their investments in them and by limited resources, they were unable at once to move into the unoccupied heartland. That great vacuum proved a mighty call to J. Hudson Taylor, and the China Inland Mission (C.I.M.) was formed for the purpose of pioneering in frontier posts.

[2] American Board of Commissioners for Foreign Missions, *Annual Report, 1927*, p. 35; Minutes of the Prudential Committee, April 26, 1927; Letter of Mary A. Walker, Librarian of the A.B.C.F.M., Boston, January 8, 1954.

Certain governments entirely excluded missions from some areas of their domains. The entrance of Protestant missions into colonies of Roman Catholic powers has usually been difficult, although French colonial antagonism to Protestant missions, other than those of French societies, has not been especially inspired by Roman Catholicism but rather by suspicion of foreign agencies. Portuguese authorities were more cordial to Protestant missions during the period immediately following the establishment of the Republic in 1910, which was marked by anticlericalism at home, but later the missions in Mozambique had much trouble and it was difficult for them to secure licenses for location and permits to acquire land.[3]

British colonial officers in Malaya would not permit Christian missions directed toward the Malays and the work there had to be restricted to the Chinese, Indians, and Europeans.[4] This was supposed to be a necessary requirement for keeping the zealous Muslim populace peaceful. Similarly the colonial officers kept missions excluded from the three northern Nigeria provinces of Kano, Sokoto, and Bornu, on the grounds that the Muslim emirs had been promised that there would be no interference with their religion.[5] A relaxation of this prohibition began to come about in the mid-1920's, and many of the missions were eager to advance into the north.[6] When the Church of the Brethren had been shut out from Bornu, an appeal was made through the International Missionary Council; and when the result of that was known

[3] Moreira, Eduardo, *Portuguese East Africa*, pp. 44, 45, 48–50, esp. ch. 5, "The State and Missions," pp. 159–69.

[4] This states the more general belief. It has been argued since the mid-1930's that the government never imposed such prohibition. See Browne, Lawrence E., *Christianity and the Malays*, pp. 68ff; MacLeish, Alexander, *A Regional Melting Pot. Religion in Malaya*, pp. 9–10.

[5] Maxwell, J. L., *Nigeria, the Land, Its People, and Christian Progress*, pp. 109, 111.

[6] *Conference of Missions in the Northern Provinces of Nigeria, 1929, Minutes of the —*, p. 8.

the Conference of Missionaries of the Northern Provinces of
Nigeria prepared in 1926 to press that case with the government and to seek freedom for advance.[7] The questioning by
the Conference brought a reply from the governor in 1929
that "it would be the deliberate policy of Government to
educate the emirs in the idea of religious freedom and to
secure progressive relaxation of the barriers to missions."[8]
The opening soon followed, but with restrictions. The Council of Missions, which had been created by the Conference in
1926, in 1932 protested a decree which restricted preaching
in public places in Muslim villages and limited the entry into
Kano emirate to one mission only.[9] Both the Church Missionary Society (C.M.S.) and the Sudan Interior Mission had
applied for permission to open work in Kano, and the government had chosen the former. The governor granted an
interview to a deputation of the Council. He informed the
missionaries that the government adhered strongly to the
policy of one mission to each emirate. Such a policy was in
effect the imposition of territorial comity by government
choice of the agency permitted to work in each emirate.
Moreover, there would be consultation with each emir before a license were granted, and the certificate then issued
would bear whatever restrictions might be indicated by the
requirements of the situation. The Dutch long kept missions
out of Hindu Bali, Muslim central and western Java, and
northern Sumatra.[10] Some powers commonly regarded as
Christian and Protestant, then, excluded missions from certain areas in their possessions just as firmly as did Muslim
governments in Arabia, Yemen, and Afghanistan, or the
Hindu rulers of Nepal, or the lamas of Tibet.

[7] *The Missionary Visitor*, June 1927, pp. 198, 199.
[8] *Conference of Missions in the Northern Provinces of Nigeria, 1929, Minutes of the —*, p. 10.
[9] *Ibid.*, 1932, p. 17; for more background material see Rowland V. Bingham, *The Story of the Sudan Interior Mission*, pp. 87–91.
[10] Rauws, J., *et al.*, *The Netherlands Indies*, p. 114.

British governmental interference with missions in matters of location was rare outside the areas where there was total exclusion. Both the colonial governments and the companies relied on the missions as civilizing agencies and depended heavily upon them for schools and medical work, subsidizing them in one fashion or another. The government sometimes placed limitations as to location of schools in areas where the missions overlapped and competition resulted. The missionaries in Nyasaland apparently came to the conclusion in 1910 that the colonial government was excluding Protestant missions from some districts in favor of Roman Catholic missions, and there was local friction in some places. The General Missionary Conference of Nyasaland in that year consequently affirmed that there were difficulties between missions as to their spheres of work, especially between Protestants and Roman Catholics in central Ngoniland. Claiming the religious liberty that was guaranteed by the Berlin Treaty, the Conference took the position that freedom must be accorded all societies to enter any sphere where the natives might desire their presence and work, unless the missions should make an agreement concerning delimitation of territory among themselves.[11] Representation was made to the governor by a deputation. The governor replied that he was aware of friction over such matters not only between Protestants and Roman Catholics but between Protestant missions also. He stated that:

> The attitude of Government is that interference in matters which relate to delimitations of spheres of influence as between different religious societies is to be avoided so long as the public safety is not endangered thereby, equal toleration being extended to all, as it is desirable that such points should be settled by the local bodies concerned.[12]

[11] *General Missionary Conference of Nyasaland, Report of the Third —, 1910*, pp. 78–79.
[12] *Ibid., 1910*, p. 84.

However, the government reserved the right always to deal with all questions involving public safety, but in case of a refusal the right of appeal to the governor was always open. The missionaries had been of the opinion that the government was deliberately excluding mission schools from Muslim villages, and on this point the governor stated that permission would not be given any mission to open a village school unless the chief, Muslim or not, gave full consent. The Natal government changed the limit between schools of different denominations from three to five miles, and the Natal Missionary Conference protested in 1933.[13] The Conference in 1936 asked the government to restore the former three-mile rule, the distance being defined as the shortest passage by foot between the two points.[14] A special committee was appointed to assemble the views and opinions of the missions. The next year it was stated that a limitation of school sites by distance in mileage had failed to prevent overlapping. A new policy was suggested to the government: that the District Native Commissioner make a survey; that when a new school was needed the new site be given to the mission with the school nearest that point; that if that point be not occupied within two years it then be assigned to another mission; and that there be a resurvey every ten years.[15]

The most notable interference by British authorities with the missions in the colonies was in those areas which were seized from Germany during World War I, which was an act of injustice that has not been forgotten even half a century later. British missions went to the assistance of the young churches of the displaced missions; for example, the Methodist and Church of Scotland missions in the Gold Coast gave help to the Basel and Bremen Society churches

[13] *Natal Missionary Conference, Report of the —*, 1933, p. 4.
[14] *Ibid.*, 1936, p. 7.
[15] *Ibid.*, 1937, pp. 11–12.

in Togo and the Gold Coast itself. American and Swedish Lutheran societies went to the assistance of the churches in Tanganyika. Considerably later the Evangelical and Reformed Church became associated with the Ewe Presbyterian Church in Togo.

Protestant missionaries frequently accused the Roman Catholic missionaries of inducing the Catholic governments to take hostile measures toward them. The accusation made against the British government in Nyasaland mentioned above is rare. There is at least one instance of a contrary position, in which a Protestant ecclesiastic took the position that the colonial government should keep out undesirable sectarians. An Anglican bishop at the 1932 meeting of the Southern Rhodesia Missionary Conference maintained that it was the business of the Conference "to see that new sects be not introduced that subvert the principles for which the Conference stood." The governor had recently allowed the Watch Tower Movement agents in the country for three months and confusion had resulted. The members of the Conference, however, took a line the exact opposite of that held by their colleagues in Nyasaland, who argued for complete freedom. They resolved: "That in the opinion of this Conference, the responsibility of decision concerning the granting or withholding of approval for the admission of new denominations into this territory, is definitely the concern of the Government, a responsibility which cannot be vested in the Missionary Conference." However, the missionaries warned the government that the utmost care should be exercised to prevent undesirable influences from operating upon native life. It recommended that in each case under consideration the government give regard to certain factors: the nature of the views held, the previous record of the denomination, the educational and other credentials of the missionaries, and the facilities of the applying mission adequately to ensure the satisfactory direction and maintenance of the work proposed.[16]

Exclusion, Separation, and Assignment by Governments

The Dutch colonial government in Indonesia, right down to the end of colonial rule, had absolute power to admit or exclude a mission.[17] Its proposed location would be one factor in approval or rejection. Each individual missionary was also required to apply for a special license for "the practise of his services," and, if granted, it could be recalled at any time. In the early period the government would not permit Roman Catholic and Protestant missions to operate in the same area, especially among primitive people.[18] Thus Soemba was Protestant and Flores was Roman Catholic, while New Guinea until 1928 was divided by an east-west line, with Roman Catholic missions only permitted south of it and Protestant missions to the north. The government, however, did not assign specific districts to Protestant missions or Roman Catholic orders. Few Protestant agencies besides Dutch missions worked in Indonesia until after World War II and independence, and nearly all the Dutch societies were Reformed in doctrine and polity. They adjusted to each other without much difficulty. Topography was one favorable influence also, since the archipelago is so vast and the population extensive. Few missions felt crowded or were tempted to interfere in the area of another. The Dutch-Indies Mission Union and the Missions Con-

[16] *Southern Rhodesia Missionary Conference, 1932, Proceedings of the —*, p. 17.
[17] Rauws, J., *et al., The Netherlands Indies*, p. 113.
[18] *Ibid.*, p. 115.

sulate related the separate missions to one another and to the government.

German colonial officers also sought to separate Protestants and Roman Catholics. Thus the mission of the Pallottine Fathers was admitted to the Cameroons in 1890 with the understanding that there would be no trespassing on Protestant territory. However, in 1898 they invaded Duala, long occupied by the Baptist and Basel Missions, on the ground that "it was impossible to obey the command of Christ to go into all the world and to teach all people and then let a river be an impassable barrier." [19] The government of German Southwest Africa in 1896 admitted the Oblates of Mary Immaculate and the Oblates of St. Francis de Sales with the restriction that they not enter the fields of the Rhenish and Finnish missions.[20] The governor of Togoland himself took the initiative in 1906 and called into conference the Bremen, Basel, and Roman Catholic missionaries. He proposed the division of north Togo, with the northeast portion being assigned to the Roman Catholics. The missions agreed. Berlin gave assent, and the decision was reiterated in 1909. This arrangement was to be in force for thirty years; it actually lasted twenty.[21]

The Congo government during the 1930's sought to separate Roman Catholic and Protestant missions also, and declared that neither might locate any form of work within five kilometers of the other. However, while this policy was supposedly in force it was applied against Protestants but seldom against Roman Catholics.

During the early period of its colonial venture, the German government feared missions and missionaries of other than German nationality. It initially favored their exclusion, and in this was supported by a portion of the German nation,

[19] Groves, C. P., *The Planting of Christianity in Africa*, vol. III, pp. 60–61.
[20] *Ibid.*, p. 68.
[21] *Ibid.*, pp. 214–215.

even by many within the churches. The authorities wished to expel the American Board missionaries from the Marshall Islands, but the German cooperative missionary agency, the Ausschuss, successfully intervened.[22] It was especially in Tanganyika or German East Africa that this was a lively issue. The missions on the scene were actually hostile to the new German government at the beginning.[23] Colonial enthusiasts wanted this largest colony especially, but all the others, too, kept as a preserve for the German churches. Some of them, including commercial interests at Hamburg, established several new organizations with a constituency quite different than the usual pietist members of the old missionary societies.[24] The great missiologist, Professor Gustav Warneck, demolished their arguments and defended the universality and supranationality of missions, as well as the rights of the English societies through prior occupation.[25] The older German societies had little alternative but to enter the new colonies in view of the activities of these newer societies and in view of Christian responsibilities toward the peoples of the colonies. Nevertheless, Roland Oliver concludes that: "The German inruption into East Africa in 1885 started a train of events which converted the missions into an important vehicle of imperialism in Europe, with consequences that vitally affected their future standing in Africa." [26]

Parts of German East Africa and the Cameroons came under the provisions of the Congo act of 1885, which guaranteed missionary freedom, and Article 10 of the German-

[22] References to troubles with the Government in American Board of Commissioners for Foreign Missions, *Annual Report, 1889*, pp. xxi, 114; *Ibid., 1890*, pp. xix, 67; *Ibid., 1894*, pp. 87–88; Bliss, Theodora, *Micronesia: Fifty Years in the Island World*, pp. 139–149; Hogg, *Ecumenical Foundations*, p. 72.

[23] Oliver, Roland, *The Missionary Factor in East Africa*, p. 96.

[24] Mirbt, Carl, *Mission und Kolonialpolitik*, p. 71.

[25] Warneck, Gustav, "Modernste Missiongeschichteschreibung," in *Allgemeine Missions Zeitschrift*, vol. XIII (1886), pp. 297–317.

[26] Oliver, Roland, *Missionary Factor in East Africa*, p. 94.

English agreement of July 1, 1890, further guaranteed it to
missionaries of both countries in the territories of both
powers.[27] The Bishop of Likoma in 1908 asserted that British
missionaries were operating unhindered under these treaty
provisions.[28] Yet there were restrictions imposed from time
to time and place to place. The C.M.S. was required to
withdraw from Mochi in Tanganyika in 1892,[29] and about
the same time the English Primitive Methodists were refused
permission to locate in the Cameroons.[30]

The French from time to time showed similar fear of foreign nationals in some of their colonies. After Tahiti was
taken the London Missionary Society (L.M.S.) was forced
out, formally withdrawing in 1886, and their churches were
largely swallowed by the Roman Catholics. The Société des
Missions Évangéliques de Paris came to the aid of the
remainder.[31] When the same society was forced out of the
Loyalty Islands and New Caledonia, the Paris Society was
also fortunately able to take over the field.[32]

The French government also long refused permission to
Protestants of other nationalities to work in Indo-China,
where the French flag had followed Roman Catholic missions. There were Reformed Churches for Frenchmen in
some cities, but the overburdened Société des Missions
Évangélique de Paris had never been able to initiate a mission to the indigenous people. The Christian and Missionary
Alliance (C. and M.A.) repeatedly sought entrance, but was
not permitted to begin work until 1911.[33] The small Swiss

[27] Mirbt, Carl, op. cit., p. 72.
[28] Pan-Anglican Congress, 1908, vol. V, p. 95.
[29] Tucker, A. R., Eighteen Years in Uganda and East Africa, vol. I, p. 186.
[30] Groves, C. P., Planting of Christianity in Africa, vol. III, p. 61.
[31] Ibid., p. 265.
[32] Latourette, K. S., History of the Expansion of Christianity, vol. V, pp.
205, 233–234.
[33] Missionary Research Library, Occasional Bulletin, vol. IV, no. 15 (December 23, 1953), p. 7; Christian and Missionary Alliance, Foreign Department, Missionary Atlas.

Brethren Mission in Laos was the only other Protestant agency admitted until the China Inland Mission sent in some missionaries to work with tribes after the exclusion of foreign workers from China. An unwritten understanding between the C. and M.A. and the Swiss Mission left the southern provinces of Laos, roughly half of that country, to the Swiss.[34] The C. and M.A. crossed the border from Cambodia into Siam (Thailand) after consultation with the Presbyterian Mission in that country and the officers of the Board in New York. The verbal agreement of about 1927 or 1928 was followed by others that extended the work in 1934 and 1947, with the result that the C. and M.A. considers itself responsible for nineteen eastern provinces.[35]

The outstanding examples of the imposition of comity, in the sense of delimitation of territory, by government decree are to be found in the Sudan and Ethiopia.

When the missions moved up the Nile from Egypt into the Sudan, comity went with them. This is largely because the government took a firm hand in the matter by limiting the number of missionary agencies and assigning them territory, but also partly because the missions there were such as had a record of friendly relations and partly because the situation stimulated them to common endeavor. The north and south Sudan are much different than most mission fields in a number of respects, and they are a contrast to each other. Since north Sudan is predominantly Muslim, the British authorities were reluctant to admit missions. It allowed only three missions with experience of other work in Muslim lands limited entry to certain towns where there were Christian communities. There the Church Missionary Society (C.M.S.), the (American) United Presbyterian Church, and the Sudan Interior Mission (S.I.M.) might

[34] Letter of G. Edward Roffe, Nyack, N. Y., January 22, 1954.
[35] Letter of A. C. Snead, Foreign Secretary, C. and M. A., New York, January 23, 1954.

establish hospitals, schools, and other welfare services primarily for the Christians, but which might also serve such Muslims as wished to use them, provided that Muslim children were exempt from Bible classes if parents requested it.[36] The C.M.S. and the Presbyterians entered in 1899, and the S.I.M. at a very much later time. In Khartoum Province all three were permitted to work in Ondurman, while the S.I.M. and the American Mission were allowed in the city of Khartoum. The two church missions were permitted to establish work in Wad Medani in the Blue Nile Province, while the American Mission was allowed at one point each in the Northern, Kassala, and the Muslim area of Kordofan provinces. The C.M.S. and the later-entering Sudan United Mission were allowed several points each in the pagan area of Kordofan Province.[37] The C.M.S. and American Mission avoided overlapping and cooperated fully from the very beginning. An Inter-mission Council was created, and in 1946 it was reorganized as Northern Sudan Christian Council.[38]

The missions admitted to the predominantly pagan south Sudan were permitted more liberty of action, but their number was kept limited and territory was assigned to them. Trimingham states: "When Lord Cromer and his staff took over the administration of the Sudan they encouraged missions to start work in the pagan South, feeling that they would be a civilizing influence and alloted to them specific areas so as to avoid overlapping." [39] This author in his booklet, *The Christian Church in Post-War Sudan*, provides a map which shows the boundaries of the mission fields. The Roman Catholic Mill Hill Fathers were given a long, thin strip of country in the Upper Nile Province, and the Verona Fathers a large region in Bahr al Ghazil and Equatoria. The

[36] Trimingham, J. Spencer, *The Christian Church in Post-War Sudan*, p. 18.
[37] *Ibid.*, p. 40.
[38] *Ibid.*, p. 31.
[39] *Ibid.*, p. 17.

C.M.S. in addition to a pagan area in Kordofan received a very large part of Upper Nile and Equatoria provinces, while the American United Presbyterians were assigned a considerable district in Upper Nile. The Sudan Interior Mission got the remaining north part of Upper Nile. The southeast corner of Equatoria was left as an "open sphere." Later comity agreements among the missions themselves somewhat modified the original boundaries. The Africa Inland Mission was permitted to occupy the "open sphere," and the station of Ler was transferred from the C.M.S. to the American Mission.[40] The Reformed Church in America entered into a union relationship in the mission with the United Presbyterians in 1948.

The Italian conquest and occupation of Ethiopia brought about almost complete elimination of Protestant missionaries from that country.[41] Before the Italian conquest there appears to have been no specific comity agreements among the missions there. After Ethiopia recovered independence, the government permitted the missionaries to return in 1941 and it allotted to each mission specific districts. Thus, in effect, the government itself established comity among the societies.[42] However, in some cases the officials inadvertently assigned the same territory to two missions. The whole country was divided into Christian and non-Christian areas, the former being those parts of the country where the national Church of Ethiopia was dominant. Mission work was supposed to be limited to the pagan and Muslim areas. However, if there were no evangelistic work included, the

[40] Letter of Dr. Glen P. Reed, General Secretary, Board of Foreign Missions of the United Presbyterian Church of North America, Philadelphia, November 18, 1953.

[41] See the World Dominion Movements survey volume for the pre-Italian Conquest situation: *Light and Darkness in East Africa; a Missionary Survey of Uganda, Anglo-Egyptian Sudan, Abyssinia, Eritrea, and the Three Somalilands.*

[42] Trimingham, J. Spencer, *The Christian Church and Missions in Ethiopia,* pp. 32–33.

missions might carry on educational and medical work in the Christian areas. There might be religious instruction in connection with these provided it be confined to such principles of Christianity as are common to all churches.[43] The territory of each church and mission in Ethiopia is reported in the book, *The Christian Church and Missions in Ethiopia,* by J. Spencer Trimingham, as it was in 1949 or 1950.[44] Some specific changes were agreed upon by the missions after that, apparently without objection from the government. For example, within the area allotted to the American United Presbyterian Mission according to Trimingham, there is a station of the Swedish Evangeliska Fosterlands Stiftelsen; and the American mission also agreed to permit the Sudan Interior Mission to operate in the area about Assosa.[45]

[43] Note the Imperial Decree No. 3 of 1944 (August 7), defining government policy toward the missions: Appendix B in Trimingham, *The Christian Church and Missions in Ethiopia,* pp. 68–71.
[44] Pp. 35–44.
[45] Letter of Dr. Glen P. Reed, refer to note 40, above.

CHAPTER VIII

Protestant Missions and the Eastern Churches

Efforts for Evangelical Revival

PROTESTANT missionaries, ranging from "high church" Society for the Propagation of the Gospel (S.P.G.) bishops to Friends, complained bitterly about the imperialistic aggression of the Church of Rome against them and of the Roman Catholic missionaries' constant interference with their people. Roman Catholic missionary theory considers heretics and schismatics to be just as much the objects of missions as are Muslims and heathen. Protestants expected no comity agreements with the Roman Catholic missionaries excepting where separation was imposed by governments, and few ever tried to achieve it. The attempt of Dr. R. M. Cust on the part of the Church Missionary Society (C.M.S.) to prevent competition in Uganda by his proposal to Cardinal Lavigerie is unusual.[1] To be sure, official policies and over-all strategy notwithstanding, many Roman Catholic and Protestant missionaries have locally resided in the same places with genuine mutual understanding and even with friendship. However, the aggressive tactics of the Roman missionaries generally served to inflame the existing fears of, and hostility toward, their church that almost universally animated Protestants during the rise of the missionary movement in the eighteenth and nineteenth centuries. Consequently, excepting for the scruples of some Anglicans at a late date about the propriety of missionary action in Latin America and the Philippines,

[1] Oliver, Roland, *Missionary Factor in East Africa*, pp. 47–48; Groves, C. P., *Planting of Christianity in Africa*, vol. II, p. 237; Stock, E., *History of the Church Missionary Society*, vol. III, p. 105.

there was seldom any question raised about meeting Roman Catholic aggression in kind and in seeking conversions among nominally Catholic peoples. Protestant missionary activities among the nonaggressive Eastern Churches, and still more in the nominally Protestant lands of Europe, raise other questions, however. It appears to be a flagrant contradiction to all the talk about Christian unity heard in missionary circles. How did the Protestant agencies justify their intrusion into the affairs of the old churchces when they were so jealous of interference in their own domains of missionary occupation? How did they explain what appeared to be an outright violation of the essential spirit of comity that they extolled?

Those Anglican missionaries, following Claudius Buchanan, who first discovered the Syrian Orthodox Christians of Malabar on the southwest coast of India wanted to help them recover from the havoc wrought by the drastic interference of the Church of Rome and the Portuguese authorities in their affairs through attempted subjugation.[2] Evangelical cells planted among them would bring revival. The separation of some of them into an Anglican community, which eventually occurred, was not the original intention. Similarly Protestant missionary action in the Near East was just as free of an aim to proselytize. The pioneer missionaries and the directors of their societies and boards had caught the same vision as Ramon Lull had seen it in the thirteenth century: those ancient churches would be revived, become again obedient to the missionary imperative, and then would themselves evangelize the Muslims with an effectiveness that Westerners could never hope to have. Those who did not have expectations as high as that, hoped that at least an evangelical movement would be set going within the Orthodox and Eastern Churches that would purify and reform

[2] Brown, L. W., *The Indian Christians of St. Thomas,* pp. 125–126, 132–139; Stock, E., *op. cit.,* vol. I, pp. 231–235.

their life and make Christianity appear far more vital and attractive (than the missionaries considered it to be) in the eyes of the Muslims. Few Protestants in the beginning had any idea of the difficulties which those old Christian communities, identified with conquered nations, had endured through long centuries under Islamic rule, or understood that their continued existence alone had been a miracle. Protestant missions deliberately intruded into the domains of these churches, then, but not to proselytize, rather with the hope of bringing about a greater and more effective Christian mission to the whole world.

The name Unitas Fratrum is not only descriptive of the close fellowship within the Moravian Church, but is also indicative of the sense of unity with the whole church of Christ felt and demonstrated by the Brethren in the course of their history. Their missionary endeavor abroad was directed toward the poor and needy, the despised and neglected, those to whom other Christians would not minister, and it had always been free from proselytism in the bad sense in which that word is currently used. The Moravian Diaspora ministry in Europe ought to establish revivifying fellowships of faith within the state churches, and had no intention of creating separate ecclesiastical organizations. This is what the Protestant missionaries would try to do in the Near East and the Balkans. (Pennsylvania also was the scene of an effort in 1741–42 by Count Zinzendorf to bring the denominations into unity.) The Moravian Unity of Brethren similarly sought fellowship with certain of the Eastern and Orthodox Churches in order that they might become agents of the Holy Spirit in strengthening those bodies and that they might cooperate with them in evangelizing the heathen.

Count Zinzendorf in 1740 sent a missionary, Arvid Gradin, to the Ecumenical Patriarch in Constantinople.[3] A sense of

[3] Hutton, J. E., *A History of Moravian Missions*, pp. 157–158.

history provided the impulse. Since Cyril and Methodius, the first missionaries to Moravia, had been sent by the Patriarch in Constantinople, the Count reasoned that there was an affinity between the Greek and Moravian Churches. Possession of the historic episcopal succession by the Moravians probably strengthened this idea in Zinzendorf's mind. He chose Gradin because he was a good Greek scholar. This missionary carried with him an address to the Patriarch, translated into Greek, setting forth the history of the Moravian Church and asking the Patriarch's intercession with the Russian Church on behalf of the Count's plans for a mission in Russian territory. The Patriarch was gracious, but he stated that he feared to offend the Russian government and to arouse the wrath of the Roman Church. Gradin returned home.

The unsuccessful Moravian mission to Persia in 1747 was directed toward Muslims, not Christians; but the mission intended for Abyssinia, yet operating in Egypt, was to the Copts. Missionaries sent out in 1752 and 1756 failed to reach their destination, and returned. Then Dr. Frederick William Hocker, the original appointee in 1752, entered Egypt again with six companions in 1768.[4] There they prospered in their practice of medicine and various forms of business, by which they supported themselves in accordance with Moravian missionary theory. They carried on a mission of good will and friendship to the Coptic clergy, discussing the gospel with them. They succeeded for some years in their object of exerting an evangelical influence with the Coptic Church, but at last opposition arose. They were finally denounced as intruders, and had to depart in 1783.

Moravian efforts were soon terminated, but other societies had the same vision and hope of the revived Eastern Churches becoming powerful missionary forces. They went

[4] *Ibid.*, pp. 161–164; Hamilton, J. T., *A History of the Missions of the Moravian Church*, pp. 32–33.

to them in hope of imparting an evangelical leaven and stimulating a zeal for witness. These societies included the Church Missionary Society, the Basel Missionary Society, the American Board of Commissioners for Foreign Missions, and the Protestant Episcopal Church of the United States.

The C.M.S. was concerned almost from its inception with the possibility of winning the heathen for Christ through the agency of the ancient churches, even though those churches appeared to the directors of the Society to be at the time obstacles to acceptance of the faith by Muslims. The subject appears frequently in the records of the Society from 1802.[5] Claudius Buchanan first brought the Syrian Orthodox Christians of Malabar to the attention of Englishmen, Scots, and Americans, and their imagination was kindled by his picture of the contrast between the lives and character of those Christians and the Hindus in India.[6] Could not the Christians of the Near East make as effective a demonstration of Christian life? Moreover, the annexation of Malta by the United Kingdom in 1814 provided a base within a British possession for such an experiment. However, the beginning preceded annexation. A Roman Catholic doctor in Malta in the year 1811 appealed to the C.M.S. to undertake the mission to the Eastern Churches which he thought the Church of Rome had now permanently abandoned after many centuries. A call for a young man was issued in 1812, and in 1815 William Jowett went forth to gather information about the state of religion in the countries bordering the Mediterranean.[7] He was instructed to investigate the best methods of propa-

[5] Stock, E., *op. cit.*, vol. I, pp. 221–235. The Report of 1812 especially indicates interest in many Eastern Churches.

[6] Early American missionary sermons abound with references to Buchanan and his *Christian Researches,* and either acknowledged or unacknowledged he seems to be the principle source of the American picture of Indian religion and culture in the first quarter of the nineteenth century. The contrast between the Syrian Christians and their Hindu neighbors was a favorite argument on behalf of missions.

[7] Stock, E., *op. cit.*, vol. I, pp. 224–227.

gating Christian knowledge. Jowett was soon joined by two other missionaries, and a press was established on Malta. These literary representatives, as they were called, received a cordial welcome from many prelates and priests, including the Coptic Patriarch of Egypt, the Greek Patriarchs of Constantinople and Jerusalem, and many Greek bishops and archbishops in Greece, the islands, and Asia Minor. The scriptures printed at Malta found ready reception, and the Syrian Jacobite Patriarch of Jerusalem went to Europe to raise funds to print the Bible in Arabic with Syriac characters. These bright prospects were destroyed, however, by the atrocities inflicted on the Greeks in Turkey in 1821, which were among the causes of the Greek war of independence. The C.M.S., therefore, after 1825 centered attention upon Egypt and Abyssinia,[8] although a few missionaries continued to work in Greece and Turkey.[9]

It was chiefly German and Swiss missionaries educated at Basel and given supplementary training at Islington who staffed the C.M.S. mission to the ancient churches of the Near East. Lieder was the outstanding member of the mission in Egypt and Samuel Gobat in Ethiopia. The Coptic Patriarch and priests were friendly, while the Greek clergy were in general rather hostile.[10] Reliance was placed primarily upon literary and educational work. A boarding school in Cairo was elevated in 1842 into a theological seminary for Coptic clergy. One of the students even became the Abuna of the Abyssinian Church.[11]

Gobat found the Abyssinian Church sunk to a very low state, but met with a friendly response. However, continued ill health forced him to leave the country. A distinguished

[8] *Ibid.,* p. 231.
[9] *Ibid.,* pp. 349–350.
[10] *Ibid.,* pp. 349–350.
[11] Dunne, J. Heyworth, *An Introduction to the History of Education in Modern Egypt,* pp. 278–280, states that none of the graduates were ever ordained, and this would rule out the supposed Abuna, if true.

group of missionaries succeeded him, but intrigues by certain Roman Catholics resulted in the destruction of the mission and the expulsion of its staff.[12] When the directors of the C.M.S. discovered that the old churches did not respond as expected, the "Mediterranean Mission" was allowed to expire. No more men were appointed to it.

Experience then led to a partial change of viewpoint about the object of missions in the area and among the Eastern Churches. When the Palestine Mission was established, in accord with an agreement reached with the American Board,[13] the C.M.S. was still firmly resolved not to carry on an aggressive policy of proselytizing among the ancient churches. However, it was just as firmly convinced as to the propriety and necessity of preaching the gospel to individuals throughout the region, even if in consequence of this they should feel constrained to seek a new spiritual home. This new mission policy was the result of a discovery by Bishop Gobat and some British consuls that among the old churches of the Near East there were many persons who were seeking spiritual illumination as the result of Protestant work in distribution of the scriptures and in education. The Chaldean Church even applied directly for scriptural instruction.[14]

The Crimean War and the efforts of the British ambassador to secure from Turkey recognition of the right of conversion for evangelicals led to the creation of a new C.M.S. mission at Constantinople (Istanbul), to which there was appointed Dr. Karl Gottlieb Pfander. He had originally been a member of the Transcaucasus Mission of the Basel Society and had served in India.[15] This mission was directed toward the Turks and was instructed to avoid trespassing on the work of the American Board's mission. Thus the C.M.S. was at length embarked on a mission to Muslims,

[12] Stock, E., *op. cit.*, vol. I, pp. 351–353.
[13] Brown, A. J., *One Hundred Years*, p. 979.
[14] Stock., E., *op. cit.*, vol. II, p. 142–145.
[15] *Ibid.*, p. 148.

which had always been its ultimate goal in the Near East, and toward which the efforts to "revive" the Eastern Churches were supposed to contribute. However, in 1864, when the work seemed exceedingly promising, the Turkish government intervened and prohibited any criticism of Islam.[16] The interpretation given the restrictions put an end to the mission, although one missionary continued for some years to reside at Constantinople.

Still another attempt to reach Muslims through a revived Oriental Church was the enterprise of the Basel Missionary Society in the Transcaucasus region that was under Russian rule. German settlements had been founded in and around Tiflis in 1819. These settlers applied to Basel for pastors. Pastors were sent to them, but with them went others who were commissioned to begin a mission to the Eastern Churches and to Muslims. Shusha became a center for work among Armenians. Again there was no intention of creating a new Protestant church, but the hope was to foster new spiritual life in the old Gregorian Church.[17] However, the Armenian ecclesiastical officials complained to the Russian government. A royal decree in 1835 forbade any further work among either Armenians or Muslims, and reserved all missionary activity to the Church of Russia.[18] Although deprived of missionary leadership, those who had been touched by the work a few years later spontaneously formed a small evangelical fellowship. They were then excommunicated by their bishop in 1861. After much difficulty the government finally permitted them to affiliate with the Lutheran Church of Russia.[19]

The original aim of the American Board of Commissioners for Foreign Missions in the Near East was just the same as

[16] *Ibid.*, p. 154.
[17] Richter, J., *History of Protestant Missions in the Near East*, p. 99.
[18] *Ibid.*, p. 102.
[19] *Ibid.*, p. 103.

these other agencies just reviewed, except that the original instruction given Levi Parsons and Pliny Fiske in 1819 was to go directly to the Jews of Palestine. While working with them, they were to study the situation with regard to approaches to the ancient churches and to the Muslims.[20] It was hoped that among the Christians in the region many "might be aroused from their slumbers, become active in doing good, and shine as lights in those darkened regions."[21] During at least the first quarter of a century there was a clinging to the hope, as expressed in the instructions given to Cyrus Hamlin on departure to his field, that through the Eastern Christians, "being so numerous and dispersed, were the mighty power of God at once to revive the spirit of the gospel in all of them, a flood of light would burst upon almost the whole Turkish empire, and would shine far up on the highlands of Asia."[22] Hamlin was charged, as were his predecessors with varying phraseology:[23]

The object of our missions to the Oriental Churches is, first, to revive the knowledge and spirit of the gospel among them; and secondly, by this means to operate among the Mohammedans. These Churches must be reformed. The fire of a pure Christianity must be rekindled upon those Christian altars. In all the professedly Christian communities of western Asia there must be living examples of the holy, happy influence of the religion of Jesus. The Oriental Churches need assistance from their brethren abroad.[24]

[20] Strong, W. E., *The Story of the American Board*, p. 80; Kawerau, P., *Amerika und die Orientalischen Kirchen*, pp. 154–200.

[21] American Board of Commissioners for Foreign Missions, *Annual Report*, *1819*, p. 230; Kawerau, *op. cit.*, pp. 291–330 on the objectives of the Board in West Asia; Walker, M. A., "The American Board and the Oriental Churches," mimeo. paper (1956).

[22] *Missionary Herald*, vol. 35, no. 1 (January, 1839), p. 40.

[23] *Ibid.*

[24] As an example of how critical a missionary might become, although sent out under such instructions, refer to Cyrus Hamlin's pamphlet, *The Oriental Churches and Mohammedans*.

And the American missionaries did regard themselves as brethren of the Oriental Christians, albeit critical brethren. They were their "brother's keeper" with a vengeance. Very few at that time who either supported or participated in the missions would have said with Eli Smith: "But in treading over again the tracks of the apostles and the martyrs, I have sought in vain for an individual that now breathes the spirit of Jesus, unless he had borrowed it from a foreign source." [25] But the "foreign source," the missionary, was believed to be the most potent and the indispensable stimulant in the whole Near East.

There was a widespread conviction that even though revived Oriental churches might not eventually take up the anticipated active witness to Muslims, any effective preaching of the gospel to Islamic peoples by Western missionaries awaited the reformation of those churches. It was thought that contempt for these subject peoples because of their character stopped the ears of Muslims. "Hence," it was declared, "a comprehensive and wise system of efforts for the conversion of the Mohammedans of western Asia will embrace efforts for the spiritual renovation of the oriental churches. Lights must be made to burn once more upon those candlesticks that remain." [26] Preachers of promotional sermons told American Christians that it was the lack of the Bible, too expensive for individuals to own, and the want of Biblical preaching and teaching by a secularized priesthood which was the root of the present low spiritual state of the old churches, and that those things could be corrected.[27]

Therefore, reformation and resulting zeal for gospel witness were the hopes, and consequently the American Board missionaries were charged not to proselytize and thereafter separate converts. As late as 1839 Cyrus Hamlin was told by

[25] Smith, E., *Missionary Sermons and Addresses,* p. 223.
[26] American Board of Commissioners for Foreign Missions, *Annual Report, 1837,* p. 76.
[27] Smith, E., *op. cit.,* p. 224.

the Prudential Committee that "our object is not to subvert them; not to pull down and build up anew." The intent, rather, was "to reform them; to revive among them . . . the knowledge and spirit of the gospel." Further, that: "it is no part of our object to introduce Congregationalism or Presbyterianism among them. . . . Let the Armenian remain an Armenian, if he will; the Greek a Greek; the Nestorian a Nestorian; the Oriental an Oriental." Evangelicals arising within the old churches would themselves correct rites, ceremonies, various errors, if the missionary should stimulate and inspire them by sticking to the expounding of the fundamental doctrines.[28]

Jerusalem and Palestine were left to the C.M.S. The bitter opposition of the Maronite clergy from the very beginning of the mission at Beirut and the opposition of the Orthodox bishops, along with the temperament and views of Dr. Jonas King, stood in the way of a friendly approach to those churches in Syria and Greece.[29] Dr. King, hostile to the Orthodox and Eastern Churches, was the exception to the rule among the early American Board missionaries. On the other hand, the missions to the Armenians of Turkey and to the Nestorians of Iran aimed solely at the revival of those churches through the creation of evangelical forces within them, and the initial response was very favorable.

The mission to the Armenians in Constantinople was begun by William Goodell in 1831. Goodell and his colleagues put great emphasis upon personal contact and literature preparation and distribution. During the first years they worshipped in Greek and Armenian churches, and even participated in services when invited. They conducted no public worship of their own. They did not at first even set up schools, showing admirable patience and restraint in feeling their way. They

---

[28] *Missionary Herald*, vol. 35, No. 1 (January, 1839), p. 41.
[29] Strong, W. E., *op. cit.*, pp. 83–85; Richter, J., *op. cit.*, pp. 187–189; Kawerau, P., *op. cit.*, pp. 522–529; Anderson, R., *History of the Missions of the A.B.C.F.M. to the Oriental Churches*, vol. I, pp. 279–314.

rather urged the Armenians to establish schools themselves. Goodell told them: "You have sects enough among you already, and we have no design of setting up a new one, or of pulling down your churches, or drawing away members from them to build up our own." [30] Alliance was made with a reformation movement that stemmed from the school of the influential teacher Peshtimaljian.[31]

Nevertheless, when all seemed to be going well, attacks on the evangelicals, who had formed a Union, began in 1839. The missionaries had given offense, too, in employing two bishops who had been disciplined for marriage, and in admitting one of them and a priest into membership in the mission church.[32] The Armenian Patriarch anathematized all persons holding evangelical beliefs in 1846.[33] Consequently the evangelical party, although claiming staunchly to be members of the one Catholic and Apostolic Church of Christ, was forced in July, 1846, to organize as a separate church.[34] The following December, the Turkish government freed the members from control by the Patriarch in civil and commercial, as well as ecclesiastical, matters. Through the efforts of the British ambassadors, Canning and Cowley, the Evangelical Church and its members were recognized as a separate *milet* by decrees of the Sultan in 1847, 1850, and 1853.[35]

The story of the American Board mission to the Nestorians or Assyrians of Iran is similar to that of the Armenian mission. Justin Perkins and his wife were instructed by the Board

[30] Strong, W. E., *op. cit.*, p. 92.

[31] *Historical Sketch of the Missions of the A.B.C.F.M. in European Turkey,* etc., pp. 12–13; Kawerau, *op. cit.*, pp. 491–492.

[32] Anderson, R., *History of the Missions of the American Board of Commissioners for Foreign Missions to the Oriental Churches,* vol. I, p. 47; Walker, M. A., *op. cit.*, p. 3.

[33] *Ibid.*, pp. 394–402; Shaw, P. E., *American Contacts with the Eastern Churches,* pp. 87–88; Kawerau, P., *op. cit.*, p. 540.

[34] Kawerau, P., *op. cit.*, pp. 496–497; Shaw, P. E., *op. cit.*, pp. 89–90; Anderson, R., *op. cit.*, vol. I, pp. 417–419.

[35] *Ibid.* pp. 479ff; 496–499.

in 1834 that their "main object will be to enable the Nestorian Church, through the grace of God, to exert a commanding influence in the spiritual regeneration of Asia." [36] Perkins, after some years of work, could still express the hope that the Nestorians would once again bear the gospel to every corner of Asia.[37] The initial response was encouraging, and there were great revivals in the years 1836, 1846, 1849, and 1855. The missionaries found some of the customs and liturgical practices of the Nestorians easier to accept than those of some of the other churches.[38] They also endeavored to win the favor and protection of influential prelates, and Bishop Mar Yohannon especially encouraged them.[39] The final outcome, however, was the same as in the case of the Armenians. Separate congregations and a general conference were created within the old church, but they could not long remain in the fold. They were gradually forced out. The final separation came the year after the American Board handed the mission over to the Board of Foreign Missions of the Presbyterian Church in the U.S.A. The first conference of the Assyrian Evangelical Church was held in 1871.[40]

Opinion about the object of the missions had been changing long before this, both among the missionaries and the officers of the Board. The missions had been experimental, and by the early 1840's it was still hoped "that among the Nestorians . . . the entire community may be brought to the knowledge and the acknowledgment of the truth (if the operations of the mission are not interfered with by other Protestant sects) with the willing cooperation of the great body of ecclesiastics." [41] As to the others, while Rufus Ander-

[36] *A Century of Protestant Missionary Work in Iran, 1834–1934*, p. 18.
[37] *Ibid.*
[38] Walker, M. A., *op. cit.*, p. 4.
[39] Strong, W. E., *op. cit.*, p. 94; Richter, J., *op. cit.*, p. 298; *A Century of Protestant Missionary Work in Iran*, pp. 21–22.
[40] *A Century of Protestant Mission Work in Iran*, p. 2.
[41] Anderson, R., *Report to the Prudential Committee of a Visit to the Missions in the Levant*, pp. 25–26.

son had been visiting in the area, it was agreed in a discussion at Beirut that

> . . . the grand aim of our mission is of course the converting of men to God; that the preaching of the gospel is the great, divinely appointed means to this end; that whenever, and wherever there are small companies of natives ready to make a credible profession of piety, they are to be recognized as churches, entitled to the ordinances of baptism and the Lord's Supper, and to such a ministry as can be given them; that the reformed churches are to have no reference to any of the degenerate oriental churches, and may be expected to combine persons from several, and perhaps all, the various sects existing in the mountains; and that the method of church organization and administration should involve the principle of throwing such responsibility on every individual member, as will develop his talents and Christian graces to the utmost possible extent.[42]

The story of the mission to Greece was quite different both because of the views, methods, and personality of Jonas King and also the nationalism rampant in Greece at the time. The mission was closed in 1844, and Secretary Anderson reported to the Board: "The Greeks have retired from us. To a most affecting extent they have become inaccessible to our preaching, our books, our influence." [43] A Greek Evangelical Church came spontaneously into being, led originally by Dr. Michael Kalopothakes, who had been a witness for Dr. King at his trial.[44] Much later the American Board returned to assist the Greek Evangelical Church and eventually to endeavor once again to seek a friendly and helpful relation to the Orthodox Church. A statement of policy drawn up by fourteen missionaries of the Near East Mission at Boston in 1923 read:

[42] *Ibid.*, pp. 25–26.
[43] *Ibid.*, pp. 6–7.
[44] Walker, M. A., *op. cit.*, p. 5.

We would state as our aim in such work in Greece:

1. To help the Oriental Church realize the spiritual significance of their founders.
2. The Bible freely distributed in the language of today.
3. An educated and morally upright clergy.
4. A place in the regular services of the church for Christian instruction.
5. Cooperation with the Oriental Church just as far as possible in evangelistic and educational effort.
6. To combat by every possible means the drift towards unbelief and moral laxness natural to such exiles. [Refers to the refugees from Asia Minor]
7. To build up a native leadership for future work among their own peoples.[45]

This statement was directed principally towards work with Greek and Armenian refugees from Asia. The language and spirit are those of the pioneers.

The efforts of the S.P.G. and of the Hermannsburg Mission while, unfortunately, directly competitive with the American Board's mission to the Nestorians also aimed at revival without schism. Both of those missions were brought to an end by a Russian invasion into that part of Persia and the subsequent accession to the Russian Church of most of the Christians in that area.[46]

The American Episcopal Church's missions to Greece and Constantinople were likewise efforts to assist toward the revival of the Oriental churches, specifically the Greek Church, to the end of awakening their missionary zeal. The mission to Greece was carried on as an educational enterprise from 1830 to 1869. Its leading missionary was Dr. John H. Hill, who made a lasting contribution to the advancement of education in Greece. However, the mission had little effect in

---

[45] *Ibid.*, p. 7.
[46] Richter, J., *op. cit.*, pp. 308–314.

stimulating the Greek Orthodox Church to new spiritual life, and it was strongly criticized at home for its lack of evangelistic purpose.[47] The Near East Mission was founded in 1839, and was intended to work with the Greeks of Constantinople and the Jacobites of Syria, but the latter work was never begun. The Foreign Committee of the Board of Missions instructed Horatio Southgate to keep steadily in view the unity of the church and the ultimate goal of the cooperation of the ancient churches in missionary action when they should become newly imbued with the spirit of Christ.[48] Southgate was consecrated bishop in 1844. Although a very able man in many respects, his time was unfortunately spent too much in controversy with his American neighbors, his outlook and policy were not congenial to his supporting constituency at home, and he was unable to get along with the missionaries who were sent out to assist him.

The very last American effort in this succession to attempt a mission of stimulation and revival was the Methodist Episcopal Mission to Bulgaria. The General Missionary Committee in 1852 had discussed, with Bulgaria particularly in view, "taking a part in resuscitating the old Oriental Churches within the Turkish empire." A mission was authorized, but the first appointments of missionaries were not made until 1857. Secretary Durbin instructed the new appointees in these words:

> Its chief object is to awaken in the Bulgarian Church, which is of the Greek rite, a desire for evangelical religion, and lead her people to seek for the same. It will be necessary for you to use all kindness and skill in approaching the people privately and publicly; and you should be well acquainted

[47] Shaw, P. E., *American Contacts with the Eastern Churches*, pp. 15–34; Kawerau, P., *op. cit.*, pp. 563–607.

[48] *Spirit of Missions*, June, 1840, pp. 176–179; Shaw, P. E., *op. cit.*, pp. 39–40.

with the doctrines and customs of the Greek Church, not for the purpose of assailing them in controversy, but, as the occasion offers, to show that they are not agreeable to Scripture.[49]

This mission had great difficulties, and it failed to achieve its stated end.

There was one American mission in the first half of the nineteenth century that was the exception to the rule in missionary policy toward the Orthodox and Eastern Churches. This was the American Baptist mission to Greece, inaugurated by Cephas Pasco and Horace T. Love in 1836. Theirs was a mission of aggression, not of revival. They were ready to, and did, defy the Greek Church.[50]

Missions to Protestant Lands

Protestant missions to nominally Protestant Europe is another question closely related to the earlier missionary efforts among the ancient Eastern Churches. This was American activity especially. Most American denominations were just as adverse to the sending of missionaries to the Protestant countries of Europe as the churches of those lands were hostile to the intrusion of such missionaries. Congregationalists, Presbyterians, Reformed, Episcopalians, and Lutherans recognized the old churches of those countries as true branches of the Church of Christ, and most older American

[49] Letter of J. P. Durbin to W. Prettyman and A. R. Long, July 20, 1857, (Mss.) *Letters from the Board of Missions*, The East-Bulgaria, 1854–1866, p. 16; On attitudes at beginning of Mission see also Missionary Society of the Methodist Episcopal Church, *38th Annual Report, 1857*, p. 21; *39th Annual Report 1858*, p. 23; *Missionary Advocate*, vol. XIII, no. 3 (June, 1857), p. 18; Barclay, W. C., *History of Methodist Missions*, vol. III, pp. 1018–1019.

[50] Shaw, P. E., *op. cit.*, pp. 129–133.

churches acknowledged them as their mother churches and paid filial respect. They took the position that Protestant Europe was not a legitimate mission field. If aid were to be given to Christians there or evangelistic work done, it was to be only through assistance rendered to those churches for the accomplishment of the task through their own agencies and their own ways. However, Methodists and Baptists took a somewhat different view.

The Methodists claimed to have entered the Protestant European countries through following their own people, on the one hand, and through a desire to do what the societies had been attempting in the Near East among the Orthodox and Eastern Churches, on the other—namely, to effect the revival of the state churches from within. Wade Crawford Barclay states:

> While the Methodist Episcopal Church was in general accord with Presbyterian and Lutheran Churches that Europe was not considered foreign missionary ground for American churches in the same sense as Africa and the Orient, it considered itself fully justified, when converts were moved, for their own spiritual welfare, to organize Societies within the more formal State Churches and to aid them as their needs seemed to require. The impetus for separate denominational organization . . . came more from within than without.[51]

This authority says that the Italy and Bulgaria missions were the exceptions to this rule.

The Methodists consequently established missions in Norway (1853), Denmark (1857–58), Sweden (1854), and Finland (1884). Scandinavian sailors who had become Methodists in the United States were in each case the pioneers. It is claimed that their spontaneous, undirected efforts

[51] Barclay, W. C., *History of Methodist Missions,* vol. III, p. 933.

brought the original Methodist groups into being, and that these in turn appealed to the Methodist Church for aid. The missions to Germany and Switzerland were earlier, the former beginning in 1849 and the latter in 1856. The incentive for the German mission came from German immigrants in the United States who became Methodists there and then wrote home glowing accounts of Methodist meetings and life. The development was then parallel to that in the Scandinavian countries. The Swiss mission was an extension of the German venture.

The Baptists gave a somewhat similar excuse to that of the Methodists in entering Germany. They were going to revive the Mennonites! Professor Sears of Newton went to Europe in 1833 in order to survey the situation in France and Germany. He reported that although the Mennonites had degenerated in doctrine and practice, they might, with the aid of American Baptists, be won again to the old paths trodden by their ancestors. He further reported that nominally within the state churches there were many Christians who were "Baptists in sentiment" but that there was no recognized church of the Baptist order in Germany. Dr. Sears immersed T. G. Oncken, his wife, and five other persons at Hamburg on April 22, 1834. The next day these persons, under Sears' direction, constituted a church, and Oncken was ordained pastor. Thus the Baptist mission was inaugurated. A temperance society was early organized, and "temperance" seems to have been an important part of Baptist evangelism. The mission was justified on the grounds that:

There was much evidence that there were here and there in the Lutheran church some who at heart desired the revival of spiritual religion, and were only held in check by fear of the clergy and government, whose combined influence sustained a heartless formal state religion, where 'every shade of

Pantheism, Deism, Rationalism, Supernaturalism, Arminian-
ism, Calvinism, etc., where pronounced to be *indivisibly*
one!' [52]

Evangelistic activity by missionaries from overseas was
bitterly resented by the ecclesiastical authorities, and the
German and Scandinavian missionary leaders denounced it
as a violation of the spirit and the letter of the comity for
which the missionary societies were striving in Asia, Africa,
and other mission fields. Gustav Warneck had reproved the
societies for such activity in his paper prepared for the
Centenary Missionary Conference at London in 1888,[53] and
Dr. A. Schreiber, director of the Rhenish Missionary Society,
spoke even more bluntly at the Ecumenical Missionary Conference of 1900.[54] He declared:

> What I have to speak is not in my own name alone, but in
> the name of our German mission people. We want to com-
> plain a little bit about some lack of comity. I am quite of the
> opinion that it is true, what we have heard this morning
> already two or three times, that outside in the fields of mis-
> sion work there is much more comity to be found than at
> home. I suppose it is true that charity ought to begin at home,
> and not alone that, but that comity ought to begin at home
> also.
>
> I make bold to give only two hints. There has been an old
> wish with us in Germany that all missionary boards, in Eng-
> land as well as in America, might be good enough to make
> clear distinction between proper mission work among the
> heathen, and evangelical work among Italians, and in Spain
> and Austria, and other parts of Europe. We do not oppose in

[52] *Baptist General Convention, Proceedings of the Eighth Triennial Meeting, 1835,* pp. 26–28.
[53] *Centenary Conference of the Protestant Missions of the World, Report
of the —,* vol. II, p. 433.
[54] *Ecumenical Conference on Foreign Missions, New York, 1900, Report
of the —,* vol. I, pp. 237–238.

the least such work, but what we are a little afraid of is that by mixing these things up, by and by you will go so far that you will consider also the whole of Germany as heathen country.

I do not care anything about the map; never mind the map, if they only understand Germany is really a Christian country. I am not going to tell you the names, but I could give you the names of very prominent men here in America who have put Germany into the same line with any heathen land, and are sending out people to Germany to convert the Heathen Germans. Now, dear friends, I only protest against that and remind you that Germany is the land where Luther came, and I remind you that during the whole century there have been lots of theological writers in Germany whose works have been translated into the English and read by thousands in England and the United States.

The interference of the Protestant missionary societies in the life of the ancient Orthodox and Eastern Churches and of a few of them in the affairs of the Protestant state churches of Europe must then be acknowledged and set alongside their own insistence upon comity and noninterference in their own affairs overseas. There is an apparent conflict between principle and policy here, but the societies did not so see it. What they did and why they did it has been shown.

The contemporary situation is quite different. The adherents of hundreds of extremely conservative denominations and nondenominational societies in the United States and British Commonwealth countries regard Europe as thoroughly pagan and both the state or former state churches there and the Orthodox Churches of the Balkans and the Near East as apostate. The newer wave of missionary effort has little connection with the historic Protestant movement described above. Eighty societies of the United States and Canada alone, maintaining 317 national units in various countries, carry on work in Europe, and only a handful of these are cooperative with the European churches.[55] The majority are chiefly concerned with the Roman Catholic countries—Spain, France, and Italy—but forty are at work in Germany, eighteen in the United Kingdom, nineteen in Switzerland, and they are spread over the whole of Europe. It is easy to understand why the Orthodox Churches which are members of the World Council of Churches and some of the European member bodies desired to have a study on "proselytism" made.

Some reference to that study seems appropriate, since it is a contribution to present comity concerns. Moreover, the Orthodox Churches are awakening to their missionary privilege and obligation and in a few places, notable in East Africa, there has been some conflict between their resentment at Protestant activities at home and their apparent interference with Protestants abroad.

The Ecumenical Patriarchate in Istanbul in 1920 issued an encyclical asking for cooperation among churches and for an end of proselytizing activities. This plea was reiterated after the formation of the World Council of Churches, and since such difficulties were affecting relationships between various member churches of the Council, the Central Committee in 1954 authorized a study of "Proselytism and Religious Liberty." After revision, a final report was submitted to the Central Committee in 1960 for recommendation to the Third Assembly at New Delhi. It is clear that the word "proselytize" now has such bad meaning that its once good connotation cannot be restored. The term "witness" is employed in the report; and it is acknowledged that: "Witness in word and deed is the essential mission and responsibility of every Christian and of every church. All disciples stand under the Great Commission of the one Lord." Coercion is

[55] Missionary Research Library, *Directory of North American Protestant Missionary Agencies, 1960.*

repugnant to the gospel for it destroys the free assent and response of a man in faith to our Lord. The spirit of Christ himself is the ground of religious liberty. Every Christian individually and in the church has the liberty to "put his whole existence under the authority of God, to believe, pray, worship, and proclaim Christ, as well as to live in accordance with His will, in the church of his choice according to his own conscience." Liberty, however, may never be exercised in a way that impairs the Golden Rule.

Proselytism is said to be the corruption of witness, "when cajolery, bribery, undue pressure, or intimidation are used—subtly or openly—to bring about seeming conversion." It occurs when there is employment of false witness, dishonest comparison, personal or corporate self-seeking replacing love. The problem has been aggravated by modern means of communication and the end of isolation, by the mobility and migrations of peoples, notably refugees, and especially by movements coming from outside or arising spontaneously within regions where legally or unofficially one particular church has been historically identified with the total life and culture of the region. Feelings have been intensified by the recent tremendous increase in the societies and independent missionaries that appeal for individual conversions in those areas, showing little church-consciousness and interest in co-operation with others.

Some basic considerations include the following: Every Christian church is required freely and openly to bear its witness, and the commandment to bear witness to the truth of Christ and to win others to loyalty to that truth is valid in relation to both non-Christians and those who have no living participation in any church. Churches have the right and liberty to speak out against abuses or errors in Christian bodies, but, in the spirit of the early missionaries, "Before they undertake to establish another church, they must humbly ask themselves whether there are not still to be found in the existing church such signs of the presence of the Holy Spirit that frank fraternal contact and cooperation with it must be sought." There are special considerations and procedures for member churches of the Council. Certain principles are recommended: mutual respect among churches whose conception and practice of church membership differ; mutual efforts at understanding and frank theological interchange; self-examination before critical utterances are made about others; recognition of the primary duty of every awakened Christian to strive prayerfully for the spiritual renewal of his own church; recognition of the right of the mature individual to change his church membership; united efforts by all churches to work for the establishing and maintaining of religious liberty in every land; disavowal of every effort

> by which material or social advantages are offered to influence a person's church affiliation, or undue pressures are brought to bear on persons in times of helplessness or stress; respect of the conscientious decision of marriage partners as to their future church allegiance; observance of due pastoral concern for the unity of the family before a young child is received into membership in a church different from that of his parents, and equal care before receiving into membership a person under discipline in another body; direct consultation between the churches when a transfer of membership is requested, but placing no obstacle in the way if conscientious motives and sound reasons are apparent.

Finally, the report makes two suggestions of principle which seem to come out of the experience of the world mission in its early days and in the present moment. One is that where the witness of a church in a given area appears to be inadequate, "the first effort of other churches should be patiently to help that church towards its renewal and the strengthening of its own witness and ministry"; and the other:

"That we should aid churches in areas where they are already at work by offering fraternal workers and exchanges of personnel as well as by sharing knowledge and skills and resources, rather than by establishing a competing mission of some other church." [56]

[56] World Council of Churches, *Revised Report of the Commission on Christian Witness, Proselytism, and Religious Liberty,* pamphlet reprinted from the *Ecumenical Review,* vol. XIII, no. 1 (October, 1960).

Chapter IX

The Near East and Africa

Developments in the Near East

The Protestant missionary boards and societies originally went into the Near East and the Balkans with the aim of reviving the ancient Orthodox and Eastern Churches, in the hope that they might become zealous in propagating the gospel among Muslims. This program involved avowed interference in the life of those churches, although proselytism was disclaimed until after the evangelicals were expelled from their mother churches. The Protestant agencies at work in the region practiced comity among themselves and strove for a policy of nonintervention in each other's affairs. However, there was one unusual experiment in cooperation in the area, that is, the Jerusalem bishopric, and there were some unhappy instances of conflict, which are exceptions to the general prevalence of comity. The mission to Muslims was so exceedingly difficult that it attracted relatively few societies, and there was plenty of room for them all.

The beginnings of comity agreements and associated practices in the Near East are very much like those in other areas. The great societies which early entered the field were staunch advocates of delimitation of territory and comity agreements. These were the Church Missionary Society (C.M.S.), the American Board of Commissioners for Foreign Missions, and the Protestant Episcopal Church. There were a few lesser efforts, some of them mentioned in the preceding chapter, in the earliest period; and later some other missions of considerable magnitude were established, such as that of the United

Presbyterian Church of North America in Egypt. The Presbyterian Church in the U.S.A. came directly into the area after the Old School-New School merger in 1870 and the transfer by the American Board of its Persian and Syrian Missions to the Foreign Mission Board of the newly united General Assembly. The New School Presbyterians had previously participated in the American Board. The missionaries of the Bible societies and of the London Society for the Propagation of the Gospel among the Jews, commonly known as the London Jews Society, were scattered throughout the entire Near East, and were helpful to all the others. Since these were very specialized societies, the Bible societies being auxiliary to all and the other being limited to the Jews, the presence of their agents in the same cities with missionaries of the societies never raised any problems. Mr. Lawrie of the London Jews Society befriended the founders of the American mission in Cairo,[1] and Robertson and Southgate of the American Episcopal Mission were received with friendship by Goodell and Dwight of the American Board in Constantinople.[2] The pioneers regularly assisted one another and advised about the location of work. Moreover, the missions very early began delimitation of fields in order to avoid conflict through mutual agreement. For example, a Scottish missionary agency which had begun work in 1802 at Karass on the northern slope of the Caucasus Mountains and at Astrakhan on the Caspian Sea, surrendered the Karass area to the Basel Mission and concentrated at the other place, when the Transcaucasus Mission was founded in 1821.[3]

There were later other adjustments made in order to accommodate new missions that wished to enter the region. The Methodist Episcopal Church entered Bulgaria at the invitation of the American Board, which thought the Danube

[1] Watson, A., *The American Mission in Egypt,* pp. 72–73.
[2] Shaw, P. E., *American Contacts with the Eastern Churches,* pp. 54–55.
[3] Richter, J., *History of Protestant Missions in the Near East,* p. 98.

region too large and promising for the resources of one society.[4] The agreement which the two American missions made left to the Methodists Bulgaria proper north of the Danube, and to the American Board the area of Roumelia south of the Danube. The most outstanding instance is that mentioned above, an agreement made in 1870 by which the American Board consented to restrict its activities to Turkey in Europe and Asia Minor, and relinquished Iran and Syria to the Board of Foreign Missions of the Presbyterian Church in the U.S.A.[5]

The course of history caused modifications in the settlement with regard to Syria, and the subsequent agreements illustrate how missions could accommodate themselves to change in territorial matters. The Mardin field was transferred to the Presbyterian mission in Syria in April, 1920, because linguistically it belonged there and was too much separated from the American Board stations in Turkey. The American Board agreed to contribute $5,000 a year for three years in order to facilitate the transfer. However, because of financial difficulties, the Presbyterians handed Mardin back to the original mission in 1927.[6] Then in the troubled times of 1923–24 many Christians associated with the Central Turkey Mission of the American Board sought refuge in Syria, and the Mission was forced to follow them with a ministry of relief and pastoral care. This was considered to be a temporary measure, with the exception of Aleppo. An agreement of 1923 set a time limit of five years upon the relinquishment of all American Board work in southern Syria and a longer range agreement covered the whole country.

[4] [American Board of Commissioners for Foreign Missions], *Historical Sketch of the Missions in European Turkey*, etc., p. 35; Richter, J., *op. cit.*, p. 167; Letter of M. A. Walker, Librarian of the A.B.C.F.M., Boston, January 8, 1954.

[5] Brown, A. J., *One Hundred Years*, pp. 46, 489, 979; Strong, W. E., *Story of the American Board*, p. 209.

[6] Letter of M. A. Walker, Librarian, A.B.C.F.M., Boston, January 8, 1954.

The work was regarded as the effect of a temporary crisis, and the understanding was that it should steadily decrease until the whole of Syria was once more left to the Presbyterians.[7] The two missions in 1933 combined their theological seminaries located at Athens and Beirut into the United Near East School of Theology at Beirut.[8] Aleppo, which had through the influx of refugees become the scene of American Board evangelistic, educational, and relief work once again after more than half a century, had been reopened by the Presbyterians only in 1922, the year before the Turkish assault on the minority peoples. Although it had been part of the territory handed over by the American Board in 1870, the English Presbyterian Church had established a school there, and the American Presbyterians had relinquished their claim at that time.[9]

Comity matters had not always had so happy a course in Syria. Because of the Druse rebellion and the massacres of the Maronites and Melchites in 1860 many Europeans had their attention drawn to the country. There was a great influx of new missionary agencies without regard to prior occupancy or to comity practices. This was to happen in other places at later times also, when there was an intrusion of new societies which had neither a notion of the historical development of Protestant missions nor a sense of having participated in a world-wide movement in which the missions were related to one another. Fifty years later Professor Richter lamented: "The waste of energy that results from the dividing of the missionary undertaking in Syria among so many small, independent missions is to be regretted. Though considerable sums have been spent, but little abid-

[7] American Board of Commissioners for Foreign Missions, *Annual Report, 1924,* pp. 78, 81; Letter of M. A. Walker, Librarian, A.B.C.F.M., January 8, 1954; Letter of M. E. Blemker, Secretary for Near East, A.B.C.F.M., October 26, 1953.

[8] Brown, A. J., *op. cit.,* pp. 1007–1008.

[9] *Ibid.,* p. 1004.

ing effect had been produced in this religiously and politically distracted country." [10] Later, after some of these
missions had become established and learned that they faced
common problems with the older missions, there were some
adjustments. The Prussian Johanniter Order, or Knights of
St. John, established a hospital in Beirut in 1861, for which
the Kaiserswerth Deaconesses provided the nurses and the
medical professors of the Syrian Protestant College (afterwards American University) contributed medical direction,
while the founding order paid the expenses.[11] Because of the
existence of that hospital, the American Presbyterians did
not institute a medical work in Beirut.[12] Two Scottish ven-
tures were later sensibly united with the American Presbyterian Mission. These were the Lebanon School Association
and the work established by the Free Church. The latter for
some time continued to pay the salary of a teacher under the
new arrangement.[13] A united mission was begun in Damas-
cus in 1843 by the Irish Presbyterians and the Free Church
of Scotland, but two years later the second party withdrew
and was replaced by the American United Presbyterians.
That partnership continued until 1877, when the American
Mission withdrew the last of its missionaries into Egypt.[14]

The Jerusalem Bishopric

Palestine, to the south of Syria, was likewise the scene of
much activity by small missions and independent missionaries. The pioneer American Board mission there had withdrawn to Syria and by agreement in 1843 left Jerusalem and

[10] Richter, J., *op. cit.*, p. 211.
[11] *Ibid.*, p. 202.
[12] Brown, A. J., *op. cit.*, p. 995.
[13] Richter, J., *op. cit.*, p. 205.
[14] *Ibid.*, pp. 207–208.

Palestine to the C.M.S.[15] It has always been relatively easy to find money for little programs in the Holy Land because many persons respond sentimentally to an appeal for support of work there. Such little missions seldom desire to cooperate with each other. The country was, however, the scene of a venture in cooperation that went far beyond the range of comity. This was the Jerusalem Bishopric, a joint English-Prussian, Anglican-Lutheran establishment.

The London Jews Society had made Jerusalem one of its chief posts, and Nicolayson, its famous missionary, resided there from 1826 to 1856.[16] A Jewish Christian congregation had slowly been gathered. When the revolting Egyptian armies defeated the Turkish forces in Palestine in 1839, the Western powers joined with Turkey in driving them out. British participation had been encouraged by some persons in high places who thought that the way would be cleared for Jews to emigrate to Palestine and settle there.[17] Prussian foreign interests and certain German missionary concerns for the Jews also had regard to this region. King Frederick William IV of Prussia sent Baron Bunsen to England to secure assistance in winning freedom for Christians in Palestine and to propose that an Anglican bishop be sent to Jerusalem as head of the whole Protestant community there and its representative before the Turkish government. Lord Shaftesbury and others warmly supported the proposal.[18]

Julius Richter attributes to the Prussian monarch the same hope that had animated the early missionary societies along with several additional aims. He wrote:

[15] Brown, A. J., *op. cit.*, p. 979. Brown is usually accurate. However, Stock makes no reference to such an agreement, nor is it found in the American Board histories and records.

[16] Nicolayson was an Anglo-Catholic and his intervention in Syria was greatly resented by the American Board missionaries, whom he tried to displace, in marked contrast to the earlier attitudes of the agents of the London Jews Society.

[17] Stock, E., *History of the Church Missionary Society*, vol. I, p. 419.

[18] *Ibid.*, p. 419.

He had four farreaching thoughts which he hoped to see realized in this way. For one thing, his evangelical heart felt impelled to create in the midst of the petrified and degenerate Oriental Churches a center of Protestant activity, the spirit of which should regenerate those Churches. He also wished to procure legal recognition and equal rights for the Protestants scattered throughout Turkey, who, up to this time had enjoyed no legal status. This he tried to effect by the means customary in Turkey, namely, through the authorization of an ecclesiastical supreme head. In the third place, he desired to provide for the Jewish Mission, which was at that time beginning to flourish, firm support and a secure centre of activity, and hoped that the episcopate would afford such a centre. He held the opinion that a firmly established Jewish mission on a large scale in Jerusalem would attract the attention of all Jews. And lastly, he particularly desired to unite the great Protestant Churches in common work for the spread of the Kingdom of God; a union of the Churches of England and Prussia, resting on the foundation of common church work, was his highest ideal.[19]

Since the Prussian State Church was a union Church of Lutheran and Reformed, this cooperative venture might relate three great Reformation traditions.

There were some Englishmen who believed that such an ecclesiastical alliance would lead to the acceptance of the episcopate by the Lutheran Landeskirchen in Germany. The chief hope among the promoters of the scheme in Great Britain, however, was to achieve the restoration of the see of St. James at Jerusalem, an independent Jewish Christian church.[20] The appointment of a Jewish convert as bishop, Michael Solomon Alexander, was in line with this hope. An Act of Parliament in 1841 made possible the creation of the diocese and the appointment of Bishop Alexander.[21] The

[19] Richter, J., *op. cit.*, p. 237.
[20] Stock, E., *op. cit.*, vol. I, p. 420.
[21] *Ibid.*, pp. 420–421.

Tractarians, or supporters of the Oxford Movement, bitterly assailed the move as an invasion of the jurisdiction of other Christian prelates, although one wonders how they might have distinguished among the conflicting claims and pretensions of the many patriarchs and bishops of the numerous Orthodox and Eastern Churches. Later they came to regard the office as a bridge of understanding between the Church of England and the Eastern Churches.[22]

This Bishop of Jerusalem was intended to be simultaneously a bishop of the Church of England and the Lutheran chief pastor in the Near East. Anglo-Catholics considered this an impossibility. The King of Prussia promised £600 a year, and the London Jews Society, which had once been interdenominational in its constituency but had become purely Anglican, raised an endowment fund to provide an equal sum.[23] The bishop was to be nominated alternately by the British and Prussian Crowns.

Bishop Alexander died after only four years in his see, and the King of Prussia then nominated Samuel Gobat, a German who had served under the C.M.S. in Abyssinia and Egypt. Gobat was not concerned with the Jews alone, and his previous missionary experience had made him determined to preach the gospel to individuals, members of the ancient churches as well as Jews, regardless of the risk of thus inducing them to leave their old spiritual home for a new one. This brought the wrath of the Anglo-Catholics upon his head. He was supported, however, by the Archbishop of Canterbury, and the four Metropolitans of the United Kingdom and Ireland issued a joint declaration in his favor.[24] Bishop Gobat turned to the C.M.S. for assistance, and that Society established its mission in the Holy Land in 1851 in accordance, however, with the comity agreement

[22] *Ibid.*, pp. 420–421.
[23] *Ibid.*, pp. 420–421.
[24] *Ibid.*, pp. 142–147.

reached with the American Board some years earlier.[25] When Bishop Gobat died in 1879, the British Crown appointed Joseph Barclay as bishop, the Germans concurring, but he died after only two years. It was again Prussia's turn to make the nomination, but there was long delay because there could apparently not be found an Anglican clergyman who might satisfactorily represent the German interests. The agreement was eventually abrogated, to the delight of the high-church party in England, and the establishment became purely Anglican. The next bishop, G. F. P. Blyth, was strongly opposed to the views of Bishop Gobat and the C.M.S. A very unhappy period ensued for the Anglican Mission, until the C.M.S. was replaced by the Jerusalem and the East Mission.[26]

It had been no easy matter for the Anglican-Lutheran Bishop of Jerusalem to satisfy sometimes conflicting Anglican-Lutheran and British-German national interests, but the bishopric had been a noble experiment. If it could have been continued, many issues in later church union negotiations would have been faced at an earlier period, and, moreover, some Faith and Order theoretical questions would have been solved in a practical situation. The causes of unity and union might both have been substantially advanced.

Some Areas of Conflict

It was Anglo-Catholic views, in addition to the acts of free-lance independents, which motivated the most flagrant instances of disregard for comity in the Near East. The Soci-

---

[25] *Ibid.*, pp. 142–147; Richter, J., *op. cit.*, pp. 242–243.
[26] Richter, J., *op. cit.*, p. 245; Stock, E., *op. cit.*, vol. III, pp. 341–343, 523–537, 659.

ety for the Propagation of the Gospel (S.P.G.) had engaged in comity agreements in some areas and had often displayed a spirit of cooperation, although by the mid-century it was sometimes acting without regard to others and by the end of the century was insisting upon the right to follow its members. The American Episcopalians who supported missions were scarcely distinguishable from other fellow countrymen in their views about missions. Outright antagonism and interference with other missions such as occurred in Constantinople and Iran were fortunately rare.

When the Protestant Episcopal Church established the Near East Mission in 1838, Robertson and Southgate were sent to Constantinople. The Foreign Committee appointed them to work among the Greeks and Syrians, leaving the Armenians to the American Board, which was already at work among them. It was specifically stated in the *Report* for 1838: "While the Committee cannot suppose that preoccupancy by one Missionary Society should of itself prevent the labors of another, they grant that circumstances may often render the yielding to such preoccupancy expedient and just. Such circumstances, they believe, exist in the present instance." [27] Yet Southgate later not only began work among the Armenians but attacked the American Board missionaries for their work among those people. He even sought the assistance of the English and Scottish primates and of the British ambassador on behalf of his cause.[28] The controversy produced several pieces of literature, and it was one of the reasons why Southgate's missionary efforts produced no lasting results. His constituency back home was also too evangelical in outlook and temperament to be happy about his actions.

Very similar to the confusion in Armenian affairs created

[27] *Spirit of Missions*, August, 1838, p. 256.
[28] Shaw, P. E., *op. cit.*, pp. 35–70, 100–105.

by Bishop Southgate's attacks on the American Board missionaries was the action of agents of the S.P.G. in Iran. There the American Board had engaged in a mission to the Assyrian Church members or the Nestorians beginning in 1834, and the Presbyterians had taken over in 1870. The leader of the new S.P.G. mission announced his intention of "protecting" the Nestorians from the American missionaries.[29] Instead of locating in unoccupied territory, Dr. G. P. Badger settled the new mission at Urumia, the central station of the Americans. Badger secured action from the authorities through the Armenian Patriarch to have the mission schools closed. The people were also ordered not to accept books from the missionaries. Badger proclaimed that the Presbyterians were "without a ministry, or any requisite of discipleship," and made disparaging reports about their work in Iran and the American Board work in Constantinople.[30] However, the controversy ended and the S.P.G was left without a field in 1898, when some twenty thousand out of twenty-five thousand Nestorians in the Urumia Plain were led into the Church of Russia through a religio-political development. The mission was transferred to the other side of the border.[31]

It was most unfortunate that other agencies also began work in Urumia when the possibilities there were so limited. The Hermannsburg Mission founded a small station in 1881,[32] and about ten other agencies carried on limited programs for shorter or longer periods.

However, the only other large and continuing missionary

[29] *Ibid.*, pp. 95–100; Richter, J., *op. cit.*, pp. 308–310; *A Century of Protestant Missionary Work in Iran*, p. 30; Anderson, R., *History of the Missions of the American Board of Commissioners to the Oriental Churches*, pp. 213–216.

[30] Shaw, P. E., *op. cit.*, pp. 95–100, esp. 99.

[31] Richter, J., *op. cit.*, pp. 310–313; *A Century of Protestant Missionary Work in Iran*, pp. 30, 109.

[32] Richter, J., *op. cit.*, p. 308; *A Century of Protestant Missionary Work in Iran*, p. 30.

enterprise established in Iran was carried on by the cooperative C.M.S. Comity was practiced between the British and American missions and eventually developed into active cooperation. Rev. Robert Bruce went to Isfahan in 1869 in order to work on a revision of the Persian Bible. A permanent mission came about when a group of converts applied to him for admission into the church. A comity agreement preventing overlapping was made by the two missions.[33] This Anglican mission has been unique in the Near East in the number of converts from Islam that comprised its membership. A further comity agreement in 1930 between the C.M.S. and the Christian and Missionary Alliance assigned the province of Khuzistan as the field of the latter.[34]

Various instances of comity agreements are reported here and there in connection with the earlier work. In northern Mesopotamia (Iraq), for example, the American Presbyterians in 1900 handed Mosul over to the C.M.S.;[35] while at Aden at the southern tip of Arabia the C.M.S. withdrew its plans for occupation when the Free Church of Scotland undertook the continuation of Keith Falconer's work.[36] Much later, after the end of World War I, the C.M.S. found it necessary to withdraw from Mosul. A united mission, going far beyond the usual forms of cooperation, filled this gap. The United Mission in Mesopotamia (later United Mission in Iraq) was established in 1922 by the joint action of the Presbyterian Church in the U.S.A. and the Reformed Church in America. The following year the Reformed Church in the United States accepted the invitation to join the union venture.[37]

[33] *A Century of Protestant Missionary Work in Iran*, p. 14.
[34] *Ibid.*, p. 15; Near East Christian Council, *News Bulletin*, December, 1930, p. 23.
[35] Richter, J., *op. cit.*, p. 163.
[36] *Ibid.*, p. 273.
[37] Brown, A. J., *op. cit.*, pp. 843, 844.

Egypt

Comity in Egypt was long confined to the interrelationship of the two largest missions, the American Mission (United Presbyterian Church of North America) and the C.M.S., insofar as formal agreements are concerned. The American Mission entered the country in 1854 just as the early C.M.S. work was terminating, and it raised up the largest single evangelical community in the Near East. The C.M.S. resumed work in Egypt in 1882, and at first some of the American missionaries regarded this as a violation of the spirit of comity. However, understanding was quickly achieved. These two missions and their associated churches from time to time entered into agreements with respect to many areas, some of them extensive and some very localized or restricted. Thus there were agreements mentioned in the years 1910, 1924, and 1927.[38] The spirit of comity was shown also by other smaller agencies that came into the country. The Egypt General Mission began work in 1898 with the expressed intention of not encroaching on the territory of any other mission.[39] The Americans, however, regarded the entrance of the North Africa Mission into the Delta as an intrusion in 1892.[40]

Probably it was because the land of Egypt was dominated, from the viewpoint of missionary occupation, by the two large missions, which dealt directly with each other, that there was not an early concern shown for an organ of arbi-

[38] Letter of Dr. Glen P. Reed, General Secretary, Board of Foreign Missions of the United Presbyterian Church of North America, Philadelphia, November 18, 1953.

[39] Watson, C. R., *The Christian Crusade in Egypt*, p. 202.

[40] Groves, C. P., *Planting of Christianity in Africa*, vol. III, p. 165.

tration or for promotion of those agreements about functional work which were developed in India and other places. The situation in the whole of the Near East was somewhat similar. There were a few large missions belonging to cooperative societies and boards, and where their interests touched they usually came readily to mutually satisfactory agreements. Problems of overlapping and competition were usually restricted to a few regions and were caused by agencies which did not share the views of the older and larger missions about priority of occupation and commonly accepted principles of relationships. Elsewhere it was concern for, and discussion of, comity matters which usually led to forms of cooperation and to regional associations. But missionary associations in the Near East arose relatively late in the history of missions in the region, and showed little concern for comity. They gave their attention to more advanced matters of cooperation in literature production for the entire Arabic-speaking Islamic world and for education. Also the conference for the entire region was created in advance of the smaller area organs, with two exceptions, and comity was not important to it, although unity was.

The United Missionary Conference of Syria and Palestine was founded in 1919. The word "Conference" was later changed to "Council," and ultimately the body assumed the name the United Christian Council for Southwest Asia. How much interest or concern there might have been for comity in the earlier years is not clear, but the *Rules and By-Laws,* as printed in 1928, state that the promotion of comity is the purpose of the Council. Article II reads:

The object of this Council shall be to promote comity between the missionary bodies working in Syria and Palestine by:

(a) Conducting investigations on lines of common interest;
(b) Laying down general principles for action on common lines;
(c) Initiating and fostering co-operative effort;
(d) Providing for the most effective occupation of the entire field.[41]

These four clauses indicate an equating of comity with co-operation, and there is no statement on inter-mission and interchurch relationships.

Egypt created an Inter-Mission Council about the same time that the cooperative body for Syria-Palestine came into being. Its attention to comity matters more nearly approximates the usual course of events in the missionary conferences of India and the Far East. This appears to be because the smaller, later-entering missions eventually traveled along the same path of experience as the older missions and also came to trust their guidance. The American Mission took the initiative in the matter. It invited the other agencies to send representatives to a general conference in Cairo in October, 1919. When the group assembled on October 15, seven missions were represented.[42] A Committee on Principles and Constitution was appointed. The Conference met at intervals of some months in order to discuss the Committee's proposals, and when sufficient progress had been made, the First General Conference was called for May 31, 1921. Nine missions participated, soon four others had joined, and year after year the membership grew.

Apparently fundamental problems of comity were sufficiently troubling the churches and missions that the Council assumed responsibility for the basic and elemental matters

[41] United Missionary Council of Syria and Palestine, *Rules and By-laws*, 1929, p. 3.
[42] *Egypt Inter-Mission Council, Minutes of the First General Conference of the —, 1921*, p. 2.

of inter-mission relationships. The Constitution included the following statement on functions:

> The object of the Council being to serve as a general means of reference and communication for the cooperating organizations in matters of common interest, it may on application of the interested parties give counsel:—
> 1. With regard to determining boundaries of Mission fields when differences arise, especially when the enlargement of work is contemplated;
> 2. To secure the avoidance of friction in the employment of payment of workers; and in general,
> 3. With a view to promoting harmonious cooperation and unity between the organizations in Egypt in all-out evangelistic, educational, medical, charitable, and philanthropic work.[43]

Types of cooperation are spelled out in the next following section of the Constitution, but territorial comity and the old associated question of uniform scales of pay were still basic.

There was further preoccupation with comity during the next few years. Mr. W. B. Smith introduced a discussion on the subject with a paper at the Second Annual Conference. In it he called for a subcommittee of the Council's Standing Committee to make a study of relationships with special reference to overlapping, standards of membership, discipline, and provision for arbitration.[44] The Conference then voted that there be made a thorough survey of the missionary occupation of Egypt by all societies as a necessary step toward arriving at a sound basis for comity and cooperation; that meanwhile any questions of comity that might arise be referred to the Standing Committee; and that this

[43] *Ibid., 1921–1922*, Appendix I, pp. 26–27.
[44] *Ibid.*, pp. 20–21.

Committee arrange retreats for the deepening of the spiritual life, "as we believe that real comity and unity in Christ are very effectually promoted thereby." Two years later, in 1923, the Council adopted the following general statement on comity:

> With sincere desire that all the missionary societies working in the Valley of the Nile should work together in truest Christian harmony and unity:
>
> We, the Cooperating Societies of the Egypt Inter-Mission Council, as a preliminary step towards a more perfect coordination of effort in the future, agree not to commence any work in a new district, or in a district already occupied by another Society or Societies without first notifying the Secretary of the Egypt Inter-Mission Council whose duty it will be to call together the Officers of the Standing Committee and the Secretaries or other leaders of other Societies interested, for consultation. If the proposed move is not considered to be in conflict with the aims and plans of other organizations, it shall go forward, but if objection is raised to the proposal which cannot in loyalty to their Societies be settled by the consultative body so called together, then the Standing Committee will be convened with sufficient time to give the Missionary Bodies concerned an opportunity of instructing their delegates; and we hereby agree to abide by the unanimous council of the Standing Committee so instructed and so convened.[45]

A more specific means of implementing this general resolution was offered to the Council by the American Mission:

> We recommend that the Mission Association in approving the above resolution endorse the following proposals as a practical application of the resolution to present conditions, and forward these proposals to the E.I.C.:
>
> (1) That we will avoid establishing congregations in towns

[45] *Ibid., 1923,* and Letter of Dr. Glen P. Reed, November 18, 1953.

and villages where another Mission or the Egyptian Evangelical Church has work in being.

(2) We agree not to receive into our respective churches and congregations persons who do not bear certificates of good standing or of honorable dismissal from the congregations of our respective bodies.

(3) We agree that we will not employ workers who come from any one of our respective bodies unless they bear certificates showing that they are workers in good standing or that they have been honorably dismissed from the body with which they have been working.[46]

Comity was apparently not much of a problem in Egypt after this. A few references appear in the annual Minutes. It was reported in 1926–28 that some cases were in process of amicable settlement.[47] Kenneth Maclennan, Secretary of the Conference of Missionary Societies of Great Britain and Ireland, gave an address on the subject at the annual conference in 1927.[48] The discussion which followed it turned to the relationship between church and missions and between their evangelists and the Coptic Church, rather than to inter-mission matters. When the constitution was revised in 1929, the articles cited above remained unchanged.[49] Nothing was said about comity in the discussions of 1939 about replacing the Inter-Mission Council with a National Christian Council. Dr. E. E. Elder commented in December, 1953:

Our problem in Egypt in recent years has not been one of comity so much as finding personnel sufficient to enable us to have greater cooperation among missions. The question of Zagazig is an illustration. We [American Mission] were unable to staff that station and, because it was adjacent to the work of the Egypt General Mission, we reached an agree-

[46] *Ibid.*
[47] *Ibid., 1927,* p. 6, *1928,* pp. 8–10.
[48] *Ibid., 1927,* pp. 11–13.
[49] *Ibid., 1929,* p. 16.

ment whereby they assumed the schools following their taking over evangelistic work. Then the time came when the Egypt General Mission, because of its shortage of workers, was compelled to give up the work there.[50]

Other local area councils of cooperation were late in developing and owe their origin to the stimulation of the Near East Christian Council. These include: the Church Council of Iran, the Supreme Council of the Evangelical Community in Syria and Lebanon, the Sudan Inter-Mission Council, and the Inter-Mission Council of Algeria. The United Christian Council for Southwest Asia was extended to cover Jordan and Israel as well as Syria and Lebanon. No comity agreements formulated by them or subscribed by their members have been found.

An organ for fellowship, counsel, and cooperative action for the entire Near East did not make its appearance until 1927. Samuel M. Zwemer and H. V. Weitbrecht attended the Indian Decennial Missionary Conference at Madras in 1902 and were inspired by it to call the Conference on Work among Moslems at Cairo in 1906.[51] The emphasis was functional and methodological, and that meeting was intended for workers among Muslims wherever they might be located. It naturally had something of the nature of a Near East conference because of the predominance of Islam in that region, but it was organized and oriented differently than a regular area conference. Its successor was not even held in the Near East, but in Lucknow, India, in 1911.[52] A continuing representative body did not emerge until 1927 when the Council for Western Asia and Northern Africa was formed as a result of a series of conferences on Muslim work sponsored by the

[50] Letter of Dr. E. E. Elder to Dr. Glen P. Reed, quoted in Letter of Dr. Glen P. Reed, December 3, 1953.

[51] *Missionary Conference on Behalf of the Mohammedan World, The First*, Cairo, 1906.

[52] *Islam and Missions: Second Missionary Conference on Behalf of the Moslem World, Lucknow, 1911*.

International Missionary Council.[53] Two years later the name was changed to the Near East Christian Council for Missionary Cooperation. It was not to be a representative body made up of regional councils, but missionary agencies in all the subdivisions of the Near East were directly to hold membership in it. It proved immediately effective in bringing a sense of unity to the Protestant forces in the Near East, although it proved difficult to enlist a majority of the agencies in formal membership. Dr. James H. Nicol, then chairman of the Council, stated in 1928 that:

> All who have had a part in the work will testify that Persia on the east and Algiers on the west and all the countries in between have been drawn together in a way never known by the simple process of meeting in council. The regional conferences have been encouraged and strengthened by their sense of this common relationship with sister groups in other Moslem lands.[54]

The Council's magazine, *The News Bulletin of the Near East Christian Council,* became a potent instrument for strengthening this sense of unity, although it was never a very large or pretentious journal. No mention of comity matters is found in its pages. This Council sought to foster spiritual unity and to stimulate cooperation in functional work, allowing comity and associated agreements to issue from such activities, rather than the usual reverse procedure.

Since the end of World War II grave problems have arisen in many mission fields through the entrance of new missionary agencies which do not practice comity, while in other areas the comity agreements of long ago may have become outmoded because of changed conditions. However, these factors have not been major ones in the Near East. Some

[53] Hogg, W. R., *Ecumenical Relations,* p. 214.
[54] *Missionary Cooperation in Western Asia and Northern Africa,* November 2, 1928, p. 7.

new agencies have entered in a manner that might be called intrusion, but disregard of comity has usually been by independent missionaries. Most trouble has come not so much through disregard of elemental comity, but through the disruption of unity caused by forces emanating from fundamentalist groups in the United States and to a lesser degree from Great Britain.

Africa

The vast continent of Africa should have provided room and ample scope for all societies which wished to work there without crowding any of them. Moreover, most of the African territories were relatively late in opening, and the pioneer agencies were usually those societies and boards which had early accepted the policy of comity and declared it necessary to the assuring of the total evangelization of any large area. Yet one cannot escape the conclusion that there was relatively little broad planning in the occupation of the continent south of the Sahara, and that in many places there was all too much overlapping. Cooperation toward ending such overlapping and adequately covering each field was declared to be an urgent call in the older areas, especially South Africa, Sierra Leone, and Liberia, in 1910.[55] That outstanding authority on missions in Africa, Edwin W. Smith, refers to "the over-lapping which is such an evil in Africa." [56] This is all the more astonishing when as late as 1910 the surveys prepared for the World Missionary Conference at Edinburgh revealed that in many regions in Africa there was still crying need for the occupation of unevangelized territory and the adequate care of underevangelized areas. It was

[55] *World Missionary Conference, 1910*, vol. I, p. 241.
[56] Smith, E. W., *The Way of the White Fields in Rhodesia*, p. 147.

affirmed that both agencies and missionaries were too few.[57]

The generally satisfactory distribution of forces in the Congo has been treated in Chapter VI, and mention has been made of the situation in Angola.

East Africa on the whole appears to have enjoyed satisfactory comity relations and to be in marked contrast to the older areas. There were only eight missionary societies in the whole of British East Africa until a very late date. The C.M.S. shared Uganda with the Roman Catholics only, and its inter-mission relationships were principally with the societies in Kenya. The survey report made to the Edinburgh Conference stated that the relations of the eight missions of Kenya and Uganda "are happily marked by an earnest regard to the principles of comity and cooperation." [58] The eight societies were the Church of Scotland, the Church Missionary Society, the Africa Inland Mission, the Friends Industrial Mission, the American Friends Board of Missions, the Mennonites, the Seventh Day Adventists, and the United Methodist Church. Thus the group included sacramental and nonsacramental churches, denominational and nondenominational societies, and even the Seventh Day Adventists, who have seldom cooperated in local matters although joining in common consultation at the home base. Apparently the original spheres of occupation had been arrived at through face-to-face consultation by neighboring missions, but in 1909 they divided the country among themselves and took responsibility for clearly demarcated areas. This action came at the end of the period of early missionary penetration and at the beginning of that which H. A. R. Philp called the period of consolidation.[59] The first inter-mission conference in Kenya occurred in 1908 in the Kavi-

[57] *World Missionary Conference, 1910*, vol. I, pp. 203–245.
[58] *Ibid.*, p. 237.
[59] Philp, H. A. R., *A New Day in Kenya*, pp. 23, 27–28.

rondo district northeast of Lake Victoria Nyanza, and it was repeated again the next year.[60] Decisions had been reached at the first conference regarding a common policy on linguistics and literature matters, including theological terms, and respecting of boundaries.

The second conference adopted a resolution calling for a united church. Later that year, 1909, the first General Missionary Conference for Kenya and Uganda convened at the Church of Scotland's Kikuyu Station. This body adopted as its own the resolution of the Kavirondo missionaries calling for a united church for the whole region. The unity of the brethren was demonstrated in a common celebration of the Lord's Supper, in which the Bishops of Uganda and Mombassa, who were C.M.S. missionaries, participated. The missionaries were so united in heart and mind that they were not content "with a bare territorial comity, each Mission representing some Home Church confining itself to its own district alone," [61] and expressed that unity in the union communion service and the steps taken toward a federation of the missions into one church. The charges which the Bishop of Zanzibar then carried to the Archbishop of Canterbury against his episcopal neighbors of Mombassa and Uganda resulted in the famous "Kikuyu Controversy." [62] The furor that followed brought external forces to bear on the local situation, and the proposals for federation consequently had hard going. Some of the missions would not agree to Anglican prerequisites and definitions. The proposals for federation were discussed at the 1913, 1918, and 1926 meetings of the Conference, but were not carried through. With the failure to achieve federation at the 1918 meeting, the missions of

[60] *Ibid.*, p. 34.

[61] Grey, H. G., *Comity in the Mission Field*, p. 6.

[62] Willis, J. J., *The Kikuyu Conference*; Stock, E., *History of the Church Missionary Society*, vol. IV, ch. XL, pp. 409–424; Groves, C. P., *Planting of Christianity in Africa*, vol. III, pp. 293–294; Philp, H. A. R., *op. cit.*, pp. 34–38.

the C.M.S., the Church of Scotland, the Africa Inland Mission, and the Methodists set up the Alliance of Missions in Kenya for their inter-mission relationships and for certain functional cooperative efforts. The more inclusive Kenya Missionary Council was established in 1924. However, the problem of basic comity for the whole country had been achieved by delimitation of spheres of occupation after the 1909 Conference at Kikuyu.[63]

Cordial cooperation and the practice of comity among the older missions was reported as existing in Nyasaland in 1910. However, the same source called attention to grave overlapping in the Shire Highlands, because seven younger missions came into an area where the one older mission could have satisfied the need most thoroughly.[64] The Anglican Universities Mission also was insisting on the right to follow its converts.

Tanganyika had been the field of a few British missions when Germany annexed the region. New German missions were organized specifically to work in the country and older German societies took a share. One authority states that the Ausschuss der Deutschen Evangelischen Missionsgesellschaften took initiative and responsibility in the division and assignment of territory,[65] but the evidence seems to indicate that the societies themselves worked out the delimitation of territory through separate agreements among themselves.[66] Thus the Berlin Missionary Society and the Moravians agreed to the demarcation of their fields in 1891, and these two made a comity agreement with the United Free Church Mission of Livingstonia.[67] The Leipzig Society and the C.M.S.

[63] Philp, H. A. R., *op. cit.*, p. 27; See map after title page and Appendix IV, on Protestant mission work by districts.
[64] *World Missionary Conference, 1910,* vol. I, p. 232.
[65] Hogg, W. R., *op. cit.*, p. 72.
[66] See Richter, J., *Tanganyika and Its Future,* for lists of the missions and descriptions of their territory in 1934.
[67] Groves, C. P., *op. cit.*, vol. III, p. 77.

came to an understanding about boundaries in Kambaland.[68]
Bishop Peel's daughter in 1914 sent to the C.M.S. headquarters "a remarkable little map" which "shows that the
district allotted by the comity of missions to the C.M.S. ex-
tends some 250 miles east and west and about 100 miles
north and south." [69] It was reported in 1910 that:

> At the very first glance the distribution of missions in this
> great territory strikes one as having been providentially
> ordered for the ultimate conquest of the land. They are re-
> mote from one another, some still in their infancy, most of
> them feeble, and, save in one district, miserably inadequate;
> but they are planted, speaking roughly, at the four corners
> of the land and in two central positions, besides the mission
> at Dar-es-Salaam, which may be regarded as the gateway of
> the colony.[70]

There was no "preconceived plan of campaign," and each
society that entered Southern Rhodesia chose its own field.[71]
However, the Southern Rhodesia Missionary Conference,
which had its first meeting in 1903, brought about a considerable degree of harmony and adjustment. Edwin Smith
reported in 1928 that there was still some overlapping, and
that some late arrivals had chosen districts already well
occupied by older agencies.[72] The older missions had a
genuine concern about the problem. Thus the East Central
Africa Mission Conference, later the Rhodesia Conference,
of the Methodist Episcopal Church in 1915 set up a Standing
Committee on Conference Boundaries and Denominational
Adjustments with full powers to act in comity matters.[73]

[68] *Ibid.*, p. 79.
[69] Stock, E., *op. cit.*, vol. IV, p. 79.
[70] *World Missionary Conference, 1910*, vol. I, p. 235.
[71] Smith, E. W., *op. cit.*, pp. 147–148.
[72] *Ibid.*, p. 148.
[73] *East Central Africa Missionary Conference of the Methodist Episcopal Church, Minutes of the —, Eleventh Session, 1915*, p. 43.

After 1922 the Comity Committee was composed of the district superintendents.[74] Henry I. James refers to what was expected of the Methodists in effective occupation by the other missions, when he defined the field of that mission in Mashonaland as bounded on the north by the Zambezi River, on the east by [Mozambique] on the south by the Sabi River, and on the west by the thirty-first meridian; [75] while an official minute of the Conference in 1913 defines the field as "a territory 220 miles long and 70 miles wide conceded to us by the Wesleyan body." [76]

Geography, along with the course of exploration and European penetration by governmental, commercial, and missionary forces, played a role in the placement of missions in Northern Rhodesia. John V. Taylor and Dorothea Lehmann, in their able study entitled *Christians of the Copperbelt*, draw attention to the fact that the place where Livingstone died and where his heart is buried appears to be the middle of Africa, and that the various lines of advance into the interior converged toward this center.[77] They describe the course of missionary occupation.[78] Seven missions, Protestant and Roman Catholic, were established within striking distance of the country in 1881 and by the end of 1890 Northern Rhodesia was ringed by mission stations on every side except the southeast, with a few toe holds within the borders. The heavy toll in manpower exhausted the pioneer societies, and new missions came in and built upon their work, advancing into the interior. Some of them were invited by the pioneers, especially by Fred Arnot of the Plymouth Brethren. The distribution of the missions is shown on the end maps in the

[74] *Rhodesian Missionary Conference of the Methodist Episcopal Church, Minutes of the Sixth Session of the —, 1922*, p. 9.
[75] James, H. I., *Missions in Rhodesia under the Methodist Episcopal Church, 1898–1934*, p. 21.
[76] *East Central Africa Missionary Conference of the Methodist Episcopal Church, Minutes of the Tenth Session of the —, 1913*, pp. 10, 87–88.
[77] Taylor, J. V., and D. Lehmann, *Christians of the Copperbelt*, p. 1.
[78] *Ibid.*, pp. 2–5, 13–28.

book just cited. An organ of missionary cooperation came into being early enough to be influential in inter-mission adjustment.

There had been a meeting in 1913 for the purpose of examining a new translation of the New Testament in Ila by Edwin Smith. This led in the next year to the calling of the Missionary Conference of North-West Rhodesia. The constitution adopted at the meeting in Livingstone in 1914 made the Executive Committee a Board of Arbitration.[79] This body eventually in 1922 became the General Missionary Conference of Northern Rhodesia. It had in its membership at some time or other, according to Taylor and Lehmann, every society in the land, including the Roman Catholic missions, and achieved an unusual degree of cooperation.[80]

Areas of occupation, called "spheres of influence," were an important item on the agenda of the first session of the Conference. Rev. S. D. Gray of the Wesleyan Methodist Mission brought before the members maps of the whole country showing the stations and outstations of the various missions. He pleaded for acceptance of the principle that there be mutual respect of all areas already occupied. The discussion that followed his presentation revealed a clear desire "to prevent the waste which is consequent of overlapping." A committee, consisting of the Anglican Bishop, the secretary, and Mr. Gray, was appointed to frame resolutions which would embody the chief factors of agreement brought out in the discussion. The resolutions adopted are a good example of a noncoercive standard of policy and procedure that could be enforced only by good will and a sense of unity. They are worth reproducing as a typical statement.

1. This Conference while recognizing that Spheres of Influence may be only temporary, yet holds strongly that at this

[79] *General Missionary Conference of North-West Rhodesia, Report of Proceedings of the First—, 1914,* pp. 4–5.
[80] Taylor, J. V., and D. Lehmann, *op. cit.,* p. 18.

early stage in the development of mission work, there is
ample room for missions to occupy distinct areas, and it
would therefore remind all the Missionary Societies of the
waste and friction that result from overlapping and urge
them to avoid this evil wherever possible.

2. This Conference trusts that any Mission wishing to open
work in a new area will first communicate with the Executive
of the Conference.

3. In the event of a new Society wishing to open up work
in the Territory, or a Society already at work in the Territory
wishing to open a new sphere, the Conference would esteem
it a favour if the Administration [i.e., the colonial govern-
ment] would refer such Society to its Executive for information as to vacant areas before granting permission.

4. It is essential in view of the above resolutions that the
map already made showing the Stations and Outstations of
the various Missionary Societies at work in the Territory,
should be kept up to date and show all the mission work
being done, it is hoped that a representative of each Society
will forward to the Secretary annually the precise details as
to the position of stations and out-stations opened or closed
during the year, so that they may be transferred to the Map.

5. The Conference trusts that no Missionary Society will
engage a native agent who has worked for another Society
in the Territory unless he possessed credentials from the
Society who formerly employed him.[81]

This resolution simply stated the consensus of the missionaries. The only provision for any degree of administration of
the stated policy was Article XI of the constitution which
provided that: "All matters of administration between Societies respecting boundaries and cognate matters may be
referred to the Executive of the Conference for consultation
and advice if both parties so desire." [82] Only two years later

[81] *General Missionary Conference of Northern Rhodesia, Proceedings of
the —*, 1922, pp. 12–14.
[82] *Ibid.*, 1922, p. 4.

there was a heated discussion about school locations and the conference-government relation in assignments. Moreover, the government had refused to admit the Dutch Reformed Church Mission into a district offered to it by the Livingstonia Mission. Since there was some question about the complete relinquishment of the latter to the district, the Conference could not act until the two missions concerned had come to a full agreement, but it adopted a resolution which affirmed: "It is within the rights of any Society to hand over its sphere or parts of it to another Society." [83]

Edwin W. Smith reported in 1928 that the influence of the Conference, with government support, had prevented much overlapping, and that, despite the interference and duplication by some latecomers, each mission occupied a well-defined area.[84]

It was difficult for Protestant missions to gain entrance into Mozambique or Portuguese Africa until the end of the monarchy in Portugal. Early efforts by the Wesleyan Methodists of England and the American Board of Commissioners for Foreign Missions (A.B.C.F.M.) had been failures. Permanent work was begun by the Free Methodists in 1885, the Swiss Mission Romande in 1887 (following the initial work of one of their African evangelists in 1881), the Methodist Episcopal Church in 1890 (by extension from its base in Southern Rhodesia), and the Lebombo Mission of the S.P.G. in 1893; but all these were small enterprises. The Revolution of 1910 brought into being the republic and a period of anticlericalism in Portugal. There was more liberalism in colonial affairs, including more cordiality towards Protestant missions, for a short period. The societies then on the spot in Portuguese Africa were able to build up their missions into more actively functioning and expanding organizations. Later Roman Catholic influence was reasserted over the

[83] *Ibid., 1924,* pp. 27–28.
[84] Smith, E. W., *op. cit.,* pp. 159–160.

colonial government, and the government became very suspicious of the aims and intentions of Protestant missions. These were charged with being dangerous to the national interests and their work and growth were hampered in many ways.[85]

The change in circumstances challenged both the missions on the spot and Protestant missions in Africa in general. The General Missionary Conference of South Africa, which considered the Portuguese territory to be within its area of responsibility, was informed by its Commission on Survey and Occupation in 1912 that:

> The largest unoccupied area in the subcontinent is Portuguese East Africa. South of the Limpopo River this area may be said to be in some sense occupied; but north of that river, as far as the Zambesi, mission work has only been commenced in certain districts. . . . North of the Sabi and south of the Pungwe we find no European missionaries, though the A.B.C.F.M. and the S.A.G.M. are doing itineration on a small but utterly insufficient scale. North of the Pungwe River the vast native population is absolutely untouched by missionary effort.[86]

Here certainly was a situation where speedy evangelization might be advanced by delimitation of territory and the acceptance of assigned responsibility by dependable missionary agencies. The Commission requested that the Conference approach those agencies already at work there with a definite request for the acceptance of responsibility for total evangelization of the region with a beginning to be made within three years. Specific mention was made of three missions with respect to the territory of the Mozambique Company, namely, the Methodist Episcopal Church, the

[85] See Moreira, E., *Portuguese East Africa*, pp. 59–69.
[86] *General Missionary Conference of South Africa, Report of Proceedings of the Fourth —, 1912*, pp. 42–43.

American Board, and the Church of the Province of South
Africa (meaning as to missionary agency, the S.P.G.); and
with regard to the rest of Portuguese Africa, the Methodist
Episcopal Church.[87] The Methodists took this to be a definite assignment or a confirmation of their concept of their
sphere of work.[88] The Methodist Episcopal Mission described its field in 1913 as: "Our territory in this field lies
between the Limpopo and Sabi Rivers, a distance North and
South of about 250 miles, and extending inland to the
Transvaal border about 200 miles. By mutual agreement and
cooperation we join the Wesleyan Methodists on the South
and the American Congregational Board on the north." [89] It
is evident from this statement that the missions named had
already at some earlier time reached mutually satisfactory
comity agreements. The official definition of the boundaries
adopted at that session of the Methodist Mission Conference
spoke of the north-south dimension as being three hundred
miles.[90] One of the missionaries was given authority to continue correspondence with the South Africa General Mission
(S.A.G.M.) on the boundary between the two fields, with
the understanding that the Mission regarded the boundary
between their two spheres as the Nyanyadzi River.[91] When
the Methodist Mission in Mozambique was set apart as a
separate Conference, at its first session in 1916, it defined
its boundaries just as its predecessor had described them,
"with the exception of the Gija Circumscription [in the
Lourenco Marques district] which by request from the Swiss
Mission and by joint agreement has been conceded to it;"
and at the same time declared that it would not open a

[87] *Ibid.*, *1912*, pp. 50–51.
[88] "This territory is conceded to us by the General Missionary Conference
of South Africa." *East Central Africa Missionary Conference of the Methodist Episcopal Church, Minutes of the Tenth Session, 1913*, pp. 87–88.
[89] *Ibid.*, *1913*, p. 3.
[90] *Ibid.*, *1913*, pp. 11, 87–88.
[91] *Ibid.*, *1913*, p. 67.

station within five kilometers of the station of any other mission.[92]

The latter proviso was necessary because there was already overlapping in this area. The Free Methodists and the Anglicans were also there. From the very outset relations between the two American missions had been cordial, and they engaged in educational projects together.[93] The Anglo-Catholic S.P.G. missionaries, however, at first rebuffed the friendly overtures of the Methodists, informing them that "in the view of our Church both you and your Bishop have a defective call to this ministry." [94] Happily the actual meeting of the missionaries of both groups in the same region led to better understanding. The Methodist District Superintendent reported to the Conference in 1915:

> While we do not and cannot expect to work in close unity and cooperation with the Church of England Mission, yet as far as possible plans have been laid so that we will not be treading on each other's toes when there is a large territory untouched as yet by either Mission. A meeting was held in the beginning of the year to plan for the removal of stations that were too close together, and that in the future neither Mission will open a station closer than five kilometers to another station. Plans were also laid that members under discipline cannot be accepted from one Church to the other without first investigating the case. In almost all instances the Church of England Mission was fair and liberal in her planning for the good of the work as a whole.[95]

The five-kilometer limitation, by separate agreements, applied in relations with the Free Methodists and the Swiss

[92] *Portuguese East Africa Mission Conference of the Methodist Episcopal Church, Official Journal of the —, First Session, 1916*, pp. 44, 57.

[93] Same sources as note 89.

[94] *Ibid.*

[95] *East Central Africa Missionary Conference of the Methodist Episcopal Church, Minutes of the Eleventh Session, 1916*, p. 9; Pasco, *Two Hundred Years of the S. C. G.*, vol. I, p. 346.

Mission, too.[96] When the Portuguese East Africa Evangelical Association was formed in 1920 by the three Methodist groups, the Anglicans, and the Swiss Mission, later joined by the Church of the Nazarene and the International Holiness Mission, that body assumed the function of a board of arbitration.[97] Thereafter the Methodist Episcopal Conference's Committee on Conference Boundaries and Denominational Adjustments would, whenever there was a question of comity, express an opinion on the matter and then request the Conference to refer it to the Evangelical Association for adjustment, with the assurance that the Conference would accept the judgment of the Association.[98] Thus in the case of a new mission begun by the Church of the Nazarene with the approval of the Association, the Methodist Episcopal Mission made a transfer of certain property and commended the people there to the new mission.[99] Moreira reported that in 1936 there were six noncooperating missions and a number of separatists, but their efforts were minor compared with those of the cooperating missions.[100]

Not a great deal can be said about the west coast. Until quite late the French territories attracted few societies. The Basel and Barmen societies agreed on boundaries in the Gold Coast and Togo, and the former made agreements with the English Methodists.[101] The C.M.S. had been party to compacts there also, but withdrew from the region in 1909, leaving it to the S.P.G. upon the establishment of the diocese

[96] Moreira, E., op. cit., pp. 25–26; Groves, C. P., op. cit., vol. III, p. 182.
[97] Ibid., p. 27.
[98] See for example: Official Journal of the Southeast Africa Mission Conference of the Methodist Episcopal Church, Eighth Session, 1924, pp. 10, 26; ibid., Ninth Session, 1925, pp. 52, 73–74; ibid., Twelfth Session, 1928, pp. 11, 34; ibid., Thirteenth Session, 1929, pp. 52, 83; and ibid., Fifteenth Session, 1931, p. 182.
[99] Ibid., Thirteenth Session, 1929, pp. 52, 83; ibid., Fourteenth Session, 1930, p. 133.
[100] Moreira, E., op. cit., p. 28.
[101] Groves, C. P., op. cit., vol. III, pp. 63, 214.

of Accra.[102] The Baptist Missionary Society (London) transferred its work in the Cameroons to the Basel Society and the German Baptists after Germany annexed the colony, and then the Basel Mission and the Presbyterian Church in the U.S.A. "amicably shared the field." [103] There were no great complaints about Nigeria in the first three decades of the twentieth century; [104] but in the decade of the 1930's there were infringements of comity and unwelcome competition by newcomers.[105] The Conference of Missions in the Northern Provinces of Nigeria was active in comity adjustments. For example, at the 1926 sessions five compacts between societies regarding changes in boundaries were reported and approved by the Conference, one case involving governmental action was reported, and missions wanting to advance into the Muslim areas recorded their desires.[106] The Rhenish Society occupied the largest area in Southwest Africa not held by the Roman Catholics, and in the north, in Ovamboland, it welcomed the Finnish Missionary Society, leaving to it the care of five tribes while it itself took four.[107] American Negro denominations which sent missionaries to, or supported African evangelists in, western and southern Africa never observed comity; and numerous new British, Continental European, and American societies which entered various parts of the continent after World War I

[102] *Ibid.*, p. 213; Stock, E., *op. cit.*, p. 64.

[103] Groves, C. P., *op. cit.*, p. 59; *World Missionary Conference, 1910*, vol. I, p. 223; Brown, A. J., *One Hundred Years*, pp. 220–221.

[104] *World Missionary Conference, 1910*, vol. I, pp. 221–223; Maxwell, J. L., *Nigeria, the Land, Its People, and Its Christian Progress*.

[105] Groves C. P., *op. cit.*, vol. IV, pp. 186, 189; *International Review of Missions*, vol. XXVI (1937), p. 65.

[106] *Conference of Missions of Northern Provinces of Nigeria, Minutes of the —, 1926*, pp. 6–8.

[107] *World Missionary Conference, 1910*, vol. I, p. 226; *Report of the Fourth General Missionary Conference of South Africa, 1912*, pp. 42, 51. The Conference hoped that these two societies could complete the occupation of the Colony.

and more especially after World War II had little regard for the rights conferred by prior occupation.

The Edinburgh Conference had singled out the older mission fields of Sierra Leone, Liberia, and the Union of South Africa as especially needing a redistribution of the missionary force for overcoming overlapping and competition and for speeding evangelization of unreached areas. A conference held in Sierra Leone in February, 1912, discussed comity, but apparently there were no noteworthy developments.[108] The United Christian Council of Sierra Leone did not come into existence until 1924, and then it was at the insistence of the British governor.[109] Four Missions—Protestant Episcopal, Methodist, Baptist, and United Lutheran—effected a comity agreement in Liberia in 1921, however. This was a welcome development in a land where the freedmen settlers had carried from the United States to Africa not only denominational differences, but denominational rivalries. Territory was delimited, and the four bodies pledged themselves to avoid overlapping. Many other missions and churches failed to enter the agreement and continued competition in that land where one writer declared: "It may be doubtful whether any other country has as many missionaries to the square inch as Liberia."[110] The missions in South Africa, however, had long been aware of the situation and its need.

South Africa

The Union of South Africa, "the oldest, the most fully occupied, and the most largely Christianized of the mission fields of the Church in Africa," was the scene of operations

---

[108] Groves, C. P., *op. cit.*, vol. III, p. 293.

[109] Fahs, C. H., and H. E. Davis, *Conspectus of Cooperative Missionary Enterprises,* pp. 98–99.

[110] Whetstone, H. V., *The Lutheran Mission in Liberia,* pp. 96–97. The quotation is from R. E. Anderson, *Liberia, America's Friend,* p. 197.

of thirty societies in 1910. The members of the Edinburgh Conference were informed that:

". . . in the almost unanimous judgment of our missionary correspondents, the number of European missionaries in the field would be adequate for the work, if only they were properly distributed and were properly seconded by efficient native workers. Almost all the correspondents bewail the extent of overlapping, which has a prejudicial influence on the attitude of the natives affected by it, and tends to neutralize that wise and careful discipline which is so necessary in the upbuilding of a native church.[111]

Excessive concentration in certain places was matched by a complete neglect in others. Many missionaries were then of the opinion that there was urgent necessity for a definite agreement among the societies to bring about a reassignment of territorial responsibilities that would advance the desired ends. James Henderson, Principal of Lovedale, said: "We are waging a warfare in which we leave no room for generalship." [112]

It was at this time that Johannes Du Plessis completed his *History of Christian Missions* in South Africa, and at its conclusion, after having reviewed the increase in societies and missionaries during the past sixty years, he added the comment that the multiplication of agencies had brought serious evils in its train, especially laxity of discipline resulting from overlapping. He remarked that it was impossible at so late a date to eradicate the evil, but "its ill effects may be largely obviated by a generous missionary comity and the unswerving determination to respect the discipline of contiguous societies." [113] He regarded the growth of a spirit of interde-

[111] *World Missionary Conference, 1910*, vol. I, p. 288.
[112] *Ibid.*, vol. VIII, p. 15.
[113] Du Plessis, J., *A History of Christian Missions in South Africa*, pp. 404–405.

nominational comity fostered by the General Missionary Conference as "one of the most pleasing features of the present missionary situation." The task that then lay ahead was the organizing of the converts into a great Christian society. Adherence to certain principles would achieve this. They were: first, no more societies should be added, for a further multiplication "would be nothing short of a calamity;" second, a more numerous and better qualified native ministry must be recruited and trained; and third, there must be established a national native church.[114]

The South Africa missionaries themselves had long been aware of the need of reform, and Du Plessis himself had been a leader in the movement. When the First General Missionary Conference met at Johannesburg in 1904, comity was on the program for discussion. The Anglo-Catholic Bishop of Lebombo opened the subject, dealing with it from the point of view of securing "comity in the matter of teaching."[115] It is interesting to find the S.P.G. missionaries sometimes in the forefront of promotion of comity and cooperation and sometimes standing aloof or even opposing such developments. The Bishop quoted our Lord's prayer "that they may all be one," and then exclaimed: "And yet it is necessary to speak about comity in the mission field!" He appealed to the motto: *In necessariis unitas; in dubiis libertas; in omnibus caritas.* The differences are nothing compared with what separates Christians from the heathen. Therefore, he proposed that all catechisms used by the churches in South Africa have two parts. The first part would be the same in all, containing the essential doctrines of the faith held in common by all. The second part should consist of a denominational section which would be separately prepared by each communion and printed in its own edition of

[114] *Ibid.*, pp. 406–408.
[115] *General Missionary Conference of South Africa, Report of Proceedings of the First —, 1904*, pp. 136–141.

the catechism. The second paper was by a Mr. Borquin, and concerned migrant workers in the towns.[116] After that date comity and cooperation were concerns before almost every triennial meeting.

The Second General Conference in 1906 adopted a Constitution, which stated its first objective to be "To promote co-operation and brotherly feeling between the different Missionary Societies," and set up a "Board of Arbitration." [117] This body was called "an unofficial Board"—"elected by this Conference to deal with all inter-mission difficulties which may be submitted to it by the official representatives of any Missionary Society labouring in South Africa." The resolutions on comity,[118] in addition to setting up this Board, requested societies mutually to arrange for the demarcation of their spheres where there was still unoccupied country and to refrain from entrance into occupied areas without prior consultation and consent. There were provisions of the usual type for recognition of visiting Christians in good standing, transfer of membership, mutual respect of discipline, and the transfer of students. The final two resolutions were curious ones having to do with stewardship and financial support, warning against countenancing "any practice giving colour to the charge that the privileges of a Church are to be bought or sold," and against "tea meetings and other social gatherings held at night under disorderly circumstances." The paper presented at the Conference on "Mission Cooperation" and the discussion recognized the need of delimitation of spheres, but stressed also the fact that the practice in South Africa with its tribal divisions involved the danger of creating little "national churches," and that the migratory workers used to the ways of one church found it difficult to adjust to the customs of an-

[116] *Ibid., First, 1904*, pp. 144–148.
[117] *Ibid., Second, 1906*, pp. 129, 131.
[118] *Ibid., Second, 1906*, pp. 125–126; may also be found as Appendix B to vol. VIII (pp. 151–152) of *World Missionary Conference, 1910*.

other.[119] Genuine unity and cooperation far beyond territorial division were urgent.

Unoccupied areas were easier to deal with than the overcrowded areas where excessive overlapping occurred. Rev. J. Du Plessis in a paper presented to the 1909 Conference pressed for action, but nothing happened except the adoption of a resolution urging the missions nearest the empty fields to move into them.[120] The Anglican missionaries were absent from this meeting because of their objections to the use in the constitution of the words "delegates" and "delegated," which seemed to give the body too official a status to suit them, and to some degree also the term "Protestant." The constitution was amended to satisfy them. Unfortunately the Anglicans did not return until 1925.

Then the World Missionary Conference at Edinburgh made its adverse comments on the overlapping in South Africa and contrasted it with the vast regions still unoccupied, and the consciences of the missionaries were made still more uneasy. Six preparatory commissions on the Edinburgh pattern were appointed for the 1912 meeting, and the first was on "Survey and Occupation." Du Plessis was the convener. The Commission was to deal with demarcation and occupation. The report treated the whole region south of the Zambesi and the Cunene rivers.[121] Unoccupied areas were found in the north of German Southwest Africa, in most of Portuguese East Africa, and in two small portions of Southern Rhodesia. It was proposed that the societies within or nearest such areas be asked to give a definite commitment to move toward adequate occupation within three years. Very few areas were listed as insufficiently occupied, and in these the societies already there would be able adequately to care for them. The congested areas presented the per-

[119] *Ibid., Second, 1906,* pp. 39–47.
[120] *Ibid., Third, 1909,* pp. 15–16, 31–37.
[121] *Ibid., Fourth, 1912,* pp. 41–54.

plexing problem. These were principally those cities where the demand for labor was great and certain native reserves and locations with dense populations. The worst congestion was found in Natal and in parts of Zululand, East Griqualand, and the Cis-Kei. There the multiplication of societies resulted in inevitable overlapping, made impossible the delimitation of fields large enough to allow for the development of a substantial native church, led to laxity of discipline through too great disrespect of neighboring churches' discipline, and tended to make each mission concentrate on the conservation of its members rather than on evangelization of the heathen. The solution of the problem was a redistribution of territory and the missionary forces. This could be achieved only by the missions themselves in direct consultation, making certain that the wishes of the native constituency have been fully consulted. If the voluntary withdrawal of some agencies was not possible, then there should be a further demarcation of fields. Perhaps a majority of the missions had already done so, but unfortunately there were still too many that were competing. If they were not able to agree among themselves, they might call in the Arbitration Board. Once lines had been established by agreement, they should be rigidly respected. Resolutions affirmed the unity of the members of the one body of Christ and a desire for reconsecration to the service of our Lord, deprecated any increase in the number of societies, called upon societies in contiguous areas to agree to demarcation of their fields, asked that some societies withdraw from congested areas in order to occupy empty fields, recommended union training schools for missions of similar doctrine and polity, and called on the home boards and societies for new missionaries to go to the unoccupied areas. An Occupation Committee of five members was appointed to carry out these resolutions along the lines of the Commision's report.[122]

[122] *Ibid., Fourth, 1912*, pp. 11–12, 15–16.

Allowance must be made for the effect of World War I on the mission work, but even then the response to the call for advance and reform had been meager. The Committee on Survey and Occupation reported in 1921 that the only advance anywhere had been the beginning of new work by the Dutch Reformed Church Mission in two districts of Southern Rhodesia that had been designated as "insufficiently occupied." Not one of the fields classified as "unoccupied" in 1812 had been attacked by any existing or newly formed mission.[123] Despairing of local initiative, the Commitee advocated inviting a special commission of the International Missionary Council to confer with the local missions and churches. There had been only four cases of exchange or evacuation of fields, and the only one relating to a large area was in consequence of the removal of the Rhenish missionaries by the government.[124]

The war had caused abandonment of the plans for the 1915 meeting, and the Fifth General Conference did not convene until 1921. The Committee on Survey and Occupation, again under the chairmanship of Professor Du Plessis, divided the fields into fourteen areas for reporting on five topics: delimitation, occupation, adjustment of fields, missionary comity, and the general situation.[125] Comity had now come to mean agreement about discipline and other matters consequent to delimitation. The report on delimitation brings together more data on territorial agreements in South Africa than can be found elsewhere. The Rhenish and Finnish societies had a clear definition of boundaries in the South-West Territory. The societies in the Cis-Kei had a general understanding faithfully observed by all but separatist churches, but no written agreements. In the Trans-Kei there was a vague understanding, not recognized "by High

[123] *Ibid., Fifth, 1921*, p. 112.
[124] *Ibid., Fifth, 1921*, p. 103.
[125] *Ibid., Fifth, 1921*, pp. 99–113.

Anglicans" and the Wesleyan Methodist Church of South Africa, which said that there was no understanding. The Swiss and Berlin missions in Transvaal had an agreement, but they were suffering from the invasion by others. The Paris Mission in Basutoland had an understanding dating from 1905 with the Wesleyan Church, but the latter had tried to withdraw in 1915 and 1918, and then had unilaterally withdrawn in 1920. As to Natal, the American Board said that the only comity was afforded by the fact that it was illegal for other missions to enter their mission reserve territory, and that outside of such areas their own stations had become outstations of a variety of other missions. The South Africa General Mission reported a perfect understanding with others about their Indian missions on the Natal coast, but not elsewhere in south Natal or in the Trans-Kei. No agreements were reported among the many missions in Zululand. The cooperating missions, with their defined relationships, in Portuguese Africa were having trouble with half a dozen agencies that did not respect comity. In Mashonaland there was a definite understanding that was generally observed except by the Roman Catholics, Anglicans, and Seventh Day Adventists. Four regional missionary conferences and some informal gatherings helped to promote comity through brotherly intercourse. The war had deprived some missions of workers, and the disruption of the German missions by internment of the missionaries had most serious consequences. By the time of the Conference, restrictions on German missionaries within the Union had been removed and they had been allowed to return to the South-West Territory. The disruption then had not been as serious as in other parts of Africa where the Germans had been removed. At the request of this committee, the Conference asked the government of the Union to remove the remaining restriction on German mission property, and it passed a resolution condemning the decision of the Peace Conference at Versailles to debar German missionary societies from re-entering their fields.[126]

The Committee on Survey and Occupation submitted a resolution which it hoped would implement its findings, calling for the creation of a "Federation" or "Alliance of Missions," which would effect delimitation of spheres, guarantee not to interfere in polity matters, and allowing freedom to visit members in the areas of others upon the reporting of intention to the agency holding that area. Further the associated churches and missions would bind themselves to recognize the status of each member of a federated church or society, respect each other's discipline, and discourage proselytism by every possible means. The Conference accepted the principle of federation and referred it to the various Mission Synods and Committees with a request for a report before March 1, 1923.[127]

Strangely there is not a word about these matters in the *Proceedings* of the Sixth General Conference in 1925. The Seventh Conference in 1928 sadly took note that "there is still injury caused to the Kingdom of God by the lack of comity in the admission of members of other churches," and reiterated the former requests for the exercise of the utmost care in matters of membership and discipline.[128] Moreover, it informed the International Missionary Council of the intention to establish a federation of the Christian forces in South Africa and asked for the assistance of that agency, in a visit by Dr. J. H. Oldham if possible. It created a Survey Committee, the old one apparently having disappeared in the course of the past six years, and requested that it work in cooperation with the I.M.C.'s Department of Social and Economic Research.[129] However, a federation was not achieved, and the National Christian Council of South

[126] *Ibid., Fifth, 1921,* pp. 15, 111–112.
[127] *Ibid., Fifth, 1921,* pp. 23, 110–111.
[128] *Ibid., Seventh, 1928,* pp. 23–24.
[129] *Ibid., Seventh, 1928,* pp. 18–19.

Africa, mentioned as a possibility in 1928, did not come into existence until 1937, and then as a result of John R. Mott's visit in 1934.[130] This Council never had the strength of the councils in Asia, and the growing tension between the British and Dutch elements of the populace hampered its effectiveness. The adjustments hoped for were never achieved to any great extent, and the multiplication of native separatist churches further confused the situation.[131]

[130] Hogg, W. R., *Ecumenical Foundations*, p. 266.

[131] The regional conferences, all interracial in contrast to the General Missionary Conference (Cis-Keian, Trans-Keian, and Natal), paid some attention to comity matters. The strictures of the Edinburgh Conference about overlapping in Natal were acknowledged as justified by the (thirtieth) Natal Conference of 1912, and it was requested that any new mission should first consult the president of the Conference before selecting a site. The Conference had a Standing Committee on Comity and Cooperation. (*Proceedings of the Natal Missionary Conference, 1912*, pp. 9, 24–29) The next year the Committee reported that it had done nothing but work on a Syllabus of Religious Instruction for Native Schools. A scheme of cooperation between three Lutheran missions was reported as working well. (*Ibid., 1913*, pp. 47–48).

CHAPTER X

Stress, Strain, and Problems

THE practice of comity had long been an almost universal characteristic of the societies and boards which comprise the mainstream of the Protestant foreign missionary enterprise. It was only in Japan that no serious effort was made to delimit territory, and even there the missionaries thought that they practiced comity, considering it to be unity of spirit expressed through cooperation. Yet territorial comity and noninterference in the spheres of occupation of others never received 100 per cent adherence in the areas other than Japan.

There were from the beginning two types of agencies and missionaries who refused to participate in the prevailing practice. The Edinburgh Conference recognized one type as comprising those bodies which are "inherently exclusive" and cannot regard as valid parts of the church of Christ any organization excepting their own. The Roman Catholic Church is the prototype, but by 1910 there were some Anglicans, even in the mission fields, who had come to hold a concept of episcopacy which caused them to take a line similar to that of Rome. Representative of such persons was the missionary in East Africa who informed his Methodist neighbor that "in the view of our Church both you and your Bishop have a defective call to the ministry." However, even such exclusivists among the Anglicans were seldom guilty of competition. More likely to be staunch exclusivists, according to the report, were "strict Baptists," "because of their personal rather than their ecclesiastical requirements." One or two Lutheran missions may also from time to time

272

have shown such an attitude on grounds of doctrine rather than of polity.

The other type recognized by the Conference was the independent or representative of some small society not related to denominations, "essentially evangelistic free lances, unwilling to be restricted to any sphere of their own, and, it may be, unwilling to leave alone the spheres or even the converts of others, not through the strictness, but through the freedom, of their concept of church polity." [1] That type of missionary has multiplied in recent years. Yet neither the exclusivists nor the free lances interfered enough to prevent the general adoption of comity. They might disturb its smooth functioning, but they could not provoke the others into abandoning it for competition. Most church mission boards and some of the older faith missions still adhere to the policy and practice of comity today. Yet despite that general adherence, there have been increasingly severe strains and stresses, and in some areas comity has been tacitly, if not explicitly, abandoned. There is a questioning especially of whether it is as appropriate to national churches as to foreign mission agencies and whether it accords with the changed circumstances of the postwar period.

The Question of "Follow-up"

The seeds of disintegration were sown very early. They were planted when the first society claimed the right to "follow" their people with pastoral ministry into the territory of another mission, reluctant to entrust them to the care of that mission or to see them join its church. A widely experienced missionary statesman said to the writer: "Follow-up is the death of comity." Certainly it tremendously weakened

[1] *World Missionary Conference, 1910*, vol. VIII, pp. 16–17.

the effect of the delimitation of territory, made possible interference and competition, and laid the ground work for the later claims to freedom of expansion by national churches. It is due in part to an increase in confessionalism among the missionaries, reflecting pressures exerted from the home base toward the end of the nineteenth century, in part to the capture of missionaries by "the colonial mind," and in part to the establishment or quasi-establishment of the Church of England in the British colonies. Follow-up forced an early modification of the rigorous application of comity.

The early missionaries in India and China, with few exceptions, regarded the denominationalism by geography created by comity agreements to be a passing phase made necessary by pioneer evangelism. The missionaries were not pastors, but evangelists, as Rufus Anderson insisted, and they were not to rule the native church as it emerged. When their task was finished, and when the self-governing, self-supporting, self-propagating church had arisen in any field, the missionaries were expected to withdraw and leave the destinies of that church in the hands of its ministers and laymen. There was quite a general expectation that as soon as that happened, the national leaders would create one national church, reformed from the European-American models in the fashion that seemed good to them under the guidance of the Holy Spirit. The missionaries of the earlier time were generally of one mind with G. V. Pope of the Society for the Propagation of the Gospel (S.P.G.), who declared at Ootacamund in 1858 that "there will arise a Church of India differing in many respects from any Christian community in Europe or America." If that were true, then there was no necessity of any mission following its people into the territory of another. Pope warned against following even an agent or a servant to his home community. The early ideas about comity were adamant against follow-up. However, after the middle of the nineteenth century the missionaries became infected with the "colonial mind" and, while still giving lip service to the Anderson-Venn formula, began more and more to act on the assumption that the young churches were to be held in tutelage and control until the missionaries and their societies should decide that they had reached maturity. Confessionalism blended with the colonial outlook; the expectation of the imminent united, national, indigenous church with a different kind of life faded; and the missionaries indoctrinated the native pastors and laity with loyalty to the denominational heritage. The sentiment which Dr. Weitbrecht discerned as held by many Anglicans in 1908 was by no means confined to members of that communion: "The reason (and a great one it is) which lies behind the shrinking from agreements on Comity is clearly the anxiety lest we should fail to hand on any essential portion of the inheritance of the Mother Church to her Indian daughter." [2] The Anglican lead in this matter stimulated other confessional groups to similar ideas.

The establishment of the Church of England in the British colonies also stimulated follow-up. Even where it might not be actually established, colonial officers and even British diplomats and consular officials in non-British territories also granted it the prestige and prerequisites of establishment. A diocese was normally coextensive with a large administrative unit, perhaps the whole country, and its responsibility was for the pastoral care of the British officials, commercial community, and probably for the families of the military, as well as for the mission churches. Churches for the white colonialists might be located anywhere in the region where there was need of them. The strangest disregard of comity because of the presence of white Anglicans in a district occurred within the Anglican communion itself. A cathedral church for the Bishop of Fukien was erected in the International Settlement in Shanghai, not only within the diocese

[2] *Pan-Anglican Congress, 1908*, vol. V, Appendix S.D.4(e), p. 9.

of another Anglican bishop, but in the very seat of the American bishop. The colonial churches of the Church of Scotland and those of the British Methodists were administered by organs unrelated to foreign missions. High-church Anglicans tended to think of their organization as covering the whole land. This seemed to them to justify follow-up.

However, it was not the Church of England missionaries who initiated the practice of follow-up, chronologically speaking, with respect to the entire missionary enterprise, although they started it in many places. The Leipzig Missionary Society very early got a reputation for chronic disregard of comity because of some occurrences in India. This Society eventually became fully drawn into the cooperative circle at the home base and it certainly made comity agreements in East Africa; but the early infractions were long remembered. It was the American Methodists to whom the Anglicans and other British missionaries ascribed the origin of the practice. This was because of the policy followed by Bishop James Mills Thoburn in India. Bishop Thoburn at the Bombay Conference of 1892–1893 had advocated not only abandonment of the old restrictions, but also the positive acceptance of his desire to follow converts and to modify very radically the tradition of territorial assignment. Under Thoburn the Methodist Church expanded in India, Burma, and Malaya in areas that were spheres of other missions. The debate against him, in which he was overwhelmed, was led by Bishop Clifford of Lucknow. This event became widely known in many fields, and again and again one finds Anglican spokesmen posing as leading advocates of comity and describing the American Methodists as the prime offenders against the practice, to the dismay of Methodists who staunchly stood by territorial agreements. Dr. Weitbrecht of the Punjab Mission of the Church Missionary Society (C.M.S.) told a session of the Pan-Anglican Congress in 1908 that the Methodists "were coming into line," and that the crystalization of missionary opinion on comity, as expressed in the Madras Conference resolutions in 1902, was largely responsible.[3]

Nevertheless, it was the Anglicans who were primarily responsible for getting the right of follow-up recognized in those same resolutions. The introductory sentence reads: "This Conference, while recognizing the right of all Christians to the ministrations of their own Communion, and to Christian liberty of thought and action, desires to affirm its opinion that, under present circumstances, the principles of territorial division should be maintained." [4] Once this privilege was accorded, others also wanted to make use of it. Efforts were then made to circumscribe it in order to lessen the possibility of interference. One finds suggestions or rules that pastoral visits be limited to a few times a year and that the visiting missionary or pastor first inform the mission into whose territory he is proposing to enter. Quite naturally, once follow-up was permitted it would not be limited to occasional pastoral visits. Little groups of communicants were organized into congregations. When this in turn was conceded, there was insistence that such churches be not made into bridgeheads for the invasion of territory belonging to others. But soon the Anglicans were insisting that each and every local church in the body of Christ has an evangelistic function which must not be inhibited or denied. They were quite right about that. Dr. Gill, the Bishop of Travancore, said: "All Christian communities are bound to be centers of missionary activity, wherever they find themselves." [5]

The Indian Statement on Comity sought to accommodate to this view and yet hold the line. It reads:

[3] *Ibid.*, pp. 1–2.
[4] *Fourth Decennial Missionary Conference, Madras, 1902, Report of the* —, p. 159 (Resolution IV).
[5] *Pan-Anglican Congress, 1908*, vol. V, p. 162.

That while the right of Christians to the ministrations of their own Communion is recognized, and while congregations or small gatherings of Christians isolated from their Communion should be expected to engage in evangelistic work on a voluntary basis, such ministrations and efforts should not be regarded as warranting isolated congregations in undertaking missionary operations that would in any way conflict with the work of the missions or churches occupying the field.[6]

However, churches grow not by addition of individual members but by the multiplication of congregations, and the faithful witness of one such isolated local church would produce new congregations. By a natural process it could be expected that there would eventually be a small group of churches of one confession existing in the midst of a larger group of churches of another confession.

The logical outcome of the practice of follow-up and of claims to the rights of pastoral care and local evangelism was the repudiation of comity agreements by the Anglican Bishops in the Provincial Synod of India, Burma, and Ceylon in 1900. The resolutions adopted by the bishops were:

RESOLVED: That the Synod recognises the gain of developing missions on a diocesan as distinct from a society basis, where local circumstances facilitate such action.

(a) In view of difficulties which have arisen from territorial agreements between different missionary bodies, the Synod holds that all members of the Church of England, whether European or Indian, wherever they may be, have a right to the ministrations of the Church to which they belong, and that it is the duty of all Christian congregations to be centers of missionary activity.

(b) That, therefore, while commending the spirit of the policy in accordance with which the Missions of different Christian bodies have endeavored to avoid coming into col-

[6] See p. 105 in Chapter III, noting Section II, item 7.

lision with one another, the Synod deprecates any such territorial agreements in the future.[7]

The Bishop of Travancore stated that this action did not
intend to "do away with the arrangements of the past," and
that the old agreements would be honored subject to the
right of Anglicans to seek and obtain the ministrations of
their church and to the evangelistic action of local churches.
Some bishops interpreted the resolutions as entirely depre-
cating all comity agreements. Practically, the question still
rested with the local missions to a great extent and depended upon the attitude of the local bishop.

Dr. Weitbrecht gathered information about the observance of comity by all the Anglican missions in India in 1908,
and found that most of them were still keeping, and some
still making, agreements. He wrote:

Taking the attitude of Anglican Missions in India as a
whole, I think that we may sum up the situation as follows:—

All are agreed that we are bound by the principles of our
common Christianity, no less than by those of our own
Church, to prize and observe the spirit of Comity. . . .

The great majority have made agreements, either explicit
or tacit, as to the adjustment of their work with other adjacent Missions, and all would agree that before overstepping
the boundaries of such work it is right to consult the neighbor.

In the great majority of instances, agreements arrived at in
a common-sense and fraternal spirit have proved advan-
tageous.

On account, however, of certain cases in which difficulties
have occurred, and in vindication of the principle that every
Christian congregation should be a centre of evangelistic
effort, the Synod of Bishops "deprecate" such arrangements.[8]

[7] *Pan-Anglican Congress, 1908,* vol. V, p. 162.
[8] *Ibid.,* p. 8.

Weitbrecht observed that the comity of missions is analogous to the comity of nations, and that while its spirit must be permanent its forms must change with circumstances. Since one third of India was then unprovided with missionaries, it was well to insist on the evangelistic witness of every local church; but there must also be resistance to the tendency to build on another man's foundations. He looked forward to a day of "interlacing Comity" gradually superseding delimited boundaries, or better still to a unity in the Church in India that would "supersede Comity itself."

The extent to which Anglicans in India would still observe comity was not known to others, and many Anglicans elsewhere took the synodical resolutions to be a complete repudiation of territorial agreements. Most persons in missionary circles viewed the action as a terrible blow to comity and unity, as did Robert E. Speer in reporting to the Foreign Missions Conference of North America.[9] The typical Anglican statement of the matter came to be either a statement of fact as the C.M.S. historian Stock put it, that "its simplicity of working only prevails in the early stages" before follow-up, or a statement of opinion that comity was only suitable to a pioneer stage of missions. The Overseas Department of the American Protestant Episcopal Church could conveniently sidestep the question when confronted with participation in comity agreements by declaring that it had no jurisdiction in territorial matters and that this was entirely in the province of the General Convention of the Church.[10] However, that Church's Liberia Mission entered into a comity agreement as late as 1921. Widespread sentiment among the Anglican missionaries was voiced by Bishop Cassels of West China when he said: "Generally, the territorial arrangement becomes less and less possible and sufficient, owing to

[9] Interdenominational Conference of Foreign Missionary Boards of the United States and Canada, *Annual Report, 1901*, p. 19.

[10] Statement made at the Cincinnati Conference of 1914: *Christian Work in Latin America*, vol. III, pp. 119–120.

extension of work and overlapping. . . . Comity should always exist on wide and simple lines, but is not sufficient—it must lead to federation and some form of unity, in order to present a common front before the enemy." [11] Unfortunately, others took the Anglican repudiation of comity to be a denial of any real and practical desire for unity and this became a stumbling block to negotiations toward union, and in all too many places Anglicans held back in functional cooperation. The strengthened confessionalism in other communions also found justification for follow-up and unilateral expansion in the Anglican position as expressed by the Indian Synod.

Confessionalism among the young churches and the missionaries received greater stimulus after World War II through the rather curious development of "ecumenical confessionalism" within the World Council of Churches. International, global, confessional organizations were strengthened or newly created, and reached out into the life of the young churches as never before. They frequently made material aid available in such volume as firmly to tie the young churches into the confessional bloc, and sent scores of young ministers and laymen abroad for study in denominational institutions. Since membership in the World Council of Churches is by churches and not by national or local councils of cooperation, young churchmen, who prize both the recognition thus given their churches and their own opportunity to speak to the Western churches in a world-wide forum, speak as denominational delegates within a confessional bloc unless they represent united churches. All of this has strengthened confessionalism to an extent heretofore unknown in Africa and Asia, and it has set in motion separatist forces that run counter to the two-century-long trend toward regional unity and union in the lands of the young churches. Confessionalism has strengthened the desire for

[11] *Pan-Anglican Congress, 1908*, vol. V, p. 167.

follow-up and it has stimulated the pretensions of young churches to being "national churches" in a territorial sense, but there is no evidence that it has led to further repudiation of comity agreements by the missionary agencies.

The Problem of the Cities

The second factor, chronologically, making for stress and strain in comity relationships was the rise of cities. Although this has been greatly aggravated during the postwar period, it began early. The great ports, the "presidency cities" in India, and national capitals were from the beginning recognized as "open ground," which might be occupied by more than one society. They were considered too big for any one society and they offered facilities needed by many. Cities became a problem in inter-mission relations when new ones suddenly arose in what had been entirely rural areas assigned to one society, which ordinarily would not have the adequate resources to provide for a new urban center of perhaps 150,000 inhabitants. Comity in the basic sense of territorial division always included the assumption (and usually the explicit assertion) that delimitation involved not privileged protection but obligation for effective and total evangelization. Any mission that failed to fulfill this obligation was bound both to incur the censure of its neighbors and the desire of others to share its field. Moreover, in such a new city or industrial complex the question of follow-up became acute where migrant laborers flocked there by the thousands from the territories of other missions which wanted to be certain that their people were receiving proper ministry. Such new cities and industrial centers came first into being in Africa, and they exerted the most obviously destructive power yet apparent upon tribal culture. This complicated the problem and heightened the anxiety of the more discerning missionaries at the same time that new agencies saw in these centers opportunity for a quick harvest. While some missions had no scruples about invading the territory of another, most of the major societies were very reluctant to do so, even when the need seemed clear. It must be admitted, too, that in some countries in Africa the missions were reluctant to get into city work, and the fact that a city was in the sphere of another society seemed to excuse them.

The question of the adequate occupation of the cities and ministry in them arose very early in Congo. Roman Catholic mission orders were prone to move into the cities in force, while the Protestants avoided the cities and sought the countryside. Mr. Frederick Beale raised the issue of this neglect in 1907 when these communities were still only towns, but towns that had not been there when the missions had located.[12] The Congo Missionary Conference of 1911 had the eyes of its participants turned toward the still unoccupied up-river areas, but Rev. A. F. Hensey, in his address "The Irresistible Plea for Advance," tried to direct them also toward the expanding cities, "neglected in the discussion of the unoccupied fields." [13] He described the situation plainly:

It is a tragic fact that the Protestant Missions have never more than touched the great centers in this land. I know that this is not a pleasant fact, and I should not feel like saying it, if my own Mission was not among those included in this statement. The station where I have spent my missionary life has never made a serious effort to evangelize Coquilhatville, though more is being done at present, and our plans for the future include something worth while, I hope. The Government plans for the Colony are for the General Government at Boma, with Vice-General Governments for the four prov-

[12] *United Missionary Conference on the Congo, The Fourth —, 1907*, pp. 164ff; see p. 181 above.
[13] *Ibid., Seventh, 1918*, pp. 18–19.

inces at Leopoldville, Coquilhatville, Stanleyville and Elizabethville. Three of these vice-governments are already in
operation. These five centers, with Matadi, Thysville, Kinhasa, and the others which commerce is forming, cannot be
left out of any survey of our unfinished task, for they are to
be to the life of this land, what the heart is to the body. And
surely I make no reflection upon the devoted missionaries,
or the work at these centers, when I say that nothing really
adequate has been attempted at these places.

This situation was reported to be repeated everywhere along
the west coast of Africa. The cities received a little more
attention at the Conference of 1924.[14] There is rapid change
in the big centers, and the "voluntary recruitment" system
was having unhappy effects. Kinhasa-Leopoldville received
a special report. D. C. Davies of the Baptist Missionary
Society said that the natives coming from the various missions were apt to get lost to the missionaries and evangelists
there unless they reported themselves on arrival; and lost to
the missionaries they became lost to the church, becoming
engrossed with material and sensual matters. He asked for
reporting by the other missions when their people went to
the city. He closed rather pathetically with the words: "I do
not know of a single missionary in our Society who would
volunteer to come and work at Kinhasa. [That speaks volumes!] Nevertheless, these urban centers are of strategic
importance to the work of the Kingdom of God." The reader
sympathizes with his sigh: ". . . there is ample scope for
work . . . if only we have proper buildings and an adequate
staff . . . to cope with it."

Yet this is the way in which it went with the growing cities
year after year in many parts of Africa. The West-Central
Africa Regional Conference at Leopoldville in 1946 declared
that: "Frequently the opportunities and responsibilities are
too great for any one mission to meet, but through coopera-

[14] *Ibid., Ninth, 1924*, pp. 13–14, 21, 138–141.

tive effort great service may be rendered to the worker." [15]
It held up for emulation the example of the United Mission
of the Copperbelt. Yet as late as 1953 the (English) Baptist
Missionary Society was still solely responsible for Leopoldville-Est and the American Baptist Foreign Mission Society
for Leopoldville-Ouest, and both were feeling most inadequate to the task. They were made all the more uncomfort-
able by the competitive activities of the Salvation Army,
which in Congo was building a separate church and discour-
aging comity. They approached a sister mission for cooperation, received a very positive response conditioned upon the
creation of an integrated comprehensive program for the
entire area, and then did not accept the offer. These two
societies' local missions, with the encouragement of the societies themselves, invited the American Presbyterian Mission
(Presbyterian Church in the U.S.) to join them in cooperative work, and met with a favorable response.[16] However,
what happened was that the Presbyterians went into some
of the satellite towns with their own separate program, and a
complete plan adequate to the whole urban complex has not
yet been achieved. A somewhat more satisfactory arrangement developed at Elizabethville, where the Methodist
Church accepted responsibility for the migrants and was
recognized as their local representative by other missions.
Unfortunately, this arrangement has broken down in recent
years, and three or four other societies have entered the
area unilaterally.

The mines of Johannesburg and the Rand probably attracted the largest variety of tribal peoples from a distance,
and, since there were no comity agreements there, piecemeal

[15] *Abundant Life in Changing Africa. Report of the West-Central Africa
Regional Conference, Leopoldville, 1946*, p. 120.
[16] Correspondence between officers of the societies, the local missionaries,
and the Africa Committee of the Division of Foreign Missions of the National
Council of the Churches of Christ in the U.S.A. in the files of the Committee,
and personal reports of missionaries in the area.

duplication of work would have been quite easy. More than forty missions might have followed their people into Johannesburg. Most of them entrusted their members to the local agencies more by default than by design, but there was multiplication of agencies without integration. The problems of the towns and the miners received some attention at every triennial session of the General Missionary Conference of South Africa from 1904 onward. There was suggested at the very first session an association of missions with a commonly recognized church membership.[17] Migrating members of each mission would be reported and entrusted to members of the association at the place to which they went. Again it was thought that formation of Y.M.C.A.'s and Y.W.C.A.'s could provide the needed supplement to ordinary mission work.[18] Apparently little was ever actually achieved in the way of a fully coordinated cooperative program that would better have provided pastoral, educational, and recreational care along with effective evangelism than was possible through a multiplicity of duplicating and overlapping churches and institutions. Yet it also seems apparent that much more was actually done about reporting on migrant workers back to the missions in the hinterland than one would have expected.

The sugar estates and refineries in Portuguese Africa also attracted workers in large numbers from across the borders and concentrated them in unwholesome mass living. Follow-up by the American Board missionaries stirred resentment among the Methodists, who considered it an infringement of comity. This led to negotiations between the missions in the field and in America which brought about agreement, but which also led to the taking of initiative by the Portu-

[17] *General Missionary Conference of South Africa, Report of the Proceedings of the First —, 1904*, pp. 144–148, 32ff.
[18] *Ibid., Fourth, 1912*, pp. 70, 72, 78.

guese East Africa Evangelical Missionary Association.[19] The Association provided for a certain amount of cooperative work on the estates, and the cooperating missions took over responsibility for members from other missions while in residence at these places. Moreira reported in 1936 that most missions accepted this arrangement, which a few supplemented with occasional visits, but that the South Africa Compound Mission and some others would not commit their members to the local missions and consequently duplicated their work.

The one new radical approach to an industrial urban area was in the Copperbelt of Northern Rhodesia. Not only the Protestant missionaries but the Roman Catholics, too, were reluctant to take seriously this enormous concentration of workers and its effect upon the total life of the land. African laymen voluntarily and spontaneously gathered congregations, built churches, engaged in evangelism, instructed converts beginning at Ndola by 1925 and then extending to the other towns. They called their congregations The Union Church of the Copperbelt. This was incorporated into the Church of Central Africa in Rhodesia in 1945. The coalescence of a number of factors led to unprecedented action in 1935: these being the activity of the Africans; the study entitled *Modern Industry and the African,* under the chairmanship and editorship of J. Merle Davis; the work of the older A. J. Cross and the younger R. J. B. Moore; and the persuasive power of G. R. Fraser with the home boards in Great Britain. The United Missions in the Copperbelt was created by the participation of the London Missionary Society (L.M.S.), the South African Baptist Mission, the Church of Scotland

[19] Moreira, E., *Portuguese East Africa,* pp. 27–30; *Southeast Africa Missionary Conference of the Methodist Episcopal Church, Official Journal of the Eighth Session, 1924,* p. 26; *Ninth Session, 1925,* pp. 74, 52; *Eleventh Session, 1927,* pp. 140, 123; *Twelfth Session, 1928,* pp. 11, 34; *Fourteenth Session, 1930,* p. 134; *Fifteenth Session, 1931,* pp. 182–183.

Mission, the Methodist Missionary Society, the Universities' Mission to Central Africa, the United Society for Christian Literature, and the South Africa Presbyterian Church. A remarkable team of men and women worked with the Union Church and stimulated its growth without exerting control over it, and sought to develop a program directed toward a total Christian approach to the life of the Copperbelt. This story and its subsequent developments are told with sympathy, understanding, and fairness to all concerned in the book, *Christians of the Copperbelt*, by John V. Taylor and Dorothea Lehmann.[20] Unhappily there were ambiguities in the plan from the beginning; there was insufficient unity among the supporting missions; some of them were more than cool to the Union Church; and there were many unresolved complications. The United Missions eventually gave way to the Copperbelt Christian Service Council. The Mindolo Ecumenical Center, founded by the Christian Council of Northern Rhodesia in 1958 with some support by the World Council of Churches, has taken over many of the earlier concerns of the United Missions.

The plight of the African urban centers came under discussion at the North American Assembly on African Affairs at Springfield, Ohio, in the summer of 1952, a study conference sponsored by the Africa Committee of the Division of Foreign Missions of the National Council of Churches. The findings spoke of the magnitude of the human needs involved in the migration from rural to urban areas and called for comprehensive, interdenominational efforts to supplement local efforts.[21] This led at the next annual meeting of the Division of Foreign Missions to a discussion of whether or not comity is a barrier to adequate evangelism and Christian ministry in the cities today. The suggestion was made in an

[20] London: S. C. M. Press, 1961.
[21] North American Assembly on African Affairs, *Africa is Here: Report of the North American Assembly on African Affairs, 1952*, p. 203.

African sectional meeting that present conditions require a new statement of principles of comity, "under which Christian bodies instead of engaging themselves not to undertake any work in centers assigned to other bodies, would rather undertake to do so only as sharers in an agreed plan of cooperation tending to maintain and develop a united Christian fellowship and community of believers." [22] The Division then referred to the Staff Council for study and consultation with others "a review of the principle of comity with reference to present day conditions." [23] Nothing further was done in the Staff Council, but the Africa Committee took up the question. At its next meeting there was drafted a "Statement on Comity in the Urban Church in Africa." [24] This document recognized "the growth of the problem involved in the very rapid migration of Africans to the cities, resulting in several instances in tasks disproportionate to the resources of those agencies, which under existing comity agreements are responsible for the Christian work and witness in the growing centers." It was stated further that "This disproportion tends to be most acute where mission-church responsibility includes general education on a large scale." The proposal previously made at the Assembly of the Division of Foreign Missions was then commended to the member boards for study and sent to the Christian Councils in Africa for their information and, it was hoped, concurrent study. Unfortunately, political complications, interracial and international tensions, and over-all educational problems appear to have diverted the attention of the local councils and nothing further was done by the Africa Committee.

There are new industrial cities in India and other places

[22] National Council of the Churches of Christ in the U.S.A., Division of Foreign Missions, Africa Committee, *Minutes*, Minute A687, January, 1954.
[23] National Council of the Churches of Christ in the U.S.A., Division of Foreign Missions, *Fourth Annual Report, 1953*, p. 25.
[24] Africa Committee *Minutes*, Minute A687, January, 1954. See note 22 above.

in Asia as well as in Africa, and the older cities are erupting over ever-wider areas, due to the population explosion and the continued immigration of rural people drawn by industry. The Conference of Provincial Christian Council Secretaries in India in 1950 took note of the growth of towns into cities and expressed the opinion that there ought to be an extension of the old comity provision on "open cities," suggesting

> that where such a city has a population of more than 75,000 and has not been declared open, churches other than those of the occupying denomination should be permitted to enter for the purpose of shepherding their own members and not for establishing institutions that would conflict with the occupying church or mission. In evangelism harmony should be maintained by close cooperation that will develop to the full the local spiritual resources. In the event of a city having a population of two lakhs (i.e., 200,000) or more, that city should be considered "open." [25]

The Executive Committee of the National Christian Council received these suggestions and appointed a Commission to revise the Statement on Comity. The newly modified Statement was adopted by the Executive Committee for the National Christian Council in 1954.[26] The right of a mission doing work in an area to extend its work into a city which is the natural center of that area was also recognized.

However, such minor modifications of the doctrine of open cities and extension of the right of follow-up do not solve the problems of adequate church-mission programs in and for the cities. These can never be solved by denominational piecemeal efforts which involve wasteful duplication

[25] Quoted by R. W. Scott in "The Evangelistic Principle in Comity," in *National Christian Council Review* (India), vol. LXXII, No. 3 (March, 1952), p. 126.

[26] *National Christian Council of India, Minutes of the Meeting of the Executive Committee of the* —, March 10–12, 1953, pp. 24–26; *Ibid.*, October 20–22, 1954, pp. 27, 47–56; *National Christian Council Review*, vol. LXXIV, No. 6–7 (June–July, 1954), pp. 293–294.

and deny essential Christian unity and mock the message that all preach about the reconciliation which God has granted men in Christ. Not one of the great cities of Asia or Africa has a plan, either long-range or short-term, for total Christian witness and ministry, and in not one of these cities do the local agencies have the resources in men and money to implement such a plan were it made, in face of the population explosion and industrialization of society.

Mobility and Migration

The stresses and strains within, and new forces of disruption exerted upon, the system of comity relationships multiplied during World War II and in the period since the war. The migration of workers from the rural to the industrial urban areas, with consequent disruption of family, tribal, and church life has been a serious problem to the churches and missions in Africa since the beginning of the twentieth century, as has been seen. The mobility of vast populations during the last twenty years is now characteristic of many lands. This has raised grave problems of comity and also far more serious problems of Christian policy and strategy in witness and ministry.

There has been almost everywhere the continued movement from the countryside into the industrial cities as industrialization has claimed ever more workers or attracted would-be workers. The prospect of better livelihood has caused thousands of farmers to seek more or better land, as in the migration from northern Luzon to Mindanao in the Philippines. Displaced peoples from European nations have increased the foreign language enclaves and churches in parts of Latin America. Political divisions and developments sent millions of refugees out of North Korea into South

Korea, in both directions across the borders of India and Pakistan, and into Taiwan and Hong Kong. The scrambling of the North and South Korean populations put an end to comity distinctions in the Republic of Korea quite naturally. It was unavoidable. Few Christians were involved in the Indian migrations, yet the hordes of refugees in West Bengal, the Punjab, and elsewhere presented relief needs which local Christian agencies could not meet separately and which called for ecumenical cooperation. There was tremendous pressure put upon churches and missions to follow their members into Hong Kong and Taiwan. Moreover, those which had few or no members to follow did have missionaries with the linguistic ability to work in those places and the urge to use them in new work was irresistible. The *Hongkong Church Directory* for 1959 lists sixty-three missions in addition to the Chinese church bodies.[27] Immediately following the war there was one native church with two assisting missions in Taiwan. The *Taiwan Christian Yearbook, 1960* lists fifty-four missions which are establishing a church in Taiwan and twenty-two other foreign, or foreign connected, societies which are not seeking to establish a church directly.[28] A very few, such as the Reformed Church in America and the United Presbyterian Church in the U.S.A., entered in cooperation with the Presbyterian Church of Formosa. Some entered in order to work independently among either the Amoy-speaking Formosa Chinese or the mountain tribes, but most of them came either to follow up their Mandarin-speaking members or to begin new work among the mainlanders. The overlapping is confusing and the competition highly injurious. The Roman Catholic Church, being fostered by an integrated group of missions, is growing by leaps and bounds. It increased from a constituency of 20,112 in 1952 to 213,764 in 1958. Despite the

[27] *Hongkong Church Directory, 1959*, pp. 85–98.
[28] *Taiwan Christian Yearbook, 1960*, pp. 90–107.

large number of Protestant missions, the total Protestant constituency was only 252,767 in 1959, and about 160,000 of those were in the Presbyterian Church of Formosa.[29]

If populations have been mobile recently, the old-line Protestant missionary societies and boards have been far from mobile in their strategy. Even those that have felt impelled to follow their members in the migrations have been hard pressed to do so. There was brought out at the Willingen Conference in 1952 what should have been long apparent, that the cooperative Protestant missionary enterprise is relatively immobile, its personnel and resources being held down by long-term involvement in institutions of Christian nurture and denominational administration in a vast system of interchurch aid rather than expended in evangelistic outreach.[30] This aid is the natural consequence of the harvest in young churches that were taught to be denominational churches on the Western model rather than passionately evangelizing agencies. The boards and societies have an obligation to the churches which they, under the Holy Spirit, have brought into being; and the *diakonia,* the mutual bearing of burdens within the body of Christ, is, indeed, a form of proclamation of the gospel of reconciliation. But the societies are involved in the maintenance of existing organizations to an extent that makes advance difficult. It is a situation somewhat analogous to that of the pioneer missions in the treaty ports of China when the interior was opened, too tied down to undertake a speedy advance into the hinterland where the new China Inland Mission then quickly penetrated. Inflation has absorbed the funds released from China without a corresponding advance in other regions. Also the reduction of the missionary force by visa refusals in India and Burma has not permitted new work elsewhere. More and more money is

[29] *Ibid.*, pp. vi–vii, 84–85.
[30] Goodall, N., ed., *Missions under the Cross,* pp. 189–191, 220–223, 234–235, 242. The consequence was a call for evangelistic advance and for a reappraisal of institutions.

given each year for foreign missions, but it is swallowed up by increased costs of maintaining the *status quo*. Financial stringency has made it increasingly difficult since the war for the British societies, for example, to exploit effectively the fields for which they are responsible by comity agreements. On the other hand, it is asserted that some churches are being built up behind comity agreements and "overfed" by boards with more ample resources. It is charged that they have become "fat and lazy" and that they do not take their fair share of the evangelistic obligation beyond their immediate borders. The prevailing system of comity, it is therefore thought by some persons, tends to reinforce the general immobilization.

The New Societies

However, if the older Protestant agencies are relatively immobile, terrible strain is being exerted upon the system of comity by the mobility of newer missionary societies which have no commitments to young churches, which put all their funds into missionary personnel, which have little regard for prior occupation by older missions, and which do not see the missionary enterprise in its totality. They have little knowledge of the history of missions. Missions is a new cause to which their supporters are as passionately devoted as are their missionaries. It is not yet generally recognized that there is now a second wave of "Protestant" missionary activity which has little or no relationship to the historic development of church missions, and which is in a large measure hostile to the churches. It has very little concern at the moment for raising up young national churches; it ignores the political, cultural, social, and economic circumstances of the present day; and it is very simple in its aims. It is missionary-centered, seeks the verbal proclamation of the gospel through all the world immediately, as did the church missions a century ago, and tries to "pluck brands from the burning" in concentration on individual conversions. While directed toward the heathen, many of these societies have no scruples about proselytizing among Christians who are the products of other missions. The supporters of these societies are "fundamentalists" in independent congregations and scattered through many denominational churches. The lure of "the regions beyond" attracts many who do not know that missions have already been at work for a hundred years in some of the areas presented as frontier posts. These organizations are mostly faith missions, patterned after the great, older faith missions such as the China Inland Mission and the Sudan Interior Mission. It is to be hoped that they will eventually grow to be more like those stable and effective faith missions in scope, methods, and relationships. These new societies have arisen chiefly in the United States and Canada, and to a lesser extent in other British Commonwealth countries, and a few in Europe. About 130—at the very least, 127—were established in the United States and Canada between 1940 and 1960.[31] They represent a very minor segment of North American and British Protestantism, but the number of missionaries whom they send out is out of all proportion to the numerical strength of their constituency.

While a number of these societies are concerned with Europe first of all, they send their missionaries all over the world. They are augmented by the independents, who locally are often indistinguishable from them. Remembering that it is these new societies which are chiefly responsible for the increase, one can get some idea of what the invasion of these missionaries disregarding comity has meant in the way of

[31] Based upon information extracted from the *Directory of North American Protestant Missionary Agencies,* fourth ed., 1960, and Missionary Research Library, *Occasional Bulletin,* vol. XI, No. 9 (Nov. 23, 1960).

local complications by comparing the number of *all missions* in Latin American countries in 1925 with the number of *United States and Canadian missions* there in 1960.[32]

	1925	1960
Mexico	21	55
Guatemala	8	19
British Honduras	2	9
Honduras	7	24
Salvador	4	9
Nicaragua	7	14
Costa Rica	7	17
Panama	9	17
Cuba	13	32
Haiti and Santo Domingo	7	33
Argentine	23	36
Chile	10	21
Uruguay	4	28
Paraguay	7	13
Brazil	23	59
Bolivia	8	27
Peru	8	25
Ecuador	3	26
British Guiana	10	20
Venezuela	10	19
Colombia	3	29

Nine North American nondenominational missionary societies which were not present before World War II have missionaries in Hong Kong, fifteen in Taiwan, and eighteen in the Philippines. There could be a place made for all in an integrated nonoverlapping plan, but, while some seek out unoccupied areas, most work where churches have long been established, and there is wasteful competition and disruption. There is much moving of members from one church

[32] Based on the *World Missionary Atlas*, 1925, and the *Directory of North American Protestant Missionary Agencies*, 1960.

roll to another, but some thousands of new missionaries have not added very many new converts to the total Christian community.

The missionary "imperialists" among the church boards, of which the Foreign Mission Board of the Southern Baptist Convention is the most widely known example, further complicate comity agreements and compound confusion. This Board once practiced comity in foreign missions, but its expansion abroad has accompanied the expansion of the denomination throughout the United States. Many of its missionaries manifest brotherliness and a cooperative spirit, but in general there is no local consultation when it begins new work. A Bible school or seminary is often established at the inauguration of the mission, young men and women reared or won by other churches are brought in as students, and after graduation employed as ministers and evangelists. This is disruptive of both comity and cooperation. Total occupation of a country is often envisaged. Thus it is reported from Tanganyika that the Southern Baptist plan there is to establish a church in every township of the land regardless of the almost solid adherence to comity agreements by others.

Partisan Strife

Schisms brought about through controversies as in Korea, through unfortunate litigation as sometimes happens in India, and through the efforts of independents who invoke the freedom of the indigenous church create further tensions. Then there are the separatist movements that confuse people and disrupt denominational church life: hundreds of little ones in South Africa, the large Iglesia ni Kristo of Felix Manalo in the Philippines, Elder Park's Korean Christian Church or "Olive Tree Church" in Korea. There is also the effect of the rivalries and dissensions introduced from abroad in the name of true "Evangelical Christianity" by Dr. Carl McIntire and his International Council of Christian Churches. All of the factors enumerated in the last few paragraphs have considerably blurred the lines of denominationalism by geography.

This writer has not not seen any evidence that there had been much disregard of comity agreements due to the establishment of National Evangelical Fellowships and the World Evangelical Fellowship through the efforts of the (American) National Association of Evangelicals under the slogan "Cooperation without compromise." This development has brought injurious division and tension among the churches and missions in some countries, but not in others. The Evangelical Foreign Missions Association (E.F.M.A.) was founded in 1945, and in 1960 had forty-nine members and associated missions, together having 5,112 missionaries in their service. One of its declared purposes is "to promote comity and cooperation on the mission field." The constitutional requirement for membership reads:

Sec. 1 *Eligibility*

[A society] must be of good repute and subscribe to and abide by the following standards of comity:

(a) *Message:* Since differences in practice and doctrinal interpretation frequently cause comity problems, there must be a mutual recognition of a message as evangelical if it presents a saving knowledge of our Lord Jesus Christ in accord with the E.F.M.A. statement of faith.

(b) *Territory:* The evangelization of fields should be by the mutual agreement of all evangelicals and insofar as possible with all concerned.

(c) *Personnel:* Missionaries or national workers under discipline by a mission or church should not be accepted by another mission or church without mutual consultation. Neither should missionaries, missionary candidates, or workers be encouraged to leave their missions or churches through offers of increased salaries or other inducements.

(d) *Presentation:* Care should be taken by each mission board and its representatives to state correctly the facts concerning its work and workers and avoid the use of pictures and illustrations from other missions without giving due credit to the respective societies.[33]

Any infringement of comity or encroachment on the sphere of another mission has been justified by appeal to the statement on "Message" and the charge that the teaching of certain missionaries is not sufficiently evangelical by the E.F.M.A. standard. Missionaries of the faith missions which are members of the Interdenominational Foreign Mission Association of North America sometimes require other missionaries to subscribe to the Statement of Faith of that Association before they will admit them to fellowship.

Spontaneous Expansion and the "Ready Harvest"

There has been a clamoring against, rather than an ignoring of, the comity system by those persons who think that it stands in the way of the "spontaneous expansion of the church" and prevents the reaping of the "ready harvest." Rufus Anderson and Henry Venn expected the rise of a spontaneously expanding native church, because in their planning it was this for which that church was being raised up, that above all else. However, in most mission fields the nerve of passion for witnessing was cut when the missionaries were captured by the colonial mind and held the young church in tutelage until maturity.

Roland Allen reacted against the prevailing state of

[33] *Constitution and By-Laws of the Evangelical Foreign Missions Association,* Article IV.

affairs, and in his books, *Missionary Methods, St. Paul's or Ours?* and *The Spontaneous Expansion of The Church,* called for methods that would leave the young church free to be *the Church.*[34] His methods were largely a restatement of those of Venn and Anderson. His unique and chief contribution was the idea that the missionary proclaims the message; the Holy Spirit effects conversions; the missionary gathers the converts into a church; he hands over to them the Scriptures, the sacraments, and the principle of church order; then he stands by as a "father in God" to aid and advise as wanted, but never to rule or control; while the new church develops its liturgy, polity, and tradition under the guidance of the Holy Spirit, and very naturally and spontaneously spends itself in evangelism. During the past ten to fifteen years there has been a rediscovery of Allen, and today there is a "Roland Allen cult," especially among missionaries of the faith missions and exceedingly conservative church boards and among national pastors who think that the missionaries have still too much influence. Few of them understand Allen, however, because they are not churchmen, and do not know that *Church* about which he is writing. Nevertheless, "spontaneous expansion" is the hope and the goal of hundreds. And Biblically, theologically, historically it is the right and proper goal. But for some strange reason it is thought that comity agreements about spheres of occupation inhibit spontaneous expansion, although examples are seldom given. Just as the revival in central and east Africa has moved on spontaneously across comity boundaries and national borders, so an advancing wave of spontaneous evangelism would move unhampered by any man-made barriers. Moreover, sending is half of the apostolate along with evangelism as the other half, and truly spontaneous expansion would result in send-

---

[34] A careful reading of Allen's books would surely correct some misunderstanding of his views among those who invoke him as their authority but who seem to know his ideas only by the report of others.

ing of missionaries as well as local evangelism. One is forced to the conclusion that many of those who cry out against comity restrictions in the name of spontaneous expansion are really advocates of denominational imperialism, and that the expansion which they envisage into the territories of others would be far more planned than spontaneous. It appears to be those who want to see some young church released from regional boundaries and made coextensive with the nation who denounce comity as a bar to the spontaneous expansion of the church.

The idea of the "ready harvest" is also closely connected with the concept of spontaneous expansion. Only one does not simply wait on God to make the harvest ready, he seeks to cultivate it if there is any sign of its appearing. The harvesting is sometimes a reaping of what has appeared apparently spontaneously, and sometimes an ingathering of that which has come out of natural developments well directed. The would-be harvesters complain about comity restrictions. A harvest appears likely in some area, but it belongs to some one society or church by a comity agreement. This prevents many from rushing in and reaping. These persons have been captivated by the views which Donald A. McGavran has set forth in his books, *Bridges of God* and *How Churches Grow*.[35] This author recalls Protestants to the strategy that was basic throughout the whole history of missions until Protestants put an undue emphasis on individual conversions, namely, the winning of the individual in the context of the largest possible social unit, contacting and winning peoples and building the church through their natural leaders, fostering and exploiting mass movements that go on rather spontaneously through particular classes or social strata, passing from one group to another. McGavran advocates the concentration of personnel and resources

[35] *Bridges of God,* London: World Dominion Press, 1955; *How Churches Grow,* London: World Dominion Press, 1959.

where the promise of such a harvest appears, withdrawing them from areas where the statistical return in conversions is small, and carrying on merely a holding operation there. Adherents of these views are likely to place too high a premium on statistics, to ascribe to men the role of the Holy Spirit, and to be impatient with the slow faithful cultivation that often seems to have been required before the Holy Spirit brings the harvest. One must remember cases such as the classical instance of the Baptist Lone Star Mission in India. Yet under the direction of the Holy Spirit, pastors and missionaries can do much toward stimulating a movement already begun, and when a bountiful harvest is reaped in the way of new converts and new churches there arise enormous requirements in Christian nurture.

Protestant missions have usually been very slow to exploit adequately any apparent or obvious sign of an imminent harvest because each mission has been accustomed to work alone in its own well-defined field and is jealous of its sovereignty. And even if cooperative aid is desired, it has not been easy to obtain. Consultation and cooperation between boards, and especially when carried on through central organs of cooperation, are still very cumbersome and time consuming. There is no central organ for coordination and central planning and action, like the Sacred Congregation of the Propagation of the Faith, which enables the Church of Rome quickly and effectively to exploit a suddenly appearing opportunity or to meet some critical need. Comity agreements can be a serious hindrance to the reaping of a harvest that is God-given if the mission in the case does not have adequate staff and resources and is too narrowly denominationally minded to invite cooperation. However, it is not difficult to meet such opportunity if there is a will to cooperate and there is proper machinery for cooperation. The United Mission in Nepal is a good example of cooperative action in meeting a need and an opportunity, and Bishop

Chandu Ray has demonstrated in West Pakistan how an interdenominational, intersociety team of evangelists can be assembled and can work together in harvesting in such a way as to stimulate the local church to its responsibility in nurture.

It is not comity in itself that is the hurdle to be overcome, rather it is the disunity of Protestantism which makes more effective action difficult. Yet the would-be harvesters decry comity, as if its abandonment would automatically bring about a harvest and make its reaping sure. There was considerable discussion of the matter in India early in the 1950's, and it was introduced at a meeting of the National Christian Council's Council on Evangelism by a study of John 4:35 and Matthew 9:37–38: "Lift up your eyes, and look on the fields; for they are white already to harvest. Pray ye therefore the Lord of the harvest, that he will send forth labourers into his harvest." Alexander McLeish reported the discussion and commented on the idea in the *National Christian Council Review*. He said that the insistence on "harvest" rather than need, on the response, was different than the usual emphasis, and that missionaries and evangelists may have been looking in the wrong direction. Much evangelistic work in India had met with no response in a generation, whereas in other areas there was an unmet response because the workers were too few. Comity confined workers to their own area and prevented their being used where there was great opportunity for reaping a harvest. Unfortunately, examples of such situations are not given. Christ sent his disciples on an evangelistic journey and gave definite instructions that where they found no response they were to shake the dust of that place off their feet and move on to another. McLeish rightly pleads for mobility of forces and a readiness to meet response where it appears. He warns against human myopia, and reminds that while the Spirit sends the evangelist, He is also preparing the response, and does that in His own way. The time is short, and the harvest, wherever it is, is to be reaped at once. Therefore, the evangelistic force ought to be mobile. The object is not vague "evangelization" but the spread of the Kingdom of God through upbuilding the church.[36]

An article on "The Evangelistic Principle in Comity" was contributed by Roland W. Scott to the same issue of the *National Council Review*.[37] He reminded his readers that effective evangelization was the whole point of comity, and that it was the practice of comity that had called forth the great achievements in cooperation. Comity "is a procedure for 'the proper interrelation of forces and methods employed' in bringing the Church into being under the power of the Holy Spirit." Comity was designed for the first stage of evangelization; is it the proper procedure in the second stage when the national church has come into being? With the emergence of the church in any place, the evangelistic function can be expressed only by the living body of members obedient to the Holy Spirit. A self-centered church cannot be the instrument of God's purpose. Dr. Scott warned that: "Since comity is intended to minimize denominational competition, it is hard to see how the principle of territorial arrangements should be changed because of the expectation of an awakened Church." The question to be explored is whether there may not be other areas, human as well as geographical, which are ready to harvest. Many a church should move out of a single caste or stratum of society into the whole community. He notes objections that comity may restrict the Church's liberty in evangelism and deter spontaneous expansion. Spontaneity, however, should not justify an undisciplined or scanty spread of a church body which ought to face its more immediate surroundings with the truth of the gospel.

---

[36] *National Christian Council Review*, vol. LXXII, No. 3 (March, 1952), pp. 116ff.

[37] *Ibid.*, pp. 120–127.

The discussions of that time in India overlooked the fact that spontaneous expansion and the reaping of the ready harvest have not depended primarily upon the number of professional missionaries and evangelists, but upon the voluntary action of zealous laymen. The remarkable growth of the Church of Christ in Korea today is the fruit of zealous devotion by voluntary laymen far more than the work of paid pastors and evangelists. Further, the recent movement of hundreds of thousands of the Scheduled Classes, the former outcastes, into Buddhism in India has been the work of Dr. Ambedkar and his followers, and it has been nearly impossible to get foreign monks and workers into India to assist that movement. Yet it continues, and objective social workers have reported on the remarkable change that has come into the lives of these new Buddhists. Comity agreements can inhibit the reaping of a harvest by a self-centered church in a local area, if it will not do the task and will not accept the aid of others. Yet the problem is not one of comity, but of unity in mission. The abandonment of comity would assure neither that unity of purpose and action nor the awakening of the laity.

Ambitions of Young Churches

The arguments against comity agreements on behalf of spontaneous expansion and harvest have been above all advanced by nationals (as the peoples of the East and Africa are now called, as if Americans and Europeans were not nationals!) and some missionaries, who want to see their denomination freed from all restraints that might prevent its becoming a national church coextensive with the national territory. Often the appeals to spontaneity and harvest appear to be made unconsciously on behalf of this more fundamental reason. This desire for denominational expansion is in part a natural consequence of the spirit of nationalism, which is as strong in the young churches as in their newly independent nations as a whole. The claim has been made possible by the loss of the ancient vision of the one indigenous church of the land that was expected to succeed the preparatory missionary period of denominationalism by geography; by the spread of the concept of the church as the spiritual ordering of society, a body concerned primarily with worship, nurture, and fellowship, jealous of rights, prerogatives, and prestige, rather than with the demonstration in its life of the gospel of reconciliation; and by the increase of confessionalism. The bent toward unity and union is still exceedingly strong in the lands of the young churches, as is made evident by the number of church unions already made and the number of negotiations now in progress. But confessionalism and outright denominationalism in the Western pattern are also strong. When a united church is brought into being it is composed of all the former denominational units in geographical districts determined by comity; and it thus becomes truly a regional or national church as were none of the units, excepting in the case of Japan where comity was not practiced. Should there be geographical gaps because certain denominations in those localities did not enter the union, there is a natural tendency on the part of the united church to desire to fill them in for the sake of solidarity, administration, and fellowship. Denominational churches confined to specific localities have, on the one hand been reluctant to allow the new united church entrance into their territory, claiming the protection of comity agreements, and, on the other hand, have wanted themselves to gain national stature and prestige through expansion. Mobility and follow-up have also stimulated both types of churches to expansion, and to chafing under comity restrictions. However, being human, the proponents of expansion and the overriding of comity agreements seldom avow their denominational ambitions openly and base their argument on evangelistic responsibility, spontaneous expansion, the harvest, and the need of follow-up.

One of the clearest examples of stress and strain due to mobility of population, church union, nationalism, and a local rather than global perspective is the Philippines. The forces within the national churches destroyed comity. The Philippines had provided the most notable instance of division of territory and assignment of responsibility prior to occupation of a country by the missionary forces. The Comity Agreement of 1901 had been an influential factor in the speedy growth of the evangelical churches and had provided the basis for far-reaching cooperation. It was very effective until the liberation of the country from the Japanese invaders and the attainment of national independence. Then problems quickly arose. Sects streamed into the land, and after the closing of China to missions that stream became a flood. Indigenous sects also appeared, mostly small compared with the Iglesia ni Kristo of Bishop Manalo. By 1949 there were not less than thirty-two new bodies in addition to the prewar churches.[38] Scarcely any of these consulted the Philippine Federation of Christian Churches or the older churches individually, and there was complete disregard of the 1901 Agreement. Moreover, that Agreement soon became a matter of contention among the cooperating churches themselves.

There was new mobility in the population, especially a movement from northern Luzon to the southern island of Mindanao, which carried thousands of Methodists into Congregationalist territory. Some of the ministers and lay leaders were eager to follow them and provide them with churches and pastors. The Bishop and the assisting Mission Board had,

[38] For 1949 see the list at the end of the document entitled *Pertinent Facts Regarding Comity Agreement* [Philippine Federation of Christian Churches], p. 47.

however, been restrained by the old Comity Agreement. The
Methodists were, therefore, restive under such restraint, and
neither Methodist nor other denominational Filipinos could
see the matter from the global perspective which had led the
mission boards and founding missionaries to desire delimitation of territory. There was a desire to be a truly national
church. Some of them even said that the Agreement was
contrary to the provision of religious liberty made in the
national Constitution. One man, during a discussion of these
matters, expressed his sentiments in these words:

1. The import of the Comity Agreement is incompatible
with the present social and economic trends in the Philippines. The improved communications and transportation
have encouraged mobility and mass migration. According to
statistics there are 800 migratory wealth seekers arriving in
Mindanao every day. Many of them come from the Ilocos
provinces and the Western Visayas. This exodus constitutes
a grave problem to the socio-religious life of the country. In
Cotabato and in Davao, a Congregational territory, it is
claimed that there are more Baptists than the Congregationalists. Likewise a great mixture of Methodists, Brethren,
Disciples, and aggressive Christian Alliance have been found
in these areas. Strictly following the Comity Agreement the
Baptists or the Methodists could not establish a church in a
strictly Congregational area. Consequently, the Baptists and
other denominations living in those areas could neither go to
church nor worship as they used to worship in their own
way. As a result many of them are being absorbed by the
wilderness without a church influence.

2. The monopolistic claim to certain areas by denominational groups has long been broken by the infiltration of the
Christian and Missionary Alliance, the Lutheran, the Seventh
Day Adventist, the Aglipayan-Episcopalian congregations,
and by other denominations not signatories to the Comity
Agreement. This continued infiltration in a distinct denominational area is a unique sign of weakness in the Comity

Agreement. For lack of teeth to enforce the Agreement makes us hope for a better and effective method of Kingdom building than the present Comity Agreement.

3. The Comity Agreement tends to promote frequent friction between denominations and the consequent denominational demarcation is likely to run counter against the Constitution of the Republic, which sanctions freedom of religious worship.[39]

However, it was the formation of a union church on almost a completely nation-wide scale that brought the discussion to the boiling point. The United Church of Christ in the Philippines was formed in 1948 by the merger of the United Evangelical Church (an earlier union of Presbyterians, Congregationalists, Evangelical United Brethren, a Methodist group, and part of the Disciples), the Evangelical Church of the Philippines, and the Philippine Methodist Church. The newly United Church contained two elements, therefore, which had been schisms from the Methodist Church, which were in the territory assigned to the Methodists by the Comity Agreement, and which henceforth would not be called Methodist. Furthermore, one of the Bishops of the United Church was assigned to jurisdiction over all of Luzon north of Manila, and he organized a Conference of the Church, comprising the former Methodists, in the territory still claimed exclusively by the original Methodist Church. These former Methodist, now United, congregations became more active evangelistically. There was most unfortunately no prior consultations between the United Church and the Methodist leaders. The Methodists regarded this action as a repudiation of the Comity Agreement by the United Church and clamored both against the "invasion" and for the right to establish churches in Mindanao. The United Church

[39] Statement of Dr. Catapusan during discussion of comity matters, meeting called by the Philippine Federation of Christian Churches, July 29, 1947. *Pertinent Facts Regarding Comity Agreement*, pp. 15–16.

people reported that they were simply organizing all elements belonging to their church. Bishop Jose L. Valencia of the Methodist Church on May 12, 1949, began a correspondence with the officers of the United Church of Christ in the Philippines about the matter, which led to an initial meeting on July 28 between the Methodists and the United Church people, and then to a serious attempt by the Federation to find a solution to the problem.[40] There was much talking to cross purposes in the early discussions, some arguing for strict adherence to the old order, others saying that the agreement was obsolete and even "a stumbling block to the speedy propagation of the gospel." Since all the churches were not represented on the Federation's present Comity Committee, a special, large committee was set up to meet on August 9, 1949. It was charged with bringing a new plan to the Executive Committee of the Federation on September 2.

The "Suggested Revision of the Comity Agreement" prepared at the meeting on August 9 was really an abrogation of the 1901 Agreement. Its import was to open the whole country to all, but to seek cooperation to avoid proselytizing, to encourage union of overlapping local congregations for strength and effective ministry, and to encourage the formation of district or provincial committees for the promotion of mutual interest and mutual cooperation. A copy of this document was sent for information to the Far Eastern Office of the Foreign Missions Conference of North America. After consultation with secretaries of participating boards working in the Philippines, Dr. Rowland M. Cross, the Executive Secretary, replied to the Federation officers on behalf of these boards that there was a consensus that the old agreement needed revision but that experience elsewhere indicated that the proposed new agreement needed far more continuing

[40] The documents, including correspondence and minutes of various meetings between May 12 and October 8, 1949, are collected in *Pertinent Facts Regarding Comity Agreement*.

supervision by the Federation.[41] A national committee with local committees related to it could still protect the legitimate interests of denominations where they had precedence and assigned responsibilities, could deal constructively with shifts in population and large-scale movements of church members, and could assist new mission agencies to locate work (such as the very recent inquiry of the Baptist General Conference of America). It was therefore suggested that the Federation consider setting up a "Comity Committee" that would be a "United Protestant Board of Strategy." These suggestions were readily adopted, and a revised document prepared for circulation among the churches and for submission to the Executive Committee of the Federation, now scheduled to meet on October 14. All the relative documents with considerable correspondence added were brought together for this meeting in a mimeographed booklet entitled *Pertinent Facts Regarding Comity Agreement.*

The Executive Committee of the Federation had invited to its meeting on October 14 a larger number of participating guests than the membership of the Committee. Discussion was frank and full, and, as the Executive Secretary of the Federation reported, "The Spirit of the meeting was excellent." [42] There appears to have been no formal abrogation of the 1901 Comity Agreement, but the new Protestant Board of Strategy created at this meeting effectively accomplished that, yet all concerned believed that they were acting in its spirit, but adapting it to present requirements. The Executive Secretary of the Federation wrote: "I suppose no comment need be made on this Agreement. It is in effect an agreement to set up a Board of Strategy, this Board undertaking to keep

[41] Letter of Rowland M. Cross, Far Eastern Office, Foreign Missions Conference of North America, to Atty. Juan Nabong, Executive Secretary, Philippine Federation of Christian Churches. (Files of the Far Eastern Office, D.F.M., N.C.C.C.U.S.A. and *Pertinent Facts*, pp. 28–29.)

[42] The minutes were issued in a mimeographed booklet entitled *Protestant Board of Strategy* by the Philippine Federation of Christian Churches, under date of October 14, 1949.

peace between denominations and guide their expansion! It will be a tremendous job. . . . After all any Comity Agreement will stand or fall on the spirit of those who make it and we are hoping for the best." [43] And: "We shall inform you of further progress in our cordial relationship between the different Churches, but we could foresee now a very definite and aggressive attitude for the total evangelization of the Philippines." [44] The Central Conference of the Methodist Church officially interpreted this action as abrogating the Comity Agreement. [45]

The document as adopted and sent to the churches was very simple:

PROTESTANT BOARD OF STRATEGY

I

The PROTESTANT BOARD OF STRATEGY shall be composed of the Head of each Church communion, together with three to seven co-opted members who shall be chosen for their cooperative spirit, wide Christian experience, and devotion to the evangelical cause.

II

The PROTESTANT BOARD OF STRATEGY shall consider the legitimate interests of denominations and churches in the areas where they are now at work, bearing in mind the denominational background of such areas, in considering new relationships and developments of their work up to the present.

III

The PROTESTANT BOARD OF STRATEGY shall meet quarterly in order to do overall planning, prevent competition among denominations, avoid congestion of churches in any area and seek ways and means of deploying Protestant Christian forces

[43] Letter of Nabong to Cross, October 24, 1949.
[44] Letter of Nabong to Cross, October 25, 1949.
[45] Quoted by Bishop Valencia, *Minutes of Christian Board of Strategy*, June 21, 1951, p. 7.

for the most intensive and systematic evangelization of the Philippines and assist Churches in finding places where they can render their best service, seeing to it that more needy though less promising areas are not entirely neglected.

IV

The PROTESTANT BOARD OF STRATEGY shall promote inter-denominational relationships, goodwill, and friendship among churches. Communions are urged to refrain from proselyting members of other churches, but should leave the choice of affiliation to the free will of their members, giving a letter of transfer whenever it may be requested.

V

The PROTESTANT BOARD OF STRATEGY may, after consultation with all parties concerned, allocate certain unevangelized geographical areas in the Philippines to Church communions which have the means and personnel to organize and carry on a strong program in such areas.[46]

The final paragraph of this document seems to indicate the feeling that comity was still desirable for pioneer areas in the early stages, but that after a period of protection it would no longer be valid.

The Biennial Convention of the Philippine Federation of Christian Churches adopted the document on January 19, 1950, and the Board of Strategy held its first meeting on April 13, 1951, with representatives of seven denominations in attendance.[47] The word Christian had been substituted for Protestant in the hope of the eventual participation of the Philippine Independent Church and the Episcopalians. Meanwhile the three Annual Conferences of the Methodist Church had voted to extend Methodist work outside their boundaries and the Central Conference had instructed

[46] Protestant Board of Strategy, *Minutes of Meeting of October 14, 1949,* between cover and p. 1.
[47] *Minutes of the First Meeting of the Christian Board of Strategy, April 13, 1951, at Union Theological Seminary.*

Bishop Valencia to visit Mindanao and make a survey. (Two of these Conferences approved the Board of Strategy, one did not.) This alarmed some people in the United Church, whom the Methodists believed to have been delaying the activating of the Board of Strategy. The Executive Committee of the United Church on April 12, 1951, had stated the adherence of the church to the old 1901 Agreement as a working basis and asked immediate activation of the Board of Strategy.[48] It was agreed that a special committee of five each from the Methodists and the United Church meet after Bishop Valencia's visit to Mindanao. In the course of that visit the Methodists instructed their people to organize churches where the United Church could not care for them, and Bishop Rodriguez on behalf of the United Church offered them the Ala Valley. When the Christian Board of Strategy next met, on June 21, there was wide-ranging discussion, chiefly about Methodist-United Church relationships.[49] The positive direction of the thinking may be indicated by several quotations: Bishop Rodriguez—"The right determination of areas unevangelized is the work of the Board of Strategy." Bishop Navarro—

> We can make progress without violating the sense of cooperation. The Board is much more than a comity organization. The Board is not a principle but an organization to work out basic principles along the lines of strategy involving comity and the strategic deployment of our resources in manpower and every other kind of power. So far we have concentrated in places where there are churches organized. Let us come to a point that we feel we are closer to each other in cooperation by making use of the Christian Board of Strategy to work out solutions to our problems.

It was voted that the principles upon which the Board had been set up and ratified by the Federation and the partici-

[48] *Ibid.*, April 13, 1951, pp. 5–6.
[49] *Ibid.*, June 21, 1951.

pating churches be the guiding rules of action and that the
Board meet as soon as possible to receive, study, and make
recommendations upon questions that have arisen between
the participating denominations. There was a general feeling that with this meeting the Board had truly been
"activated."

Considerable progress seemed to have been made at the
next meeting on November 21, 1951, where actions were
taken encouraging the continuation of work by any church
of a cooperating denomination already established in a community; requiring approval for another church in such a
community by a regional subcommittee of the Board of
Strategy, subject to ratification by the Board itself; calling
for regional subcommittees in Luzon, Mindanao, and the
Visayas; authorizing a survey and plan for the organization
of churches in communities and municipalities where none
then existed; and asking the cooperating churches to promote an interchurch plan for evangelizing the unreached
communities of the country.[50] But a year later the Board was
marking time, because the Central Conference of the Methodist Church had not yet officially accepted the Board of
Strategy, and because of the reluctance of some to accept
developments that could not be reversed. The General Conference of the Methodist Church, meeting in San Francisco
in April, 1952, extended the jurisdiction of the three Philippines Annual Conferences over the whole of the nation,[51]
and, in consequence, the Philippines Central Conference in
November, that same year, declared that it was no longer
able to approve the principles and procedures of action of
the Board of Strategy.[52] However, it affirmed: "The Metho-

[50] Reported in *Ibid.*, June 21, 1951.
[51] *The Methodist Church, Journal of the 1952 General Conference of—*,
p. 1735.
[52] *Philippines Central Conference of the Methodist Church, Official Record
of the Fifth Regular Session of the —*, 1952, pp. 49–51, see also pp. 22, 39–
40.

dist Church in the Philippines in extending and expanding its work is doing it not in the spirit of competition with other churches, but in the spirit of cooperation with and goodwill to all religious denominations and institutions." Nevertheless, this action by the Methodists sounded the death knell of both comity and the Board of Strategy. In light of this development, the sessions of the Board, of October 15, 1952, and thereafter, accomplished very little and it soon ceased to meet.[53]

The United Church of Christ in the Philippines at its Third General Assembly in 1952 accepted the principles upon which the Christian Board of Strategy had agreed in its meeting of November 21 of the previous year. However, it added a vote "That should it be necessary, we be prepared to take up such problems as cannot be solved by the Christian Board of Strategy with the Federation for a larger hearing and possible solution in line with the above principles which we have approved."[54] It was also voted to overture the sister churches in the Republic seeking a conference for the advancement of the Church Union movement which, if successful, would naturally eliminate comity problems. In line with this, the Executive Committee of the Federation voted the next November to create a Committee on Comity; in the March 1953 sessions it took some actions relative to Comity; but in the amendments to the Constitution of the Federation made in March, 1954, the standing Committee on Comity was dropped because it had been replaced by the Christian Board of Strategy.[55] However, the Board of Strategy was really defunct. It had been established principally to resolve

[53] Christian Board of Strategy, *Minutes,* October 15, 1952.

[54] *United Church of Christ in the Philippines, Minutes of the Third General Assembly of the —, 1952,* Vote 52–49; also 52–50 and 52–51.

[55] *Philippine Federation of Christian Churches, Minutes of the Fourth Post-War Biennial Convention, March 11–12, 1954,* pp. 86, 92, 93, 94, 104, 108. See pp. 132–134 for the Constitution as amended.

the tensions between the United Church and the Methodists, and having failed to be accepted by both sides, it speedily vanished.

The discussions in the postwar years revealed that the national leaders in the young churches regarded denominational relationships much in the same light as their counterparts in the older churches in the West, yet manifested a much more thorough sense of underlying unity and dedication to cooperation, but lacked the historical perspective that had been general in the missionary movement a half century earlier. The discussions and the attempts at solutions certainly contributed to the maturing of the national leadership and have had their part in producing the recent movement to change the Federation, which is committed to ultimate church union, into a Council of Churches in which the Episcopalians, the Philippine Independent Church, and others may accept membership. Yet this could certainly have been achieved by a slight amendment to the constitution.

The very same sentiments about freedom of expansion for national churches had been operative in India, partly cloaked in concern for spontaneous expansion and reaping the harvest. Even the Syrian Churches had awakened. The Mar Thoma Church was active in evangelism from Kerala northward to Nepal and eastward to Singapore. The Orthodox Syrian Church was acknowledging its evangelistic obligation. McLeish quoted a bishop as saying that territorial comity had no relevance to his church, that all India was its proper field, and if they had been negligent of their duty in the past, the Syrians were now determined to make up for lost time.[56] The great union Church of South India had come into being as a genuinely regional church of the whole southland with the avowed intention that union should be

[56] *National Christian Council Review,* vol. LXXII, No. 3 (March, 1952), p. 117.

for the sake of evangelism. The North India Church Union scheme was making progress and bringing about the advent of a similar regional church for the northern half of the subcontinent. The Kerala Christian Council declared that comity agreements were "not to be construed as binding on the conscience of a church which feels in duty bound to its Lord to preach the Gospel;" and the Bihar Christian Council in the name of spontaneous expansion recognized the desire of some long-established and populous church to reach out into new areas.[57] Following the discussion of comity in the Council on Evangelism, mentioned above, the topic was taken up by the next meeting of the Conference of Provincial Christian Council Secretaries, and that body forwarded to the Executive Committee of the National Christian Council some recommendations for the revision of the Statement on Comity, last revised in 1937.[58] The World Dominion Movement office in India was requested to make a factual study. The National Christian Council meeting at Guntur in 1953 had the suggested revision before it, and gave authority to the Executive Committee to approve the Statement after publication and reception of comments. The publication was made, with an introduction by Roland W. Scott, in the summer issue of the *National Christian Council Review* in 1954, prior to final action by the Executive Committee in October of that year.[59] The changes were particularly intended to meet the situation "created by the initiative and spontaneous growth of churches." A comparison may be made with the 1938 document on pages 102–109 in Chapter III above.

[57] Reported by R. Scott in *Ibid.*, pp. 123–124.
[58] Reported by A. McLeish in *Ibid.*, p. 116. Appointment of Special Committee in *Ibid.*, vol. LXXIII, No. 4 (April, 1953), p. 145.
[59] *National Christian Council of India, Minutes of the Executive Committee of the —,* October 20–22, 1954, pp. 47–56, 27; *National Christian Council Review,* vol. LXXIV, No. 6–7 (June–July, 1954), pp. 288–295.

A new first paragraph was added to the Introduction:

The principles of comity have developed through the long experience of churches and missions working in the same or contiguous areas, and with similar aims. Comity continues to be essential to the churches in their divided state, but it should not be considered a reason for them to remain apart. Closer cooperation and agreement should become means whereby the churches realize the importance of considering together how to make their oneness in Christ more manifest to the peoples of India.

There was added with respect to territorial arrangements a second paragraph under II.1 providing that when more than one church or mission wished to enter a new area the local Regional Council should set the terms of comity. Carefully drawn maps were requested to be added to the written records of boundary agreements, under II.6, along with a periodic review by the Regional Council. Follow-up was somewhat limited by the explicit statement that while the rights of Christians to the ministration of their own communion is recognized, "this should be allowed by the Church concerned only in the case of those who have conscientious convictions that do not permit them to accept the ministrations of the church in that area." Section II.9 declared cities of 200,000 to be open.

A new Section III, inserted between II and the former III, sought to satisfy most fully the conditions caused by the emergence of independent churches. It reads:

III. Expansion of the Churches

With the development and organization of churches and local congregations which recognize their responsibility for evangelizing the people of the neighbourhood and those farther afield who have racial, social, or cultural affinities with them, it is desirable that comity allow for their spontaneous growth.

A distinction should be made between this kind of expansion which occurs largely through the activities of Christian people among their relatives and friends of the same social group, and the 'missionary operations' of isolated congregations mentioned in II (7), or the activities of new missionary bodies seeking to begin work in an area.

It is agreed that:

1. In the present divided condition of the churches comity is essential to their evangelistic outlook.

2. While churches and missions should continue to adhere to the principle of making and abiding by territorial arrangements, this should not be so interpreted as to impede the spontaneous expansion of long established and populous churches into adjacent territory. Any expansion which involves territory previously assigned by agreement to another church or mission should be carried out only in consultation and, if possible, in agreement with the occupying church or mission.

3. Where Christians of one church emigrate in considerable numbers to an area previously assigned to another church or mission a natural expansion may be possible among those of the same social or racial origin who have emigrated to that place. While the right of this expansion to take place should be recognized by the occupying church or mission, it should not, except by previous agreement, be allowed to interfere with the established institutions or the evangelistic work in the area.

4. The Regional Council or Councils may be asked to explore the possibility that previously accepted territorial arrangements may be revised so as to allow for the growth of churches, while at the same time permitting full scope for the work of the occupying church or mission.

5. Agreement by consultation of the bodies concerned, with the knowledge of the Regional Council, should be the normal way of meeting these situations. Where necessary the

Regional Council or Councils should be asked to arbitrate as
in Section I above.

This attempted solution appears superior to the course
followed by the churches in the Philippines, where the barrier
to a perhaps better judgment was the fact that the tension
was between two churches of approximately equal strength
and the course followed could not be the consensus of a
large number of churches. There is one apparent danger in
the liberty for expansion allowed in the Indian document,
which is, that denominationalism by castes may replace the
old denominationalism by geography. For even though caste
is supposed to be outlawed from the body of Christ, it still
lives on in the so-called communities within the Church
which will not intermarry or have certain other relationships.

Finally, there is one other consideration with regard to a
possible revision of the scheme of comity that should be mentioned. Noninterference and protection were always secondary to effective occupation as goals of comity. A person would
be hard put to it to define effective occupation today in any
but a very few areas. Robert E. Speer's once excellent and
adequate definition is no longer applicable in areas of population explosion and rapid industrial urbanization, and in a
time when the welfare state has taken over from the missions
the education of youth. There are twice as many persons who
have never heard of Jesus Christ in parts of Asia, if not of
Africa, today than there were fifty years ago. The removal
of comity restrictions and the multiplication of numerous
little missions will not make it certain that Christ will be
presented "to every individual with such clearness and com-
pleteness as to place upon him the responsibility of acceptance or rejection of the Gospel." Too many agents, it can be
clearly demonstrated in many places today, simply drown
out each other's voices. But the challenge is there to a new

understanding of evangelism and a more effective strategy for implementing it.

In Retrospect and Prospect

The Protestant world mission was developed and promoted in unity from its inception—interdenominational and international unity, spiritual unity in Jesus Christ. The unitive tendency in the mission expressed itself quite early and rather spontaneously in the system of mutual adjustment known as comity. Through consultation by two or many agencies responsibilities for evangelistic occupation in specific assignments were accepted, looking toward the goal of proclaiming the gospel to every last man on the globe and of fostering a native church in every part of the earth. Noninterference in one another's affairs, along with respect for each other's discipline and the adoption of common standards and procedures, were essential features of the system. Comity, therefore, involved active cooperation from the very beginning. Experiences in the course of its practice gave rise to manifold manifestations of the underlying spiritual unity and to ever more extensive and effective forms of cooperation in study, policy formation, and action. Comity has been the very bedrock of unity upon which all other unitive practices were erected.

The practice of comity was so fundamental to the Protestant missionary enterprise and so universal in it, that it came to be regarded by some as a term embracing every aspect of cooperation and effort to express unity up to actual organic union of churches. Others so took it for granted that they called it negative cooperation, or primary cooperation, or the first rung on the ladder of unity. The wide range of content which was eventually put into the term is illustrated by the definition given by Rev. Dr. H. M. King, Chairman of the Executive Committee of the American Baptist Missionary Union at the Ecumenical Missionary Conference in New York in 1900. He said:

> Missionary comity is, in its essence, the spirit of Christ manifesting itself in all the forms, and methods, and activities of foreign evangelization, and in all the intercourse and relations of those who are seeking to prosecute it. It is the illustration of that spirit which evangelization is professedly seeking to realize in all human society. It is the expression of that courtesy and thoughtful regard for the rights, and the feelings, and the convictions of others which should ever and everywhere characterize the intercourse of Christian gentlemen.
>
> In a word, missionary comity is born of the love of Christ shed abroad in the hearts of His disciples, and is the manifestation of the life of Christ in the lives of His followers. It is inculcated with great frequency in the Scriptures, as in the language of the Golden Rule; in Christ's commandment to His disciples, "That ye love one another as I have loved you;" and in His sacerdotal prayer for all believers, "That they may all be one, as thou, Father, art in me, and I in thee, that they also may be one in us," a prayer which may not necessarily include organic union, but must involve a unity of spirit and of life that shall in some manner make itself visible and felt in the world, and be a convincing evidence of the divine nature of Christ and the superhuman character of the Christian religion, "that the world may believe that thou hast sent me." [60]

Such a definition, however, could both cover every kind of positive Christian action in mission and be a pious nod to brotherliness which excused inaction. Dr. Weitbrecht of the Church Missionary Society's Punjab Mission succinctly

[60] *Ecumenical Conference on Foreign Missions, 1900, Report of —,* vol. I, p. 233.

put the whole of the positive intent of such a broad definition in the sentence: "By comity we understand fellowship such as may exist and should manifest itself between different bodies apart from organic union." [61]

The Edinburgh Conference of 1910 stripped the subject down to the bare bones of the matter, stating:

> Under the general heading of "Comity" we propose to consider those aspects of our subject which relate to co-operation of a negative rather than of a positive kind. . . . These principles are concerned with such matters as overlapping or intrusion, the transfer of agents, the standards of Church membership, and the discipline of the Church.[62]

Yet comity was never a mere matter of these bare bones. It was always clothed in the flesh of positive intention and action and animated by the spirit of unity for effective ministry. It aimed at total evangelization, the elimination of confusing differences among young Christians, and the eventual union of the separate parts in a new young church of each land which would be indigenous and different from the churches of the West, but join with them in the common task.

The recent stresses, strains, and problems have not robbed the system of comity of the glory of its achievements. The radically changed circumstances of the present do not call for the rejection of the fundamental intent and purpose of comity, but rather for the urgent search for the adaptations and new forms and institutions which can effectively implement that intent and purpose in a new "world mission" of young and old churches together.

An editorial in the *Christian Century* in 1951 assumed that "comity [is] out the window in most areas," that there cannot be a return to it, and asked the question: "After

[61] *Pan-Anglican Congress, 1908, vol. V, Appendix* S.D.4(e), p. 2.
[62] *World Missionary Conference, 1910,* vol. VIII, p. 8.

comity, What?" [63] Comity is certainly not "out the window" in most regions; and the mission boards and societies which have long practiced it will not repudiate it. Repudiation or drastic modification of the practice may be expected to increase, however, to whatever extent young denominational churches strive to become nation-wide churches themselves rather than units in national union churches. The initiative lies with them rather than with the mission boards, although the latter have still great influence in enlarging the vision of the young churches and stimulating them to action. Both young national churchmen and the missionaries of the second wave of missionary action need to study history and to see their situation in the context of the whole course of the expansion of Christianity and in the perspective of the whole globe. They will learn that the present world-wide Protestant community and the flowering of young churches in what were once mission fields were the result of ever-increasing unity and cooperation, not of competition and rivalry.

Territorial comity was intended first of all to assure responsible evangelistic occupation everywhere and then to be a preliminary step toward a united, independent church in every land. The process should have brought about one church with great diversity within it, enriched by the traditions of many Western churches accommodated to, and transformed through, indigenous forms, if the hopes of most of the pioneers were realized. As long as there is not a single church in any land, there is still a place for cooperative assignment of locations to sister churches in unoccupied rural areas and in the churching of the expanding cities, just as there is in the churching of American cities and suburbs. However, even far less than in the United States is that an adequate approach to the evangelistic and pastoral task in the exploding urban industrial complexes. Comity agree-

[63] *Christian Century,* vol. LXVIII, No. 23 (June 6, 1951), pp. 677–678.

ments of the future can only be a part of a comprehensive and integrated plan which pools and effectively relates all resources, energies, and devotion to the doing of a task that even all the churches working simultaneously, but piecemeal and separately, cannot accomplish. The population explosion and the erupting industrialized urban complexes, with their drastic revolution in culture, present a gigantic challenge to a Christian community which is a dwindling minority. Duplication, rivalry, and cutthroat competition are not only wasteful and self-defeating, but they deny the gospel that God has in Christ reconciled the world unto Himself.

Today the secularized intellectuals of Asia and Africa reject all religions as superstition, while the adherents of the resurgent religions aggressively attack Christianity. Their publications are full of denunciations of our faith as being responsible for imperialism, colonial exploitation, war, and the threat of atomic annihilation. They each claim to have the spiritual basis for a new stable, just, and peaceful world order. This writer in numerous interviews with the clerical and lay leaders of the Asian religions during the past five years has heard much about the intolerance and foreignness of Christianity and even more about its divisiveness and unbrotherliness. Nationalists fear any element that introduces a threat to national solidarity, and their fear about the divisive effect of Christianity upon the national culture is compounded when they observe that it tends to be virulently divisive within itself. The aloofness and indifference of some denominations toward others is difficult of understanding by those who know something of the Bible's teaching about unity and brotherhood, but bitter controversy, competition, disruption, and litigation among Christians actually frighten them. This appears inimical to national welfare. Our divisiveness strikes at the heart of the gospel of reconciliation that we preach.

The Protestant missionary enterprise stands today at the

point which the pioneers envisaged: there are almost everywhere young churches able to discharge the responsibilities of the Church of Christ. This is the day when they expected them to build upon the foundations of denominationalism by geography a united church of the land, different in many respects from the churches in Europe and America. Organic union is a matter for the young churches to decide for themselves; but there is a unity given of God, which was inherent in the scheme of comity, that they dare not deny. It is for them to discover under the guidance of the Holy Spirit what forms it should take. It involves even greater cooperation than the missionary societies achieved. It cannot be achieved by discarding comity for competition. In one thing the pioneers were wrong. There are now no "regions beyond" into which the missionaries can advance as they withdraw from lands completely evangelized. There are no such lands of either kind. The frontier lines run through every land in a single mission of the Church to all the unreconciled world. Young and old churches together are called by God into a new unity, beyond even partnership, in proclaiming and demonstrating the gospel of reconciliation to men who are hungry for reconciliation. If the missionary enterprise could more than a century ago in an era of intense denominationalism achieve the unity that was expressed in its system of comity and cooperation, what greater and truer expression of spiritual unity ought not emerge in an ecumenical age!

Bibliography

ABEEL, DAVID. *The Missionary Convention at Jerusalem; or an Exhibition of the Claims of the World to the Gospel.* New York: Taylor, 1838.

ALEXANDER, ARCHIBALD. *Objections Obviated, and God Glorified by the Success of the Gospel among the Heathen.* A sermon preached at Albany, N. Y., Oct. 7, 1829, at the Twentieth Annual Meeting of the American Board of Commissioners for Foreign Missions. Boston: Crocker and Brewster, 1830.

American Board of Commissioners for Foreign Missions. *Annual Report.* Boston. From No. 1, 1810 to present.

——. *Outline of a Plan of Missions for the Board.* Boston: A.B.C.F.M., 1843. Also in *Annual Report, 1836,* pp. 108–117.

——. [Sandwich Island Mission]. *The Duty of the Present Generation to Evangelize the World; An Appeal from the Missionaries at the Sandwich Islands to their Friends in the United States.* 2nd ed. Buffalo, N. Y.: Charles Faxon, 1847.

ANDERSON, RUFUS. *History of the Missions of the American Board of Commissioners for Foreign Missions to the Oriental Churches.* 2 vols. Boston: Congregational Publishing Society, 1872.

Andhra Christian Council, Minutes of the Fourth Biennial Meeting of the —, 1929.

BARCLAY, WADE C. *History of Methodist Missions.* 3 vols. (in progress) New York: Board of Missions of the Methodist Church, 1949–1957.

Bengal and Assam Representative Council of Missions, Proceedings of the Third Meeting of the —, 1916; Fourth, 1917; Fifth, 1919.

BINGHAM, ROWLAND V. *Seven Sevens of Years and a Jubilee. The Story of the Sudan Interior Mission.* Toronto and New York: Evangelical Publishers, 1943.

BRAGA, ERASMO. *The Republic of Brazil.* London: World Dominion Press, 1932.

BROWN, ARTHUR JUDSON. *One Hundred Years. A History of the Foreign Missionary Work of the Presbyterian Church in the U.S.A., with some Account of the countries, peoples, etc.* New York: Revell, [1936].

329

Brown, Leslie W. *The Indian Christians of St. Thomas; an Account of the Ancient Syrian Church of Malabar.* London: Cambridge University Press, 1956.

Browne, Laurance E. *Christianity and the Malays.* London: S.P.G. and S.P.C.K., 1936.

Browning, Webster E., John Ritchie, and Kenneth G. Grubb. *The West Coast Republics of South America. Chile, Peru, and Bolivia.* London: World Dominion Press, 1930.

Burton, John W. *Missionary Survey of the Pacific Islands.* London: World Dominion Press, 1930.

————. *Modern Missions in the South Pacific.* London: Livingstone Press, [1949].

Camargo, G. Baez-, and Kenneth G. Grubb. *Religion in the Republic of Mexico.* London: World Dominion Press, 1935.

Carpenter, George W. *Highways for God in Congo; Commemorating Seventy-Five Years of Protestant Missions 1873–1953.* Leopoldville: La Librairie Évangélique au Congo, [1952].

Centenary Conference on the Protestant Missions of the World, Held in Exeter Hall (June 9th–19th) London, 1888, Report of the —, ed. by James Johnston. 2 vols. London: James Nisbet, 1888.

A Century of Protestant Missionary Work in Iran (Persia), 1834–1934. A Record of One Hundred Years of the Work of the Iran (Persia) Mission of the Board of Foreign Missions of the Presbyterian Church in the U. S. A. Beirut: American Press, [1936].

China Centenary Missionary Conference Records. Report of the Great Conference held at Shanghai, April 25th to May 8th, 1907. Shanghai: Centenary Conference Committee, 1907. American edition, N. Y.: American Tract Society, [1907].

China Continuation Committee. Milton T. Stauffer, secretary and editor. *The Christian Occupation of China; a General Survey of the numerical strength and geographical distribution of the Christian Forces in China,* made by the Special Committee on Survey and Occupation, China Continuation Committee, 1918–1921. Shanghai, China Continuation Committee, 1922.

————. *Proceedings of the Fourth Annual Meeting of the —, Shanghai, 1916; Fifth, Hangchow, 1917; Sixth, Shanghai, 1918; and Seventh, Shanghai, 1919.*

The China Mission Yearbook. 1910–1939. Shanghai: Christian Literature Society, 1910–1938/39, excepting 1927.

The Chinese Church as Revealed in the National Christian Conference Held in Shanghai, Tuesday, May 2, to Thursday, May 11, 1922.

Editorial Committee, Rev. F. Rawlinson, chairman. Shanghai: Oriental Press, [1922].

The Chinese Recorder. 1867–1941. (Until 1910 title reads *Chinese Recorder and Missionary Journal.*) Foochow, 1867–1872; Shanghai, 1874–1941.

The Christian Movement in Japan. See *Japan Christian Yearbook.*

Christian Work in Latin America. 3 vols. N. Y.: Missionary Education Movement, 1916. Report of the Panama Congress, 1916.

Church Congress, Held at Nottingham, 1897, The Official Report of the —; ed. by the Rev. C. Dunkley. London: Benrose, 1897.

Church Missionary Intelligencer. London: Church Missionary Society, 1849–1906, when merged with the *Church Missionary Review.*

Church Missionary Record. London: Church Missionary Society, 1830–1875; published with *C. M. Intelligencer,* 1876–78, and merged with it in 1879.

[CLARK, N. G.] *Discourse Commemorative of Rev. Rufus Anderson, D.D., LL.D.* Boston: American Board of Commissioners for Foreign Missions, 1880.

CLARK, N. G. *The Message and Messenger.* pam. [Boston: American Board of Commissioners for Foreign Missions, 1887]. Also in *Annual Report, 1887.*

———. *Missionary Comity.—Methods and Means for Carrying forward the Work in the Foreign Field.* pam. [Boston: American Board of Commissioners for Foreign Missions, 1886].

———. *True and False Economy in Missions.* pam. [Boston]: American Board of Commissioners for Foreign Missions, [1891].

COCHRANE, THOMAS. *Survey of the Missionary Occupation of China.* Shanghai: Christian Literature Society for China, 1913.

Conference of Missions in the Northern Provinces of Nigeria, Minutes of the —, 1926; 1929.

Conference on Federation Held at Peking, China, September 28 to October 1, 1905, The Records of a —. Yokohama: Fukin Printing Co., 1906.

Conference on Missions Held in 1860 at Liverpool. London: Nisbet, 1860.

Congo Mission News. Coquilhatville and Leopoldville, 1913 —. Organ of the Conseil Protestant du Congo and of its predecessor, the United Missionary Conference of the Congo.

[Congress on Christian Work in South America, Montevideo, 1925]. *Christian Work in South America: Official Report of the Congress on —;* ed. by the Committee on Cooperation in Latin America. N. Y.: Revell, [1925].

Conseil Protestant du Congo. *Constitution,* revised and ratified 1955. [Leopoldville: La Librairie Évangélique au Congo, 1955.]

————. *Minutes of Meeting No. 13, 1935; No. 19, 1941; No. 21, 1945; No. 23, 1948.*

The Continuation Committee Conferences in Asia 1912–1913. A Brief Account of the Conferences together with their Findings and Lists of Members. N. Y.: The Chairman of the Continuation Committee, 1913.

CURTEIS, G. A. *Bishop Selwyn of New Zealand and Litchfield.* London: Kegan Paul, Trench, 1889.

Decennial Missionary Conferences, India. *General Missionary Conference Held At Allahabad, 1872–73, Report of the –,* Madras: C. Foster, 1873.

————. *Decennial Missionary Conference, Held at Calcutta, 1882–83, Report of the Second –.* Calcutta: J. W. Thomas Baptist Mission Press, 1883.

————. *Decennial Missionary Conference, Held at Bombay, 1892–93, Report of the Third –,* 2 vols. Bombay: Education Society's Steam Press, 1893.

————. *Decennial Missionary Conference, Held in Madras, December 11–18th, 1902, Report of the Fourth –.* Madras: Christian Literature Society, [1903].

DIBBLE, SHELDON. *Thoughts on Missions from a Missionary to His Classmates.* N. Y.: American Tract Society, [1844].

DOVEY, JOHN WHITSED. *The Gospel in the South Pacific.* London: World Dominion Press, [1950].

DU PLESSIS, JOHANNES. *A History of Christian Missions in South Africa.* London: Longmans, Green, 1911.

Ecumenical Missionary Conference, New York, 1900. *Ecumenical Conference on Foreign Missions, Held in Carnegie Hall and Neighboring Churches, April 21 to May 1, Report of the –.* 2 vols. N. Y.: American Tract Society, 1900.

Egypt Inter-Mission Council, Minutes of the Annual General Conference of –, 1921; 1922; 1923; 1927; 1929.

Evangelical Foreign Missions Association. *Constitution and By-Laws of the Evangelical Foreign Missions Association.* Washington, D. C.: E.F.M.A., [1951].

FAHS, CHARLES H., and HELEN E. DAVIS. *Conspectus of Cooperative Missionary Enterprises.* N. Y.: International Missionary Council, 1935.

Faith and Order. Proceedings of the World Conference, Lausanne, August 3–21, 1927; ed. by H. N. Bate. N. Y.: Doran, 1927.

FINDLAY, G. G., and W. W. HOLDSWORTH. *The History of the Wes-leyan Methodist Missionary Society.* 5 vols. London: Epworth Press, 1921–1924.

Foreign Missions Conference of North America, Report of the Annual Meeting, 1893–1950. Originally named the Interdenominational Conference of Foreign Missionary Boards of the United States and Canada. It became in 1950 the Division of Foreign Missions of the National Council of the Churches of Christ in the U. S. A.

FOX, C. E. *Lord of the Southern Isles. Being the Story of the Anglican Mission in Melanesia, 1849–1949.* London: Mowbray, 1954.

FREYTAG, WALTER. "Mission and Unity." A mimeographed prepara-tory paper for Group I at the International Missionary Confer-ence, Willingen, 1952. London: International Missionary Council, 1952.

General Conference of the Protestant Missionaries of China, Held at Shanghai, May 10–24, 1877, Records of the —. Shanghai: Presby-terian Mission Press, 1878.

General Conference of the Protestant Missionaries of China, Held at Shanghai, May 7–20, 1890, Records of the —. Shanghai: Presby-terian Mission Press, 1890.

General Conference of Protestant Missionaries in Japan, Held in Tokyo, October 24–31, 1900. Tokyo: Methodist Publishing House, 1901.

General Conference of the Protestant Missionaries of Japan, Held at Osaka, Japan, April, 1883, Proceedings of the —. Yokohama: R. Meikeljohn, 1883.

General Conference on Foreign Missions, Held at the Conference Hall, in Mildmay Park, London, in October 1878, Proceedings of the —. London: John F. Shaw, 1879.

General Missionary Conference of Northern Rhodesia, Proceedings of the —, 1922; 1924.

General Missionary Conference of Northwest Rhodesia, Report of the Proceedings of the First —, 1914.

General Missionary Conference of Nyasaland, Report of the Third —, 1910.

General Missionary Conference of South Africa, Report of the Pro-ceedings of the First —, 1904; Second, 1906; Third, 1909; Fourth, 1912; Fifth, 1921; Seventh, 1928.

GIDNEY, W. T. *History of the London Society for Promoting Christian-ity amongst the Jews from 1809 to 1908.* London: L.S.P.C.J., 1908.

GOODALL, NORMAN. *A History of the London Missionary Society 1895–1945.* London: Oxford University Press, 1954.

————. ed. *Missions under the Cross. Addresses Delivered at the Enlarged Meeting of the International Missionary Council at Willingen, in Germany, 1952; with Statements Issued by the Meeting.* London: Published for the International Missionary Council by Edinburgh House Press, 1953.

GOODSELL, FRED FIELD. *You Shall Be My Witnesses.* Boston: American Board of Commissioners for Foreign Missions, 1959.

GREY, H. A. *Comity in the Mission Field.* London: Longmans, Green, 1914. (pam., Kikuyu Tracts series)

GROVES, CHARLES P. *The Planting of Christianity in Africa.* 4 vols. London: Lutterworth, 1948–1958.

GRUBB, KENNETH G. *The Lowland Indians of Amazonia.* London: World Dominion Press, 1927.

————. *The Northern Republics of South America.* London: World Dominion Press, 1931.

————. *Religion in Central America.* London: World Dominion Press, 1937.

HAMILTON, J. T. *A History of the Missions of the Moravian Church during the Eighteenth and Nineteenth Centuries.* Bethlehem, Pa.: Times Publishing Co., 1901.

The Harvest Field. See *National Christian Council Review.*

HAMLIN, CYRUS. *The Oriental Churches and Mohammedans.* Missionary Tracts, No. 11. Boston: American Board of Commissioners for Foreign Missions, 1853.

Historical Sketch of the Missions of the American Board of Commissioners for Foreign Missions in European Turkey, Asia Minor, and Armenia. N. Y.: Gray, 1861.

HEYWORTH-DUNNE, J. *An Introduction to the History of Education in Modern Egypt.* London: Luzac, n. d. [1939?]

HOGG, WILLIAM RICHEY. *Ecumenical Foundations. A History of the International Missionary Council and Its Nineteenth Century Background.* N. Y.: Harper, 1952.

Hongkong Church Directory, 1959. Hongkong: Council on Christian Literature for Overseas Chinese for the Hongkong Christian Council, 1959.

HUTTON, J. E. *A History of Moravian Missions.* London: Moravian Publication Office, [1923].

IGLEHART, CHARLES W. *A Century of Protestant Christianity in Japan.* Rutland, Vt., and Tokyo: Charles E. Tuttle, 1959.

————. "Comity and Cooperation in Japanese Christianity." A mimeographed paper prepared for the Conference of the North American Missionary Boards in Japan, New York City, 1934.

IMBRIE, WILLIAM. *Church Unity in Japan.* Tokyo: Kyo Bun Kwan, 1914.

Interdenominational Conference of the Foreign Missionary Boards of the United States and Canada, Annual Report of —. See Foreign Missions Conference of N. A.

The Island Mission: Being a History of the Melanesian Mission. London: Macintosh, 1869.

JAMES, HENRY I. *Missions in Rhodesia under the Methodist Episcopal Church 1898–1934.* Old Umtali, S. Rhodesia; Rhodesia Mission Press, 1934.

The Japan Evangelist. Tokyo, 1893–1925. Superseded by the *Japan Christian Quarterly.*

The Jerusalem Meeting of the International Missionary Council, March 24–April 8, 1928. N. Y. and London: International Missionary Council, 1928.

KAWERAU, PETER. *Amerika und die Orientalischen Kirchen.* Berlin: Walter de Gruyter, 1958.

LATOURETTE, KENNETH S. *A History of Christian Missions in China.* N. Y.: Macmillan, 1929.

———. *A History of the Expansion of Christianity.* Vols. IV-VII. N. Y.: Harper, 1937–1945.

LOVETT, RICHARD. *The History of the London Missionary Society, 1795–1895.* 2 vols. London: Henry Froude, 1899.

MACGILLIVRAY, D., ed. *A Century of Protestant Missions in China (1807–1907), Being the Centenary Conference Historical Volume.* Shanghai: American Presbyterian Mission Press, 1907.

MAXWELL, J. L. *Nigeria, the Land, Its People, and Christian Progress.* London: World Dominion Press, n. d.

MCGAVRAN, DONALD A. *The Bridges of God; a Study in the Strategy of Missions.* London: World Dominion Press, [1955].

———. *How Churches Grow.* London: World Dominion Press, [1959].

MCLEISH, ALEXANDER. *A Racial Melting Pot. Religion in Malaya.* London: World Dominion Press, 1940. pam.

Methodist Episcopal Church, East Central Africa Missionary Conference, Minutes of the Tenth Session of the —, *1913; Eleventh, 1915.*

Methodist Episcopal Church, Portuguese East Africa Mission Conference, Official Journal of the First Session of the —, *1916.*

Methodist Episcopal Church, Southeast Africa Missionary Conference of the —, *Official Journal of the Eighth Session, 1924; Ninth, 1925; Eleventh, 1927; Twelfth, 1928; Thirteenth, 1929; Fifteenth, 1931.*

MIRBT, CARL. *Mission und Kolonialpolitik.* Tübingen: J. C. B. Mohr, 1910.

Missionary Conference on Behalf of the Mohammedan World, the First, Cairo, 1906. *The Mohammedan World of Today, Being Papers Read at the First Missionary Conference on Behalf of the Mohammedan World at Cairo, April 4th–9th, 1906;* edited by S. M. Zwemer, E. M. Wherry, and James L. Barton. N. Y.: Revell, n. d.

Missionary Conference on Behalf of the Mohammedan World, the Second, Lucknow, 1911. *Islam and Missions: Being Papers Read at the Second Missionary Conference on Behalf of the Mohammedan World at Lucknow, January 23–28, 1911;* edited by E. M. Wherry, S. M. Zwemer, and C. G. Mylrea. N. Y.: Revell, 1911.

The Missionary Herald. Boston: American Board of Commissioners for Foreign Missions, 1805–1951.

Missionary Research Library. *Directory of North American Protestant Foreign Missionary Agencies.* 4th ed., 1960. N. Y.: Missionary Research Library, 1960.

————. *Occasional Bulletin.* 1950–.

Missionary Review of the World. Princeton and N. Y.: 1878–1939.

MOREIRA, EDUARDO. *Portuguese East Africa. A Study of Its Religious Needs.* London: World Dominion Press, 1936.

Natal Missionary Conference, Report of the —, 1933; 1936; 1937.

National Christian Council of China, Annual Report of the —, 1922–32; Biennial Report, 1932–1937.

National Christian Council of India, Executive Committee, Minutes of the —, 1924–59.

National Christian Council of India, Proceedings of the —, 1–10 (1924–1946).

National Christian Council Review, 1880–, published as *The Harvest Field, 1880–1924.* Journal of the National Christian Council of India.

National Council of the Churches of Christ in the U. S. A., Division of Foreign Missions, Annual Report of the —, 1950–.

National Missionary Council of India, Burma, and Ceylon, Proceedings of the Second Meeting, 1915; Third, 1916; etc.—*Ninth, 1923.* (The national Continuation Committee Meeting held by Dr. Mott in 1914 is considered to be the First.)

Near East Christian Council News Bulletin., 1926–1927. Beirut.

North American Assembly on African Affairs. *Africa Is Here. Report of the North American Assembly on African Affairs, 1952.* N. Y.:

Africa Committee of the Division of Foreign Missions, National Council of the Churches of Christ in the U. S. A., [1952].

OLIVER, ROLAND. *The Missionary Factor in East Africa.* London: Longmans, Green, [1952].

ORCHARD, R. K., ed. *The Ghana Assembly of the International Missionary Council, 28th December, 1957 to 8th January, 1958. Selected Papers, with an Essay on the Role of the I. M. C.* London: Published for the I. M. C. by Edinburgh House Press, 1958.

The Oxford Conference (Official Report); edited by J. H. Oldham. Chicago and N. Y.: Willett, Clark, 1937.

PAIK, L. GEORGE. *The History of Protestant Missions in Korea, 1832–1910.* Pyeng Yang, Korea: Union Christian College Press, 1929.

Pan-Anglican Congress, 1908, Report of the —, vol. V, being Section D. "The Church's Missions in Non-Christian Lands." London: S.P.C.K., 1908.

PASCOE, C. F. *Two Hundred Years of the S.P.G.: An Historical Account of the Society for the Propagation of the Gospel in Foreign Parts, 1701–1900.* 2 vols. London: Published at the Society's Office, 1901.

[Philippine Federation of Christian Churches]. *The Evangelical Church in the Philippines: A Factual Statement.* Mimeographed for distribution at the Bangkok Conference, 1949, by representatives of the Philippine Federation of Christian Churches. [Manila: The Philippine Federation of Christian Churches, 1949.]

Philippine Federation of Christian Churches, Minutes of the Fourth Post-War Biennial Convention of the —, March 11–12, 1954.

[Philippine Federation of Christian Churches]. *Pertinent Facts Regarding Comity Agreement.* Golden Jubilee of Protestantism in the Philippines, 1889–1949. Manila: Philippine Federation of Christian Churches, [1949]. Mimeo. pam.

PHILP, H. A. R. *A New Day in Kenya.* London: World Dominion Press, 1936.

Punjab Missionary Conference, Held at Lahore in December and January, 1862–1863, Report of the —. Lodiana: American Presbyterian Mission Press, 1863.

Punjab Representative Council of Missions, Proceedings of the Second Annual Meeting of the —, 1914; Third, 1915; Sixth, 1918.

RAUWS, JOH., H. KRAEMER, F. J. F. VAN HASSELT, and N. A. C. SLOTEMAKER DE BRUINE. *The Netherlands Indies.* London: World Dominion Press, 1925.

Regional Conferences in Latin America, Reports of a Series of Seven Conferences . . . 1916. N. Y.: Published for the Committee on

Cooperation in Latin America by the Missionary Education Movement, [1917].

RHODES, HARRY A., ed. *History of the Korea Mission, Presbyterian Church U. S. A., 1884–1934.* Seoul: Chosen Mission, Presbyterian Church, [1934].

RICHTER, JULIUS. *History of Protestant Missions in the Near East.* N. Y.: Revell, [c.1910].

———. *Tanganyika and Its Future.* London: World Dominion Press, 1934.

ROOME, W. J. W. *A Great Emancipation.* London: World Dominion Press, 1926.

The Second World Conference on Faith and Order held at Edinburgh, Aug. 3–18, 1937; edited by Leonard Hodgson. N. Y.: Macmillan, 1938.

SHAW, P. E. *American Contacts with the Eastern Churches, 1820–1870.* Chicago: American Society of Church History, 1937.

SKINNER, THOMAS S. *Thoughts on Evangelizing the World.* N. Y.: John S. Taylor, 1836.

SLADE, RUTH M. *The English Speaking Missions in the Congo Independent State (1878–1900).* [Bruxelles: Académie royale des Sciences coloniales, 1959.]

SMITH, EDWIN W. *Life and Times of Daniel Lindley.* London: Epworth Press, [1949].

———. *The Way of the White Fields in Rhodesia: A Survey of the Christian Enterprise in Northern and Southern Rhodesia.* London: World Dominion Press, 1928.

SMITH, ELI. *Missionary Sermons and Addresses.* Boston: Perkins, 1833.

South India Missionary Conference, Held at Ootacamund, April 19th–May 5th, 1858, Proceedings of the –. Madras: Society for Promoting Christian Knowledge, 1858.

South India and Ceylon, The Missionary Conference of –, 1879. 2 vols. Madras: Addison, 1880. (Bangalore Conference)

South India Missionary Conference, Held at Madras, January 2–5, 1900, Report of the –. Madras: M. E. Publishing House, 1900.

Southern Rhodesia Missionary Conference, 1932, Proceedings of the –.

SPEER, ROBERT E. *Report on the Japan Missions of the Presbyterian Board of Foreign Missions.* N. Y.: Board of Foreign Missions of the Presbyterian Church in the U. S. A., 1897.

Spirit of Missions. N. Y.: Domestic and Foreign Missionary Society of the Protestant Episcopal Church, 1836–1939.

Standing Committee of Cooperating Christian Missions in Japan, Ninth Annual Meeting of the –, 1910.

STOCK, EUGENE. *The History of the Church Missionary Society: Its Environment, Its Men, and Its Work.* 4 vols. London: Church Missionary Society, 1899–1916.

STONELAKE, A. R. *Congo: Past and Present.* London: World Dominion Press, 1937.

STOW, BARON, ed. *Missionary Enterprise. A Collection of Discourses on Christian Missions.* Boston: Gould, 1846.

STRONG, WILLIAM E. *The Story of the American Board; an Account of the First Hundred Years.* Boston: Pilgrim Press, [1910].

Taiwan Christian Yearbook, 1960. Taipei: China Sunday School Association, 1960.

TAYLOR, JOHN V., and DOROTHEA LEHMANN. *Christians of the Copperbelt. The Growth of the Church in Northern Rhodesia.* London: Student Christian Movement Press, 1961.

TEMPLE, WILLIAM. *The Church Looks Forward.* London: Macmillan, 1944.

THOMAS, WINBURN T. *Protestant Beginnings in Japan. The First Three Decades, 1859–1889.* Tokyo and Rutland, Vt.: Charles E. Tuttle, 1959.

THOMPSON, H. P. *Into All Lands: The History of the Society for the Propagation of the Gospel in Foreign Parts, 1701–1950.* London: S.P.C.K., 1951.

TORBET, ROBERT G. *Venture of Faith. The Story of the American Baptist Foreign Mission Society and the Women's American Baptist Foreign Mission Society 1814–1954.* Philadelphia: Judson Press, 1955.

TRIMINGHAM, J. SPENCER. *The Christian Church and Missions in Ethiopia (Including Eritrea and the Somalilands).* London: World Dominion Press, 1950.

————. *The Christian Church in Post-War Sudan.* London: World Dominion Press, [1949].

TUCKER, JOHN T. *Angola. The Land of the Blacksmith Prince.* London: World Dominion Press, 1933.

Union Missionary Convention, Held in New York, May 4th and 5th, 1854, Proceedings of the —. N. Y.: Taylor and Hogg, 1854.

United Missionary Conference on the Congo, The First, Leopoldville, 1902; Second, Leopoldville, 1904; Third, Kinchassa, 1906; Fourth, Leopoldville, 1907; Fifth, Kinchassa, 1909; Sixth, Bolenge, 1911; Seventh, Luebo, 1918; Eighth, Bolenge, 1921; and Ninth, Leopoldville-Est, 1924. (The name of the conference varied slightly in the early years.)

United Missionary Council of Syria and Palestine. *Rules and By-Laws, 1929* [Beirut].

VAN DUSEN, HENRY P. *One Great Ground of Hope. Christian Missions and Christian Unity.* Philadelphia: Westminster Press, 1961.

WARNECK, GUSTAV. "Modernste Missionsgeschichtschreibung," in *Allgemeine Missions Zeitschrift*, Vol. XIII (1886), pp. 297–317.

WARREN, WILLIAM. *These for Those: Our Indebtedness to Foreign Missions; or What We Get for What We Gave.* Portland, Me.: Hoyt, Fogg, & Breed, 1870.

WATSON, ANDREW. *The American Mission in Egypt, 1854–1896.* Pittsburgh: United Presbyterian Board of Publication, 1898.

WATSON, CHARLES R. *The Christian Crusade in Egypt.* Philadelphia: Board of Foreign Missions of the United Presbyterian Church of North America, [c. 1907].

West China Missionary Conference at Chungking, January, 1899, The Records of —. Shanghai: Presbyterian Mission Press, 1899.

[West Central Africa Regional Conference, 1946]. *Abundant Life in Changing Africa. Report of the West Central Africa Regional Conference, Leopoldville, 1946.* N. Y.: Africa Committee of the Foreign Missions Conference of North America, [1946].

WHETSTONE, HAROLD V. *The Lutheran Mission in Liberia.* N. Y.: Board of Foreign Missions of the United Lutheran Church in America, 1955.

WILLIAMS, JOHN. *A Narrative of Missionary Enterprises in the South Sea Islands.* London: Published for the author by J. Snow, 1837.

WILLIS, J. J. *The Kikuyu Conference. A Study in Christian Unity.* London: Longmans, Green, 1914.

World Council of Churches. *Revised Report of the Commission on Christian Witness, Proselytism, and Religious Liberty.* Reprinted from The *Ecumenical Review*, Vol. XIII, No. 1 (October 1960).

World Missionary Atlas; edited by Harlan P. Beach and Charles H. Fahs. N. Y.: Institute of Social and Religious Research, 1925.

World Missionary Conference, 1910. 9 Vols. Edinburgh: Oliphant, Anderson, & Ferrier, 1910.

Index

Abeel, David, 56, 111
Abra, 138, 139
Abyssinia, see Ethiopia
Accra, 261
Afghanistan, 191
Africa, 16, 29, 36, 38, 39, 43, 49, 52–57, 59, 64–66, 78, 164, 177–187, 188, 189, 190–195, 196–198, 199–202, 203, 206, 248–271, 280, 282–289
Africa Inland Mission, 201, 249, 251
African Methodist Episcopal Church, 156
Aguas Calientes, 144
Albay, 137, 139
Aleppo, 230, 231
Alexander, Archibald, 23
Alexander, Bishop Michael Solomon, 234, 235
Algeria, 246
Allahabad Decennial Missionary Conference, 1872–73 (India), 88
Allen, Roland, 299–300
Alliance of Missions in Kenya, 251
Amazon Valley, 155
American Baptist Foreign Mission Society, 11, 21, 117, 136–139, 144, 178–179, 182, 218, 221–222, 285
American Bible Society, 21, 56, 111, 117–118, 137, 149, 155
American Board of Commissioners for Foreign Missions (A.B.C.F.M.), 21, 25, 36, 39, 43, 47–59, 60, 63, 77, 92, 111, 112, 113, 119, 135–139, 167, 189, 197, 207, 209, 210–217, 228–231, 237–238, 256–258, 286
American Friends Board of Missions, 249
American Indian Missions, 18, 19, 20, 25
American Marathi Mission, 92

American Negro Churches, 261
Amoy, 38, 111, 113, 115
Ancachas, 153
Anderson, Rufus, 32, 51, 55, 58, 60, 215–216, 274, 275, 299, 300
Aneityum, 61
Anglicans, 19, 20, 21, 27, 29, 30, 39, 61, 62, 64–66, 78, 88, 91–93, 112, 127, 128, 136, 140, 141, 145, 155, 156, 166, 169, 191, 194, 198, 199–210, 217–218, 228, 229, 232–239, 240ff, 249–250, 251–252, 256, 258–259, 260, 262, 264, 266, 268–269, 272, 274–281, 317
Angola, 59, 188–189
Anhwei, 128
Anju, 162
Antananarivo, 65
Anzoateguia, 153
Apure, 153
Arabia, 191
Aragua, 153
Araucanian Indians, 154
Arbitration, 87, 90–91, 94ff, 103–104, 118–119, 133, 145, 146, 171–172, 180, 185, 254, 265, 267
Arequipa, 154
Argentina, 146, 155, 296
Armenian Church (Gregorian), 210
Armenians, 210–214, 237
Arnot, Fred, 253
Arthington, Robert, 67–68
Associate Reformed Presbyterian Church, 144
Assyrian Evangelical Church, 215
Assyrians or Nestorians (Iran), 213, 214–215, 238
Astrakhan, 229
Asunción, 155
Athens, 231
Ausschuss der deutschen evangelischen Missionsgesellschaften, 77, 251

341